FIRECLAY

An Autobiography
Thomas R. Bowerman, Sr.

Artex Publishing

About the Cover

The picture on the cover depicts a forest fire. Fighting a forest fire was my first CCC duty assignment in the CCC near Leavenworth, Washington in 1940. The title Fireclay is the code word used by my brother to identify himself when he sent me penny post cards from hospitals where he was a patient using an assumed name to avoid payment of hospital bills.

Copyright © 1996 by Thomas R. Bowerman, Sr.

ISBN: 1-57745-009-4

Library of Congress Catalog card Number:

Artex Publishing
1601 North 8th Street
Sheboygan, WI 53081

Printed in the USA.

FOREWORD

This book is dedicated to my four sons:

Charles Henry Bowerman by my first wife, Mae Brucke.
Thomas Roy Bowerman, Jr., Terry Adrian Bowerman, and Barry Lynn Bowerman by my second wife, Frances Erline Johnson.

It would be presumptuous of me to consider my life to be significant enough to warrant an autobiography, and I am not a presumptuous person. However, I lived during an interesting period, surrounded by interesting people and events. This is their book!

I also dedicate this book to my Sister, Juanita Bowerman Berman, and to my Mother, Eunice Bales Bowerman. Both had profound influence on my life and are responsible for whatever small degree of success I may have had in life.

This book is based largely on my memory and it is not perfect therefore certain dates and events may have to be flip flopped occasionally to be fully understandable. It has been said that "If you want to tell the truth, write a novel and if you want to tell lies, write your autobiography." All I can say is that I removed all of the lies I found. Hopefully, I got all of them. I resisted the temptation throughout to make myself look good and told the truth, even when it hurt.

This book was originally written as an electronic book. The electronic book had provisions for "jumping to supporting data" and if I failed to remove any of those during my conversion it will appear to have duplication. Just consider it to be a "flashback."

May the power be with you!

Table of Contents

Foreward	3
Chapter 1 My Parents	7
Chapter 2 My Brother Herman and Sister Juanita	12
Chapter 3 The Smackover Connection	20
Chapter 4 My Childhood Days	27
Chapter 5 Youth	47
Chapter 6 The Civilian Conservation Corps	59
Chapter 7 The U.S. Navy and World War II	87
Chapter 8 The U.S. Army and return to Civilian Life	129
Chapter 9 Charles Henry Bowerman, my first son.	141
Chapter 10 Life after Marriage	144
Chapter 11 The Army Air Force	146
Chapter 12 The Formative Years	150
Chapter 13 University of Alabama	156
Chapter 14 Graduation, Gen. Accounting Office and Army Audit Agency	162
Chapter 15 Courting Caton	178
Chapter 16 Tommy	187
Chapter 17 Terry	191
Chapter 18 Barry	194
Chapter 19 Anniston Army Depot	198
Chapter 20 Retirement	261
Chapter 21 Bulletin Board Systems	263
Chapter 22 The Declining Years - Waiting for the Fat Lady to Sing	265
Reference Data	269
Genealogy One	271
Genealogy Two	271
Tuscaloosa High School	277
Civilian Conservation Corps	278
Armed Guard Gunnery Officer Log - S.S. Charles Sumner	279
Armed Guard Gunnery Officer Log - S.S. Lewis Luckenbach	295

Test of a Manager

The test of a Manager is the fight that he makes
        The grit that he daily shows.
The way he stands on his feet and takes
        Fate's numerous bumps and blows.
A coward can smile when the risk is small,
   When theres nothing his progress to quench.
But it takes a man to stand straight and tall,
   And never give an inch.

It isn't the victory after all,
        But the fight that a brother makes.
The manager who, driven against a wall,
   Still stands erect and takes
The blows of fate with never a flinch,
   Is the man who'll win in the by and by,
For he'll stand his ground what ere the fight
        And never give an inch.

It's the bumps you get and the jolts you get
   And the shocks that your courage stands.
The hours of sorrow and vain regret,
   The prize that escapes your hands
That test your mettle and prove your worth.
        For it isn't the hours of toil at the bench,
But the blows you take on the good old earth,
   That show your stuff, so—
NEVER GIVE AN INCH!!

(author unknown)

Chapter One

My Parents

My parents were William Henry Bowerman and Eunice Bales Bowerman. Dad had been married before and had a son named Clyde, who was an evil person and eventually was sent to prison for life. My Mother had never been married before. There were three of us children, Herman, Juanita and myself. I was the youngest and Herman was the oldest. The world regarded us as poor White trash. Juanita and my Mother proved them wrong over and over and over again.

My Father was born in Paducah, Kentucky in 1882 and was 16 years older than my Mother. He was always foreman or superintendent of a heading mill and was an alcoholic. He was not your average alcoholic in that he often went six months to a year without drinking alcoholic beverages. Once he started he could not stop drinking until he had spent all the money he had and then sold everything he had and spent that money. Once he was broke and could not raise any more money he would sober up. We never knew when the next alcoholic binge would begin.

I suppose I was the only one in the family who loved my Father. Dad had a second grade education and had educated himself in the school of hard knocks. I think I understood my Dad and his total inability to do anything other than what he did. He was hard on the family but never abusive and I learned early that Dad talked tough but would not hurt a fly. I guess it is understandable that my Dad loved me more than he did my Sister or Brother.

Dad was a very large man, usually weighing anywhere from 225 to 275 pounds and with the height to handle about 225

Mrs Eunice Bowerman

William H. Bowerman

without appearing fat. He always wore the same size clothes and when he was down to 225 or less he appeared to have enough room in the seat of his pants to keep an orchestra there. My brother coined the nickname of Sag for Daddy because of this. Dad was usually called Stall by everyone who knew him and I leave it to your imagination as to why he would be called Stall.

My Mother was born in Sheridan, Arkansas in 1896 and was 16 years younger than my Father. Her Mother, Lula Bales, ran a boarding house and my Mother vowed to marry the first man who asked her. That man was William Henry Bowerman.

My Mother was 18 when Herman was born and only 24 when I was born but I can never remember her as seeming young to me. She always seemed to be an old person. I know now that this is not true but it surely seemed that way. I suppose living through what she did with my Father and my Brother is enough to make anyone old. Mother never smiled and I guess she had little to smile about. She married Dad to get away from boarders and in no time he saw to it that she had 24 of her own to cook for and to wash for and to clean up after.

Mother had four brothers, Ross, Loys and William Otto and Joseph. She was the only girl. Ross was the oldest and married a girl named Beatrice and lived in Stamps, Arkansas. Loys married Lura and lived in and around Smackover. William Otto, or Bill as he was always called, was married a short time and divorced and lived with his Mother most of his life. Bill finally married again when he was in his forties and his Mother took him out of her will. Joseph married and lived in Monroe, Louisiana. He was gassed with mustard gas by the Germans during World War I and did not live long after the war. We considered his wife to be fabulously wealthy because she received his $10,000 insurance. In those days anyone with $10,000 was much like a millionaire today. They had three children, two girls and a boy. The girls both graduated from college and one was a dietitian and the other a pilot (among other things I suppose). The pilot had a good job during World War II ferrying war planes from the factory to their destination. The boy was caught by police riding his motorcycle while standing on his head, and at an excessive speed. The judge gave him the choice of jail or the Army and he joined the Army.

Much of the above may not appear to be background information on my Mother, but it really is. My Mother cared very much for her family. When her Mother got cancer there were many, many relatives living near her in Smackover, Arkansas that could have taken care of her. My Mother was running an upholstery shop in Tuscaloosa, Alabama, a long way from Smackover. My Mother did not think twice about it. She immediately closed her shop and went to Smackover and took care of her Mother until she died. After she died her will left everything she had to my Mother and my Mother's brother, Loys. My Mother and Loys knew that their brother Bill had built all the houses my Grandmother had and they signed it all over to Bill. Bill sold out and spent it all in less than three months, but that was his right. My Grandmother once had the most beautiful place in Smackover and now it is nothing but a paved Church parking lot.

Chapter Two

My Brother Herman and Sister Juanita

My brother was Herman Henry Bowerman and my Sister was Juanita Bowerman. We were stereotyped as "poor white trash" when we were young, always living on what was termed as the "wrong side of the Tracks", which used to mean the same side the Blacks lived on.

Herman was born in Harriman, Tennessee in 1916 and was 6 years older than me and 3 years older than my Sister. Herman had asthma from the day he was born.

As far as I know, Herman only had one White friend; the rest of his friends were Black. We always lived in areas that were prejudiced towards Black people. They were referred to as niggers, nigras, coons and apes. Herman never understood that prejudice and preferred to be with them. He saw no difference between Black and White other than he felt more comfortable with Blacks.

Our Mother always had twenty or more boarders, usually around 24. Herman lived with the boarders. Most were alcoholics and by the time Herman was 11 years old he was also an alcoholic. He left home the first time at 11, with a boarder named Perrin Pressley. They left on a freight train. They got off the train somewhere around Chicago to bum something to eat. When another train came through Perrin told Herman to grab a ladder as the train went by and he would make sure Herman was okay and get on the next car. Herman made it all right and looked back to see if Perrin was okay. He did not see Perrin so he jumped off and walked back. He found Perrin laying beside the track. One leg was cut almost off, just dangling by a small piece of skin. Perrin told Herman to reach in his pocket and get his knife

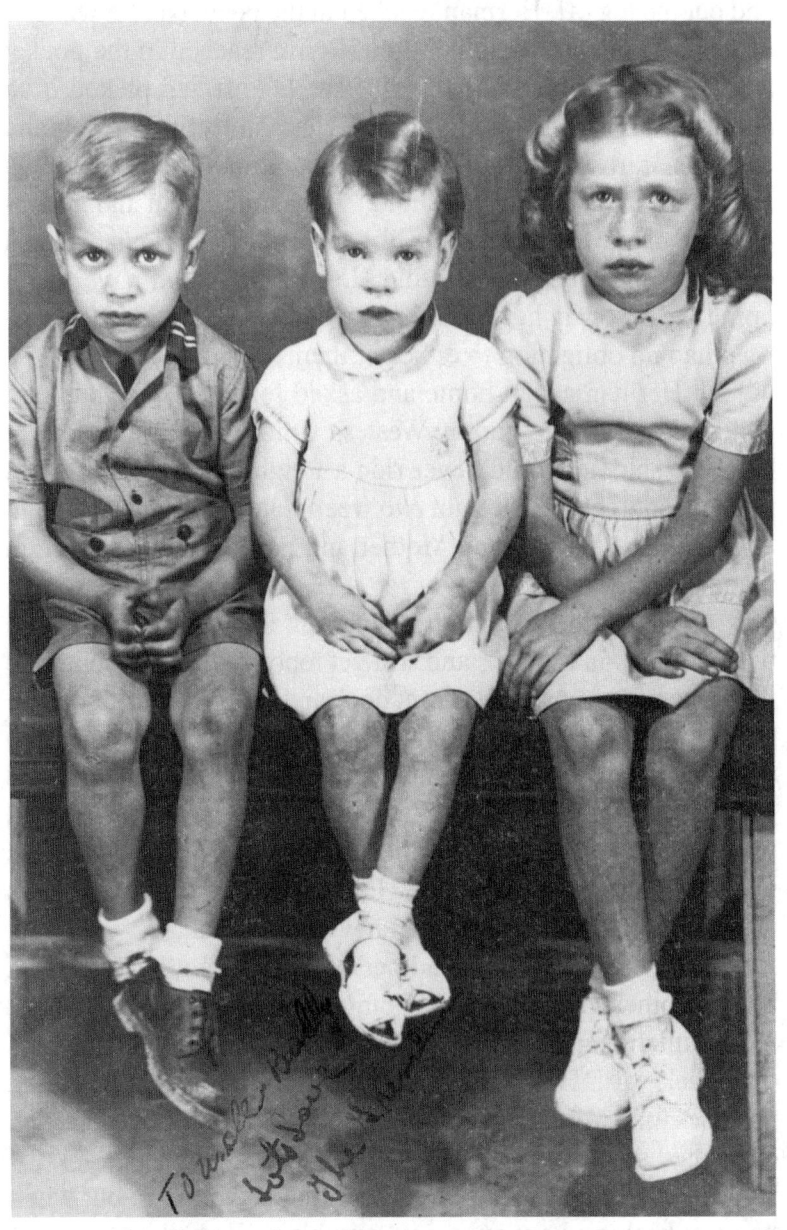

Children of Herman and Jimmie Mae

and cut the leg off. Herman reached in the pocket and it was full of thick blood. He could not do it. Perrin reached in the pocket and got the knife, finished cutting the leg off and picked it up and threw it in a ditch. He did get Herman to find a stick and took his shirt off and made a tourniquet to stop the bleeding. Herman found someone and told them about Perrin and an ambulance came for him. The railroad paid for Perrin's medical expenses and a peg leg but told Herman he would have to get home the best way he could. They were trespassers and the railroad had no obligation to either of them.

Herman called home and asked for money for bus fare and Daddy sent it to him by Western Union. When Herman got home he said he would never ride a freight train again. He left town on another freight train two weeks later. He came and went as he pleased and nothing Mother and Father could say to him made any difference.

My Mother would drive or walk Herman to school and watch him go in the door and still get reports he was absent. She found he was going in the front door and dropping his books on the floor and going out the back door. The principal decided to whip Herman one day and called him in and locked the door and got his paddle. Herman took the paddle away from him and whipped him. Herman said the principal was clawing in his pocket for the key to the door. Herman was expelled. That was in the eighth grade and Herman never went back.

Herman was not a bad person. I could not have found a better brother. He was always doing something for me. He built me a miniature golf course so I could play "Putt Putt" golf in my own back yard. He bought me a pair of shoes once when I had no shoes for several months. All I had to do was mention I needed or wanted something.

When Herman was sober he was scrupulously honest but when he was drinking he would steal anything. We had been out of food for a week once and Herman came in with a bag of groceries in each arm. My Mother asked him what it was and he said he got a little job and bought some groceries with his first pay check. He set the bags on the table and Mother started unloading them. He had two bags of nothing but dog food. He then admitted he had seen a lady putting them in her car and when she went back inside he stole them. Mother started looking around and found a black leather doctor's bag. She took it to the doctor in Southside and asked him to try to find out who it belonged to and return it. It was his.

When we were in Smackover once my Grandmother heard a truck and then a lot of noise. She looked under the house the next morning and there were 20 to 25 shovels under there. Herman had stolen a WPA truck and put the shovels in the back of it under the house. All of them had WPA burned into the handles. My Grandmother was so afraid he would be arrested that she cut them up and threw them in the outdoor toilet. She had three houses she rented out and when one was vacant Herman would steal everything in them and sell it, including the sink and wood stove. Grandma would try to find out where he sold the stuff and buy it back if she could.

Herman was always getting hurt when he was drunk. He walked across Jensen Drive in Houston, Texas and was hit by seven different cars. It was easier to count the bones that were not broken than those that were. Herman was in casts almost from head to foot and barely able to move. In less than a week he walked out of the hospital when no one was watching and went back to work. His boss did not want to let him work but finally decided to put him on piece work. Herman made less than a dollar the first day but in a week or so was making more than he had before.

A bus driver spotted Herman laying by the side of the road in Houston and picked him up and drove him to the hospital. He had been stabbed and the doctor said he did not have enough blood left to fill a fountain pen. He was given many pints of blood and he walked out of the hospital without telling them he was leaving two days later. It developed that his wife had stabbed him.

Herman was very dark skinned and had coal black hair

Juanita Bowerman

and never weighed more than 145 pounds. He was very strong though and I have seen him handle my Daddy when Daddy weighed around 250 pounds. Herman could work around the clock and never take a break or slow down. He never had a cold or a headache in his life. Asthma was the only affliction he had and he never had it in Houston, only in Mississippi or Alabama.

Herman went to sleep drunk in a hobo camp on a cold night, next to a barrel full of burning cross ties. The barrel turned over during the night and the cross ties fell across his chest. He suffered terrible burns. Daddy found out about it and got him out of the hospital and put him on a freight train to come to stay with my Mother and me. Daddy bought him a new overcoat but when he got there he had on a nasty, dirty jacket. I asked him about the overcoat and he said there was a poor old colored boy on the train about to freeze and since the cold never bothered him he just swapped with him.

Herman and Jimmy Mae had four children and after he healed from his burns we bought him some clothes and took him to the freight yard to catch a train back to Houston. We knew if we bought him a ticket he would cash it in and spend the money for whiskey or bay rum or anything to drink. He blinded a passenger train (rode on the outside between the cars) and left for New Orleans, on the way to Houston. After he left I found a tablet he had been writing in and he had written over and over, "My children are calling another man daddy." Herman fell off the train in New Orleans and was run over by five trains before they found him. Identification was made by his social security number tattooed on one arm. My Mother was making a set of slip covers when the telegram came from the coroner in New Orleans and I read it to her. My Mother was a very unemotional person and she just said, "I'm not surprised." and kept on sewing. His wife refused to come to the funeral and said she was glad he was dead and hoped he went to hell.

Juanita was born in Hope, Arkansas, three years after Herman was born and three years before I was born. She died from Leukemia in Montgomery, Alabama and part of me died with her. I loved Juanita so very much and she was such a wonderful sister and person. I cried at Juanita's funeral, the second time I cried in my life. The only other time I ever cried was when I learned that Charlie, a programmer at Anniston Army Depot, whom I had treated better than any of my four sons, had plotted behind my back and convinced my boss to oust me and give him my job. But that is another story, one much harder to write.

I think maybe when your life is a succession of town after town, school after school, church after church, very short term friendships, an alcoholic parent, living in what people decide is the wrong side of all the towns, often hungry of body, always hungry of soul, seeking the answers to unknown questions, brothers and sisters are very close and seek comfort from one another. Herman was more like a second Father and Juanita and I clung to one another spiritually. If anyone had ever hurt my Sister I would have killed them without even thinking about it. She represented all that was good in life to me. I knew I was weak and subject to temptation but Juanita was the stalwart, the weak yet strong one. I still miss her so much. I have had less desire to live since Juanita died.

When we were in high school Juanita had one more year to go to graduate. My Mother was making five dollars a week making slip covers for H L Kincaid. We rented a one room apartment from Mrs. Kincaid for $3.75 per week and the $1.25 per week left after paying rent was all we had. It became obvious that one of us had to quit school and try to get a job and I decided to quit. Juanita would have no part of that. She told me she planned to get married and her education was not as important and she was quitting and I was going to finish. Mother felt the same way and Juanita quit and went to work in a downtown department store.

Juanita met Harry Simon Berman, Jr. and when Harry went in the Army in World War II Juanita went to Louisiana and they were married there. She stayed with Harry until he went overseas to the China, Burma, India theater of operations. If I had conducted a nation wide search and selected a husband for Juanita, it would have been Harry. Harry was the greatest guy I ever knew and he was more of a brother than a brother-in-law. I loved Harry Berman and when he died I cried for the third time in my life. I always knew that as long as Harry Berman was alive nothing really bad could happen to me as Harry would not allow it. Then suddenly Juanita died, a short time later Harry died and then a short time later my Mother died. Harry understood my inability to handle personal finances and told me he was going to put me in his will and if he had anything left I would get enough to pay my debts and he wanted me to stay current. He never got around to it but I know he intended to. He died unexpectedly after what should have been routine surgery.

Wherever Juanita is now, the angels there have more cause to sing and I know she is happy and the angels there are happy. I miss my sister and the sadness will linger as long as I am here. The sadness is much greater because I realize I have not led the type life necessary to be able to join her. I am the weak one. I will be found lacking on the judgment day. I derive what satisfaction I can from the knowledge she and Harry will be there with my Mother. God bless them both.

Chapter Three

The Smackover Connection

My Grandmother, Lula Bales, lived in Smackover, Arkansas. She had four houses on one large lot. She and my Uncle Bill (William Otto Bales) lived in one of the houses and she rented the other three when she could. My Uncle Bill built all four houses. Bill was primarily a paper hanger but was also a good carpenter and plumber and did concrete and brick work as well.

When my Father got on one of his extended drunks he had usually lost his job by the time he sobered up. He was always penniless and out of a job before he would even attempt to quit drinking and sober up. He would somehow find a way to take the family to Smackover and leave us until he found another job and worked long enough to get enough money to rent a house and come get us.

The problem with being dumped in Smackover was that my Grandmother and Uncle Bill were poor and had enough problems taking care of themselves. Three or four more mouths to feed was a real hardship. Grandma never complained if Daddy left immediately but Uncle Bill complained long and hard and let us know he did not like it. He would get infuriated if my Mother gave me a dime to go to the movie. It was not a short complaint. It went on for days and days. My Mother would try to sneak me a dime so Bill would not know but he always found out one way or another.

Daddy dumped us in Smackover one time and there was just no food and no extra blankets and we were all hungry. My Mother went to the relief agency and they told her she should

**Back: Lura and Loys Bales.
Front: Charles and Jimmy Bales**

Son Bales

not have come from Mississippi to Arkansas and to go back to Mississippi and ask for relief there. We were desperate. My Mother called Washington, D.C. and asked to speak to Franklin Roosevelt and was told he was not available. She got insistent and she says she did talk to him personally. Perhaps it was him or maybe someone in desperation told her he was President Roosevelt. Regardless, a few hours later a station wagon arrived at my Grandmother's house and they unloaded canned vegetables, canned beef, cheese, potatoes and many other grocery items. A little later they came back with blankets, quilts, sheets and clothing. The man who came said it was by direct order of President Roosevelt. My Mother adored President Roosevelt and anyone saying anything bad about old Franklin got cut down by her real quickly.

On one particularly bad trip to Smackover Daddy found my Grandmother had a house vacant and stayed. He decided to open a grocery store in Smackover. Capehart's Grocery was in the next block and there was a vacant lot next to it. Daddy talked the owner into building a grocery store and then rented it and somehow got it stocked - on credit I am sure. The most used form of advertising was to get flyers printed and send small boys all over town delivering them. Daddy waited until Capehart had his flyers printed and then used the same items with lower prices. Mr. Capehart had new flyers printed with lower prices and so did Daddy. The next week the same thing happened and the week after that Mr. Capehart came out with flyers with lower prices and Daddy lowered them even more. Finally Mr. Capehart had really ridiculous prices and many more items on the flyer, so Daddy cut his prices to the bone and showed some items as free. Mr. Capehart did not deliver his flyers and posted Dad's flyers all over the store and if people tried to buy from him he told them to go next door and get it free or almost free. That broke Daddy and he had to close the store. What made it rough for me was that Sonny Capehart was my best friend in Smackover. However, Mr. and Mrs. Capehart treated me like their own son and never had an unkind word to say about Dad.

Smackover, Arkansas

I had other friends in Smackover. Junior Princehouse lived across the street. His father was a doctor and he had a jigsaw puzzle with dinosaurs on it and we put it together so many times we started putting it together with the plain back side showing to make it a little harder. They had a storm house in their back yard that was lined with steel and had food and water stored in it. Everyone else had a storm pit but they all had dirt floors. I was very impressed by such affluence. One day a car ran off the bridge over Smackover Creek and Doctor Princehouse arrived there just as they pulled a woman out of the car. She was covered with oil as a lot of crude oil was dumped in the creek. Doctor Princehouse worked on her more than an hour trying to revive her and finally realized there was no chance. He cleaned her face off and found it was his daughter he had been working on. I was always impressed that he did not continue to try and revive her. It indicated to me that he had given all he had when he thought she was a stranger.

There will always be a soft spot in my heart for

Smackover. The people were kind to a ragged-ass little boy who had nothing more than a burning desire to survive and succeed. I had nothing to give, I was a taker, and they gave to me love and friendship. Maybe it was because this was the only town we ever lived in when I was a kid that we lived on the right side of the tracks, I don't know. I never remember even having a pair of shoes when we were in Smackover. The streets were mostly all dirt and in the summer they were powdery soft layers of pure dust and when an occasional car went by the dust billowed high and took a long time to settle. When it got that bad they would bring in truck after truck of crude oil and finally there would be several inches of it until the car wheels beat it down to an appearance of cheap asphalt. I would run across that crude oil, blazing hot from the sun, until my bare feet were coated with it. When I got home my Grandmother either had a great perception or had been watching for me because when I opened the door all I saw was a hand come out with a pan of soapy water and a rag. She would tell me to sit down and scrub till I got every dab of it off my feet before I came in her house.

Tommy Patterson lived two houses from us and his Dad had an old nehi bottling plant behind their house. It was no longer in operation but it was a very tall structure with all kinds of neat places to climb. We could also pretend we were running a bottling plant. We played in there hours and hours, day after day. The house between his house and my Grandmother's was a cottage usually rented out and one time it was rented to Charles Chapman, a well known bank robber. There was an old trunk outside and we were playing there one day and opened the trunk. It was half full of bullets and shotgun shells. Mr. Chapman came out and told us to get lost and if we told anyone about the trunk he would track us down and slit our throats.

I was told that they were looking for oil in Arkansas and had tried many places with no luck. They had been at that particular site several times but had not tested it. Finally someone did test it and discovered the largest oil field in the world. Someone remarked they had looked all over the state and had been smack over it all the time, so they named it Smackover. I have also heard that this story is not true, that someone just made it up. Smackover is about 12 miles from Eldorado, Arkansas and I have met several people around the world who told me they lived "near Eldorado." I always asked them if they meant in Smackover and they were always astounded I had heard of it, and yes, that was where they were from.

Smackover, Arkansas was somehow a sign of defeat for us as we only went there when there was no other place to go. However, I have many precious memories of Smackover and the kind people there. I remember it now as a more pleasant place than it seemed at the time.

Chapter Four

My Childhood Days

I was born in Pensacola, Florida in an area called Gaulding. I thought I was born April 5, 1922 and celebrated my birthday April 5th until I needed a birth certificate to join the Navy when I was 20 years old. I found there was no record for a Thomas Roy Bowerman anywhere but there was a record for a male child, surname Bowerman, no given name, April 6th, 1922. What a shocker! You know all your life that all great people are born on April 5th and suddenly you have to readjust your thinking. I had a sneaking suspicion all along that April 6th was really the greater day, and I was right of course.

When I was very young we kept moving from town to town. Many of the towns were just repetitions of other towns we lived in, with nothing significant happening. I have selected only the towns where something significant happened. It is also worth mentioning that we moved back to Jackson, Mississippi several times and that we usually went to Smackover, Arkansas between towns. I went to more than a dozen different schools before I got to high school.

My earliest memories begin in Jackson, Mississippi. I can remember almost everything since I was five years old. One of my earliest memories is when I was around five and was sexually abused by a man. I remember telling my Dad about it. Dad went to the police and there was a trial. I had to tell the judge what happened and the man said something while I was talking. He ran up to the judge to say it and the judge reached across and hit him on the head with his gavel. They finally decided he had mental problems and put him in the asylum. I do not remember it ever being a great embarrassment or causing me any problems. Maybe it will show up in later life. After all, I am only 74 as of the time I am writing this.

We lived on South Gallatin Street in Jackson. There was a commissary that Dad was a partner in and our house was next door to it. It was a very large frame house and built like many of the day. The front was fairly close to the ground and as you went back it got higher and higher off the ground and at the very back an adult could walk under it without bending over. The yard was dirt, with no grass at all and one end of the lot had hedges about 12 to 15 feet high. There were several china berry trees and a low wooden fence about the middle of the house on one end running over to the hedges. The back yard was fairly level and there was a garage in the back. The front of the lot was about four feet above street level and the dirt bank was great for digging tunnels and roads for play cars. There was very little traffic on South Gallatin Street.

The house had a large porch all the way across the front and there was a swing on each end and a lot of chairs. Mother had 24 boarders and they sat on the porch a lot at night. There were windows opening on to the porch and you could sit inside behind the curtains and listen without being seen. I sat in there a lot listening to Dad and the boarders talking. Most of these men were alcoholics, many afflicted with what was called Jake leg, said to be caused by drinking vanilla extract. These were truly men with broken dreams and it was amazing to hear the experiences of some of them. One had been a doctor and one had been a lawyer and several had been white collar workers with good jobs and were well educated. It was a liberal education in itself to listen. I thought they might be just telling lies but became convinced that most were telling the truth.

Juanita and I shared a bed when we were very young and later shared a room. Herman stayed with the boarders. They had cots very close together to make the best use of the space available. We had a large radio and Dad would always come home and eat supper, then listen to Amos and Andy, Fibber Magee and Molly and similar programs after he had read the newspaper from front to back. We were not allowed to speak or make any noise while Daddy was reading the paper. Dad just had a second grade education but he had taught himself how to read, write and handle math. Dad was not an ignorant person; he was very intelligent. He was a Mason and belonged to several organizations.

Dad had what was called a carbuncle, on the back of his neck and it gave him a lot of problems. He told the doctor to come by the house and remove it. The doctor came in and I asked if I could watch and Dad said it was okay. Dad pulled the bed out from the wall and sat down on it and leaned back against the low headboard. The doctor opened his bag and got a bottle of whiskey out and gave it to Dad and he drank the entire contents in one long drink. The doctor got behind the bed and shaved Dad's neck and wiped it off with something and started cutting. Blood went everywhere but it did not seem to bother the doctor. He cut really deep into Dad's neck. He finished up and bandaged it and Dad went to work the next day as though nothing had happened. He had an awful scar on his neck the rest of his life but the carbuncle was gone forever and never bothered him any more.

Part of the time in Jackson my Mother cleaned house, washed and ironed clothes, cooked and washed dishes for the family and all the boarders. This was a back breaking job when you consider that we had no washing machine, just large tubs and a rub board. The sheets alone were more than enough for one person. Part of the time my Mother worked at the commissary and a Black lady named Laura did the cooking and house work. Another Black lady named Charlotte helped out. I loved them both. Laura was young and fat and cheerful all the time and Charlotte was much older and thinner. She was my favorite and we talked a lot about almost everything but the difference between whites and blacks. Charlotte would not talk about that but she did tell me once that the black would not rub off on me. She had a son named Feazell and I liked him, too. Feazell told me once that if I was ever black for just one Saturday night I would never want to be white again. I do not want to give the impression I was not prejudiced. I can remember always thinking as a child that I was better than blacks, that they were like a lower form of life. My Mother was also prejudiced but she had a conscience. Bill Harrell was the other partner in the commissary and when a black came in for a single plug of chewing tobacco Bill would often charge them for a box of 12 plugs and make them put their X on the ticket. My Mother would watch for this and the next time they came in she would give them the other 11 plugs and tell them they had paid for it.

    Eugene Graham owned the heading mill. He was a real fat man, weighing somewhere around 400 pounds. He had a daughter named Emma who weighed between two hundred and fifty and three hundred pounds. Mr. Graham had a special car with one large door on one side and extra springs on that side. Bill Harrell was a really nice looking man, trim and well built. He married Emma to get the Graham money. I do not think he thought either of them would live very long. Mr. Graham did die young but he lost all his money in the stock market crash and died a pauper. Dad told me many, many years later that Emma looked like she would live forever.

    Bill Harrell and Dad had a partnership agreement that stated either one could sell to the other at any time for a stated price and if the other would not or could not buy them out then that partner could buy the other out for the same amount. Bill waited until Dad finished one of his binges and had spent everything he had and could not raise a penny and offered to sell out to Dad for five hundred dollars. Dad's half was probably worth ten thousand or more but he could not raise five hundred dollars. Bill gave him five hundred and bought out Dad. Dad had always gone back to Mr. Graham when he sobered up and Mr. Graham would fire him and Dad would tell him he could not fire him, he worked there. Sooner or later Mr. Graham would laugh and tell him to get to work. This time Mr. Graham introduced him to a man named Kellogg and told Dad it was all over, Kellogg was the new foreman. Dad came home and got all the Kellogg cereal out of the pantry and jumped on it and threw it out of the house.

We were never allowed to have Kellogg's in the house after that.

Marion Simmons was my best friend and anywhere you saw one of us you saw us both. In Jackson, Marion and his folks lived across the street from us. Marion had two sisters, Ruth and Bettye, and a younger brother named W.J.. I guess I was always in love with Bettye but she never took me seriously as she considered me to be too much like family. Their mother was Mattie Simmons and their father was Earl Simmons. Earl was much, much older than Mattie. Earl was also the best Christian I ever knew. When he got really frustrated he would say "dad dum it" and then ask forgiveness for that. I never heard him curse. He was very strict with his children. I remember Marion getting a fake cigar once that had some glittering red stuff on the end and Earl went out and got a switch and switched him real good. Marion was yelling it was a fake and pressing it on Earl's arm to prove it but Earl told him it was wrong to have it because it showed you wanted to do it.

The Simmon's made less money than our family and were at poverty level. The Edward's Hotel in Jackson had a big Christmas party for the under privileged every year. They somehow got a really tremendous tree in the lobby and stood it up in the center of a spiral stair case. The children got a good meal, talked to Santa and Santa gave each of them a very nice present. I was not going to be able to go because Dad made too much money and I was really disappointed. Then Dad handed me a ticket and told me to have a good time. I had a great time and remembered it for years as the best party ever. Then Herman told me Dad had told Earl Simmons he would have to give me one of his tickets and Ruth did not get to go. I was really hurt and embarrassed when I found out and I guess Ruth hated me all those years and I was not even aware of it.

Earl Simmons was a man of many talents. He could draw great cartoons, had been in vaudeville and was an electrician, could re-wind motors and many more things. He used to have hooks in the floor and would put on his vaudeville act. He had rings in the heels of his shoes and could fasten them to the floor hooks without you being aware he was doing it and lean any direction almost to the floor. Earl also knew a lot about radio and he dabbled with inventing. He came up with an idea for a slanted radio. All radios had been straight up and down and a pain to stoop down to tune. Earl designed a special cabinet and wrote a cartoon about what he called "No stoop, no squat, no squint" radios. He sent it to Philco with the assumption they would pay him for the idea. A few months later they came out with the model and used his slogan and cartoons to advertise it. After he heard nothing he sent his idea in for a patent and wrote Philco. Philco claimed to him they had the idea in the mill for a long, long time but the patent office told him Philco got a patent a few weeks after Earl mailed them his material. Earl was also a song writer and you still find some of his hymns in church hymnals. Earl wrote a special song to be sung only at his funeral.

When I was about eight years old, my best friend, Marion, was much older. Marion was a full nine years old. We were really close friends. Every evening about eight PM Marion and I headed North on South Gallatin Street to the railroad tracks and then up the tracks into Jackson. The downtown area was maybe 3 or 4 miles from our homes (across the street from one another) depending on how much out of the way we went exploring things. When we got downtown we headed to the Jackson Clarion-Ledger and bought our newspapers for three cents apiece. We had to decide how many we could sell as we had to "eat" the left overs. We then headed to our block assigned to us by the Clarion-Ledger. Marion always sold three or four times as many as his side of the street had a cafe and mine had nothing but the Governor's Mansion. Very few people walked that side of the street but you better believe that if they had a nickel when they hit my block they had a paper when they left it.

We usually sold papers until two or three in the morning or until we sold out (not often) or until some new policeman thought we ought to be at home. If we had a real good night we would go by the all night bakery and buy a sack of day old cookies. We could get a sack the size of a large grocery bag almost full for 25 cents.

We would head for the tracks and work our way back to South Gallatin Street. Sometimes we picked out a track and stuck to it. If there were box cars side lined on it we went up and over and down the other end. Often this included going down into and through gondolas.

We would get home somewhere between three and four AM and sometimes we stayed at my house and sometimes we stayed at Marion's house and at times we just stayed up all night talking. We were at a tender age but our parents never seemed to worry about us. If someone had mentioned drugs we would have thought they were talking about Grove's Chill Tonic or Syrup of Pepsin or maybe Carter's Little Liver Pills.

I remember so much about Jackson. My memory has dulled very little. There was a small house behind the commissary and a childless couple named Sledge lived there. They used to get in terrible fights but if anyone mentioned the noise they always said they were "killing roaches." When other people got into arguments they got to where they said they were killing roaches. Sometimes if you wanted to fight someone you would ask them if they wanted to kill roaches.

Mr. Sledge was really a nice man and he loved children. He took us fishing in the Pearl River a lot of times. I remember one time I went fishing with Mr. Sledge and he decided there was a better spot on the other side. The Pearl was shallow enough to walk across in a lot of places and was very deep in other places but Mr. Sledge knew the river for miles around Jackson. He told me to follow him and we started across and about the time he stepped in a hole up to his chest I went in over my head and the current took me down river. I could not swim then and cannot swim now as I have no flotation at all. I must have been taken half a mile when I hit a stump and grabbed and held on for dear life. Mr. Sledge had been running, crawling and swimming trying to catch me and when I hit the stump he was right behind me. He took me to the bank but fishing was over for the day as all the equipment was gone.

Many, many years later I read an associated press release about two children drowning in the Pearl River and it mentioned Mr. Sledge's name. I called someone in Jackson and found out it was the same Sledge who used to take me fishing. I guess I lucked out. I cannot recall Mr. or Mrs. Sledge ever being employed. I am sure one of them must have been but it seems he was always available when anyone wanted to go fishing. One thing is for sure; he was a nice man and never molested any of us.

The Commissary delivered groceries and also had to pick up meat and other items around Jackson. They had a Studebaker spring wagon and a horse. My brother Herman did most of the delivering and picking up. He would hitch that horse to the wagon and go charging off at a full gallop. The horse hated Herman and bit him on the chest once. Herman picked up something to hit the horse with and before he knew what had happened Dad appeared and took it away from him and hit him with it several times.

I remember also in Jackson that Black people were often arrested for looking at white women "in a lewd manner." Blacks were supposed to look at the ground when they were around white women. When you are raised in these surroundings and under these conditions I think it is impossible to be totally unprejudiced. I know I have some prejudices and maybe more than I realize. I never claim to have Black friends. I am acquainted with several Black people that I like very much and enjoy being with them and talking to them but friendship is more than that and I would not say they are true friends that I share confidences with and support and defend like a friend. I guess I am a bigot to a certain extent. I know I can not deal with inter racial marriages. The thought of a Black guy making love to a white woman turns me off totally but the idea of the reverse does not sound as bad. Yes, I guess I am a bigot, but on the other hand I am not a hypocrite. No, I would not want my Sister married to one. On the other hand, if I was Black I am sure I would be militant and would probably feel whites were inferior. No one would stop me from doing anything a white was allowed to do.

Many things happened in Jackson and when I sit down and concentrate I can remember event after event and even many, many conversations. I just recalled a large sign board on South Gallatin Street, 3 or 4 blocks North of our house. It was very high and had several support cables. Someone had loosened one of the cables and put a short pipe around it and fastened it back but with a lot of slack in it. The pipe had a ring welded to it and a rope tied to the ring and to the top of the sign board. We used to climb up the sign board and take the rope and pull the pipe to the top, then hold on to it and ride down the cable. We had to hit the ground with our feet just right and start running and turn loose or we would slam into the post the cable was fastened to.

There was also an old mill close to our house that had been run by steam engines and belts and pulleys. There was one wheel still in its bearings that must have been ten feet in diameter. We would climb up and put our hands on a rafter that ran above the wheel and work ourselves over until we were above the wheel and drop on it and then start walking to turn the wheel and see how fast we could get it going. Sometimes two of us would get on it facing opposite directions and one walk backwards and one walk frontwards. And sometimes one of us would get thrown off and wind up on the ground hoping we did not get under the wheel. How do kids keep from getting killed doing things like that? I surely do not know.

The one close White friend Herman had in Jackson was eventually Chief of Detectives in Jackson and Herman was eventually an alcoholic and wino. How do things like that happen? I do not know. I do know that Herman would not go to Jackson after he got so bad as he did not want to do anything that would embarrass his friend. Herman was often arrested wherever he was.

There was a small town just outside Jackson and I remember Dad telling about this woman driving through there doing fifty miles an hour or some other outlandish speed for the time. There was a speed breaker at each end of town and she hit that breaker and bounced in the air and made an awful ruckus. The police nabbed her and took her to the Justice of the Peace and he fined her $10, a really big fine in those days. Dad said she handed the Justice a $20 bill and started out and he said, "Hey, wait for your change." Dad said she looked at him and said, "Keep it, I will be coming back through on the way to Jackson in an hour or two and it will save me a stop. "

The only kids I knew in Jackson who ever really physically mistreated Blacks were the Walls brothers. One was named Ralph and I forget the name of the other. They always carried glass milk bottles with them and if they met a Black kid and he did not get off the sidewalk until they passed one of them would break a milk bottle over his head. If one said anything the other would break another bottle over his head and tell him to shut up or he would kick him in the heel where he kept his brain. The Walls boys always said, "If you really want to hurt a Nigger, kick him on the foot ." I suppose the Walls boys eventually became Bubbas.

There was one thing I did for the first time in Jackson that I have never told anyone about because I have felt no one would ever believe me. I did it several times there and also later in Bonita, Louisiana and in Aberdeen, Mississippi. I would lay down on the bed and concentrate on what I called floating. If I could concentrate enough without being distracted by anything I could get my body to raise a foot or so off the bed. I thought at first that I just imagined it or even dreamed it but I know it happened. I often dreamed, and still have the same dream, that I did this and caused my body to move around the room. I cannot remember ever actually moving any direction except vertical but I know that did happen quite a few times. I also know that I have been out in a field and marked a spot to jump from and ran to the spot and jumped and appeared to become almost weightless and jumped as far as fifty feet. I cannot explain this and it sounds so stupidly impossible I have never told anyone about it. About once or twice a month I still dream I am walking and my feet go into the air and I fold my arms and put my hands under my head and move feet first horizontally. It feels real. I do know I was able to distinguish between dreams and the real thing when I was a kid.

Holly Ridge, Louisiana was a totally new and different experience for us. In Jackson my Father had been foreman of the mill and a partner in the operation of the company commissary. Only "the Nigras" had to trade at the Commissary. Whites could trade where they wanted to but if a Black did not trade at the Commissary then he did not have a job with the company any longer. In Holly Ridge we were required to trade at the Commissary, along with the Blacks. My Father never drew a dime while we were in Holly Ridge, just a "balance due" the company store.

Holly Ridge just has to be the smallest town in the world. When we went there, there was a frame hotel with a small post office downstairs, a gas station, a heading mill, a school with grades one through four, and four company houses. The houses were in a row behind the hotel and were identical. The houses were frame, set on stacks of rocks, and had tin roofs. They were not sealed inside and you could see the studs and outside boards from the inside and could look up and see the tin roof. The floors were rough lumber worn smooth from walking and the outside boards had holes you could see through. Herman used to say there were holes big enough to throw a cat through and there were. The floor also had holes. This meant that rats as large as cats could come in freely.

There was no bathroom, just an outdoor toilet supplemented by what were called slop jars for inside use. The only heat was a wood stove in the front room and a wood stove in the kitchen. When the fires went out at night the house rapidly came to the same temperature as outside. We took a bath once a week in a tub beside the wood stove. Several of us would share the same water but since I was youngest I was usually told to bathe first. This had to be the most miserable living conditions. There was no electricity, just kerosene lamps and when you walked in the kitchen with a lamp the walls would be thick with roaches and they would scurry for dark corners. We worked on getting rid of roaches all the time we were there but it seemed to be a hopeless job.

My Mother always got up first and built a fire in both stoves and then cooked breakfast and woke everyone. Everything we had came from the commissary. Daddy would buy a side of bacon and a side of white fatback every week but he was the worker and the meat was for him. We ate gravy made from his meat grease. Dad always insisted on having biscuits every day of the year. They had to be made as there was no such thing as canned biscuits. Herman was working in the mill by this time. He started working full time when he was about fourteen years old. Juanita and I had to ride the school bus, driven by an alcoholic named Smith, about eight or ten miles to Rayville every morning. Mother fixed us a lunch. Juanita's was put in a sack, usually a biscuit or a sandwich, and mine was put in a bucket. I usually had syrup and corn bread and an onion. I loved to have an onion so that I could find Juanita talking to what I referred to as her ritzy friends and sit down with them and open my bucket and drag out the corn bread and syrup and my big onion. Juanita would get mad and tell Mother on me and she would tell me to leave Juanita alone and next day I would just try to get a larger onion. The school bus had long seats from front to back, with storage space underneath and we would raise the seats and see dozens of whiskey bottles. Mr. Smith was usually only slightly inebriated on the morning run but was really on a good toot by afternoon. He left at the precise time, never checking to see if everyone was there. If we were a minute late in the morning we just did not go and if we were a minute late in the afternoon we had to walk home. The bus was in bad condition and the back door had long since been lost and the opening was covered with an old coca cola sign. Some of us kicked the sign off one day and sat down in the doorway with our feet hanging out the back. Mr. Smith grabbed two of us by the hair and banged our heads together so I told Dad about his drinking to get even with him. Dad met the bus the next afternoon and looked under the seats and saw the whiskey bottles. He grabbed Mr. Smith and smelled his breath and drug him off the bus and beat him half to death. He told Mr. Smith he would get a daily report on his condition and he would get another beating every time he had been drinking. It was amazing how fast that alcoholic recovered.

The Simmon's family usually followed Dad wherever he went and they came to Holly Ridge. Marion and I missed the bus one day and Marion said we could just catch a freight train and jump off when it slowed down going through Holly Ridge. We caught the freight train all right but that sucker did not slow down at all going through Holly Ridge. If anything, it speeded up a few miles per hour. It did not slow down enough to get off until it got to Delhi, probably fifteen miles the other side of Holly Ridge. The only phone was in the company office and we called and told them where we were and asked them to tell Mr. Simmons to come get us. Mr. Simmons had an old Nash and came after us but he chewed on us all the way back. The collect call to the Company was billed to Dad and he was not very happy about that.

The only exciting thing that ever happened in Holly Ridge was when the hotel burned. The hotel was a two story frame building with wood as dry as gun powder. Each room had a wood stove for heat and the occupants were all mill workers. Every room was stacked with piles of what was called clippings. Barrel tops are made of wood that has been dried in a kiln. The "joiners" press the boards against drills and drill out holes for pins. The "pinners" drive wooden pegs in the holes and then use a pinning axe to clip the ends of the pins to make a diagonal cut and then hammer the boards together after sticking a strip of flag across the pins. They wind up with a large square board and the turners cut it into a circle. The two ends cut off by the turners are called clippings. Some people called them goose necks. The workers usually took an arm load of clippings to their hotel room every day and most rooms were stacked with them. When the hotel caught on fire it went up like a sky rocket. The only fire protection was a few hoses and these were all used to try to save the company houses. The company houses were all scorched pretty bad but the tin roofs probably saved them. The most exciting thing was to go where the post office had been and look at the melted change. All the pennies, nickels, dimes and quarters were one large chunk of melted metal. People would come for miles around and someone would say, "There she is" and someone else would say, "Yep, shore is." How exciting can one stand it?

This was one place Daddy left without getting drunk. We were there about two years or longer and he still had never received a dime in pay; just an envelope with a little slip of paper that gave a balance forward, net pay, and balance due the company store. He went to the company store and bought all they would let him have and one night we got in the car and drove off without looking back. He took us to Smackover and set out to find something better. The next place he found was Bonita, Louisiana.

There was nothing at Holly Ridge for kids to do. It was not even a wide place in the road. It was Dead End, USA. We did not have electricity or a radio and television had not even been invented. One man owned everything in town. There was not even enough to tempt motorists to slow down, much less stop. It was existence, no more. A few years ago, when I was in my fifties, I drove to Texarkana, Texas and I passed near Holly Ridge and decided to stop and take a look. The gas pumps were still there but the gas station was boarded up. The mill was closed. The four company houses were overgrown with brush and unused. The school was the only thing left that looked operable and it appeared to be closed. The town of Holly Ridge was gone. I thought of my Mother wasting some of her adult life in this God forsaken place and I wanted to cry but I could not. I wondered how my Father could have ever brought my Mother to this place that was not a place. I thought of the rats and roaches and the outdoor toilet and my Mother building fires in below freezing weather in a house that was not even sealed, with a tin roof and holes in the floor and walls. I drove on to Texarkana silently and saddened beyond belief.

Bonita was another wide spot in the road. If you blinked your eyes at the city limits you were apt to drive right on through without ever knowing you had been there. It did have a small downtown with a drug store, grocery store, clothing store and several bars.

We had left what junk we had in Holly Ridge so Dad found a house in the country owned by a little old lady named Mrs. Faith. He rented half of her house and bought all new furniture. The house was not fancy but it was sealed and warm and had no rats or roaches and we thought it was just like Heaven must be, with its inside bath and kitchen with new linoleum on the floor. We were so fortunate. Daddy took me downtown and introduced me to people as his "good son." He asked this one lady to show me the town and where everything was. I did not realize it at the time but she was the town whore. Regardless, she was a really nice lady and loved children and she took me in every building in town and I believe I met everyone that lived there. I met several whores when I was a child and I generally found them to be more generous, more forgiving and more compassionate than the Christians.

Bonita was great only when compared with Holly Ridge. If Holly Ridge had not existed I am sure Bonita would have been a hell hole. It was not too long until the Simmons family arrived in town and that made it some better. Mrs. Faith had a barn behind her house and it had a large loft filled with hay. When it rained we used to go up in the loft and lay on the hay and look up at the cracks in the roof. The roof was shingles and the sun had warped them badly. You could see the sky through the large cracks but when it rained not a drop of water ever came in. We pondered that a lot and discussed it to death and vowed some day to do some research as to why it did not leak, but of course we never did. It seemed we were always vowing to find out answers to things when we grew up but somehow the research never took place.

There was a large tank in the loft at one end of the barn

and we used to wonder what it was for. We decided maybe it was a water tank but there were no pipes running into it or out of it. We were wondering one day if it might be where Mrs. Faith kept all her money. There were two openings in it about three or four feet apart but they had some kind of caps screwed on them. We got one cap off and took turns looking in but could not see anything. We managed to get the other cap off and Marion told this kid with us to look in one hole and he would light a match and stick it in the other one. He did and Marion did and there was a real loud noise and this other kid was sitting there with his hands over his eyes. We pried his hands loose and he was holding one eye in the hand. The tank had once had gasoline in it and there were enough fumes to blow the kids eye out.

That was about the extent of the excitement in Bonita. Juanita and I went to school and Herman worked with Daddy at the mill and my Mother did everything else. The school, like most Louisiana schools of the time, required everyone to go to the auditorium for an hour every morning and sing Stephen Foster songs like 'Camptown Racetrack' and 'I Dream of Jeannie with the Light Brown Hair'. One day no one was singing other than two or three dumb girls and the superintendent of education stood up and asked everyone who was not singing to stand up. I knew everyone would stand up so I jumped up and looked around and there I stood all by myself. He called me to the stage and said okay I was going to sing all by myself. My singing is atrocious but I decided to bluff it out so I started singing all alone with all those kids staring at me. And laughing. And snickering. My voice is horrible. I knew I had to do something or I would be the laughing stock of the school so when the superintendent could stand no more of it and told me to take my seat I told him I had not sung them all yet. I went down on one knee and began another song. He kept telling me that was enough and I started running around the stage singing the next one and then went into another. It was soon obvious to even him that they were now laughing at him so I just kept singing till he escorted me to my seat. Then I started another and he dismissed assembly and I kept singing. Everyone told me I was great.

Daddy went on another binge and went from bar to bar drinking. He would order a drink and pay with a five or ten dollar bill and walk off and leave his change. Herman started following him around picking up the change. Daddy kept drinking and Herman kept getting the change but Daddy remembered it and took it away from him. Daddy got fired and we packed and left. Mrs. Faith told Daddy he never had paid her any rent and threatened to call the police. Dad told her he was giving her all the furniture and she was happy. My Mother told him he had never even paid the first payment on the furniture and he told her the experience would be good for the old lady. Dad took us to Smackover and dumped us and left.

Aberdeen, Mississippi was a thriving metropolis after Holly Ridge and Bonita. It must have had more than five thousand people. I liked Aberdeen and it was in Aberdeen that Herman met Jimmy Mae Cook, whom he later married.

Dad found a house at the edge of town, very close to the City swimming pool. We lived next door to a family named Hagedorn. They had a girl named Obion Hagedorn, a natural blonde, and a boy named Murl but they were closer to Juanita's age. Obion was always a good friend of Juanita but she finally moved to Denver, Colorado and they lost touch with one another. Murl was okay but we were not interested in the same things. Then the Simmons family came to town and Marion and I were back together again.

There always seemed to be a lot to do in Aberdeen. Actually all the rest of the family got there several months before I did. When Dad sent bus money to Smackover there was not enough for everyone and I was left in Smackover. I did not have any shoes and they would not let me go to school in Smackover without shoes. I got to Aberdeen in late February and the school officials told Dad it was too late for me to start as there were less than three months to go and I could never pass. I told Dad I knew I could pass so he went to the school and told them I would be admitted or he would kick butt.

When I got to school all the teachers and the principal were angry with me and made it clear in a meeting that morning that I was wasting time. I was just a skinny little ragged ass kid to them from the wrong side of the tracks. At recess that morning the school bully, Goat Robinson, told me I was a no good bum and he stuck a broom handle between my legs and a crony of his grabbed the other end and they started banging that broom stick up and down, which causes great discomfort to the scrotum and its contents.

Suddenly I was just enraged at the injustice of it all. I find a town I like and some ratty ass kid is going to make it miserable for me. Goat weighed 30 or 40 pounds more than I did and could easily kick my butt but I decided while he was getting a full meal off of me I was going to get a sandwich off of him. I yanked the broom handle away from him and broke it over the head of his crony and then launched myself into Goat. I remember hearing kids screaming that Goat was beating up the new kid and that made me mad and I hit him with everything I had. Several teachers ran up to us and looked at us and then turned around and walked off. I made Goat say Uncle and Calf Rope and several other things and then told him to say Buddy whipped Goat (I was Buddy) or I would kill him. He said it and I told him when he saw me coming he was to go to the other side of the hall or other side of the street or I would whip him again.

Now I am sure that 99 times out of 100, Goat would have kicked me all over the school ground but he tried me when I was really frustrated. I knew that but Goat didn't know it. When I went in the school my teacher took me to the principal's office and there were other teachers there. The principal told me he would never tolerate another fight and I would be expelled if I fought. But then he smiled and said Goat had been picking on kids there for a long time and the teachers had come to pull him off of me. When they saw I was on Goat they left and pretended they did not see it. He then told me they were going to help me make up the school time I had missed. They did, too, and at the end of May, after going to school for just three months, I was promoted two grades, not just one.

As for Goat, he came by my house and told me he wanted to be my friend. I agreed but told him he would stop bullying small kids or I would kick his butt and to my surprise Goat said okay. I found out many years later that when World War II started, Goat was the first in Aberdeen to volunteer and went in the infantry and was one of the first to be killed in action in the Pacific theater.

Dad found another house in Aberdeen and we moved closer into town. It was only three or four blocks from town. Like most houses in those days the electric meter was in the hall just inside the front door. Herman decided to save on the power bill and put jumpers on the electric meter. All you had to do was get two heavy pieces of electrical wire and bend them in a U shape and plug them in the top and bottom of the meter. The power then went around the meter instead of through it. Unfortunately, he forgot to take them off when they came to read the meter. The power company sent a crew the next day to move the meter outside the house where it could be seen from the street. The problem was that when anyone saw a meter on the outside of a house they knew you had been cheating and it was a stigma. He just did it for a lark as he was not paying the bill anyway.

The Tombigbee River was near Aberdeen so Marion and I had more to do. We went down there a lot. We went one day and decided to walk across the railroad trestle to the other side. It was fairly long and we were in the middle when we heard a train coming. There was not time to get to either side and not enough room to take a chance on the train missing us as it passed. We went over the side and held on while the train passed. I think that must have been the longest train in the world and I never knew those trestles shook and vibrated like that when a train went across. I was afraid I was going to lose my grip. We were dangling in the air and just holding on with our hands. It finally got across and my hands felt numb and I was sure I was going to drop into the river. I told Marion I could not get back up and he kept saying I had to and somehow I did and then I just lay there.

Marion said he heard another train and that got me up and running.

Marion and I both had old plain hound dogs. Mine was a female named Dot and Marion's was a male named after the current heavyweight boxing champion. I remember it was Max Baer once and Max lost and he renamed the dog. He did this about three times and then Joe Louis became champ and Marion said he was not going to name his dog after a Negro and just called him Dog after that. The dog was brown and I tried to get him to name him Brown Bomber but he did not go for that.

Aberdeen had artesian water with high iron content. Water pitchers turned brown looking after being used awhile. There was an artesian well on the main street flowing into a horse trough and there were several places in town where places were provided to hitch horses. Aberdeen was not a bad little town at all and we enjoyed living there. Juanita and Mother were both involved in women's Christian groups. Juanita was always involved in religion, but not a fanatic.

Daddy lost his job and was so broke he left us there. Mother had to face the bill collectors and find a way to get something for us to eat. We had absolutely nothing. A man told me if I would go out to his farm he would give me all the turnip greens I could carry. I had a red wagon and Dot and I went out and I loaded up the wagon way above the top. On the way back to town Dot ran out in front of a car and was killed. I put her on top of the turnip greens so I could bury her when I got home. Some joker passed by and slowed down and yelled "Hot dog and turnip greens" and I was really ticked off. When I got home I buried Dot in the back yard and my Mother asked me how I got her home. I told her I put her on top of the turnip greens and she made me throw them away. It was a bad day for me.

We finally got money from Daddy to use for bus tickets to go back to Smackover. I hated to leave Aberdeen.

Chapter Five

Youth

We moved to Smackover, Arkansas from Aberdeen, Mississippi, and then to Tuscaloosa, Alabama when I was junior high school age. We lived in 26 different apartments and houses in Tuscaloosa. That was Dad's answer to the age old question, "Whatcha gonna do when the rent comes due?" We stayed until evicted and then found another place where they did not know us. Most of my life had been tough. Whatever happened though, we knew the love of our Mother would see us through. I always had the utmost faith in my Mother. She was a solid rock in a paper world.

We eventually got to Tuscaloosa, Alabama and after we had been there a month or two my Mother told me that she had found the place she had been looking for and if my Father lost his job here he would leave alone as she was staying in Tuscaloosa. She meant what she said and when Dad left he left alone.

Times were really getting tough about the time we moved to Tuscaloosa but I will cover that later. This is about Tuscaloosa. Tuscaloosa is located in the Western part of Alabama and this was pretty obvious as it seemed at times that half the businesses in Tuscaloosa started with West Alabama, such as West Alabama Cleaners, West Alabama Furniture Company, etc. Tuscaloosa is close to the Mississippi border. It is also located along the Black Warrior River.

Tuscaloosa is the home of the University of Alabama and the Bryce Insane Asylum. Tuscaloosa is named after Indian Chief Tuskaloosa and you frequently see it spelled with a K instead of a C but the C is the correct spelling. Tuscaloosa is home of Stillman College, a predominantly Black college. Tuscaloosa

Tom and Juanita Bowerman

is progressive and tends to do things on a more permanent basis than many cities in Alabama, such as overpasses over railroad tracks instead of the lower cost crossings. Tuscaloosa is a friendly town and Tuscaloosa is a town where people tend to care about other people. Tuscaloosa may well be the greatest city in America.

The Warrior River is primarily the boundary between Tuscaloosa and Northport. Northport is on the low side of the river bank and tends to flood during high water and Tuscaloosa is on the high side of the river bank and tends to be high and dry regardless of the state of the river. Tuscaloosa is Tuscaloosa and there is no other like it. People in Tuscaloosa tend to know why, such as Radio Station WJRD is named after James R Doss and Radio Station WTBC is Tuscaloosa Broadcasting Company, owned by Bert Bank, who was a Japanese prisoner of war in the Bataan Death March.

You may have been able to detect that my Mother was

not the only one crazy about Tuscaloosa. I loved it the minute I saw it. I love it now. I have lived in Anniston in the Eastern part of Alabama, near the Georgia border, for 40 years but I still love Tuscaloosa. I will always love Tuscaloosa.

Tuscaloosa is the home of the foundry in Holt, Tuscaloosa is the home of BF Goodrich Tire Company. Tuscaloosa is the home of Gulf States Paper Company and Bemis Bag Company. Tuscaloosa is the home of many of my remaining high school classmates. Tuscaloosa will always have a special place in my heart. Tuscaloosa is where I was young and Tuscaloosa is where I had dreams of fame and fortune. Tuscaloosa is where I sat under the stars and plotted a course for the future. It is the place I found integrity and said, "Hey, this is for me." Tuscaloosa is where I saw my sister blossom from an awkward girl to a beautiful woman. Tuscaloosa is where I was baptized for the remission of sins at the age of 15. It is the memory of Brother Long and Elder O.J. Henley. Tuscaloosa is where I was prayed for and where I was given brotherly love like I had not known existed, and where I discovered who I was and who I wanted to be. Tuscaloosa is where I learned to cope with the realization that all my dreams would not materialize on earth. Tuscaloosa is where everything my Mother loved remains. Tuscaloosa is where I hoped and dreamed and where I began to make the necessary arrangements for the trip through life. Yes, I will always love Tuscaloosa, but not enough to leave the area where I met and courted and won my wife and where our lovely children were born. I must be satisfied with Tuscaloosa as a memory, like a first love.

Marion Simmons was the only true friend I ever had before we moved to Tuscaloosa. In Tuscaloosa, William Hoggle, Roy Schmarkey, Bill Miller, and L.B. Hughes became very close friends. Champ Lewis, Eugene Barlow and Druid Beavers were also close friends. I loved Brother Long, who baptized me for remission of sins and Brother O.J. Henley, Elder of the Central Church of Christ. I was very close to H. L. Kincaid and Dave Underwood. Sue McLeod, teacher of Boy's Social Problems and

Rubye Gulleye, algebra teacher were also very close friends. I considered Mr. Harry Simon Berman, Sr., Father of my sister's husband to be a dear friend and one of the finest men I ever met.

Dad was foreman of the tight barrel heading mill and Mr. Schmarkey was foreman of the slack barrel heading mill. The Schmarkey's ran a rooming house for college students and we stayed with them awhile when we first moved to Tuscaloosa. That is how I met Roy Schmarkey, who was about my age. Bill Hoggle, Bill Miller and L.B. Hughes were friends of Roy and became my friends.

Roy Schmarkey was slightly heavy but not what you would call fat. Roy chewed tobacco and was crazy about the Warrior River. His Mother would not knowingly let Roy go to the river so Roy invented a club called The Bent Door and always told his Mother we were going to The Bent Door when we left for the river. No one ever asked where I was going so I did not have to lie. It was not that no one cared, it was just that my parents trusted me. In all my life, my parents never asked me where I was going or where I had been. Anyway, I liked Roy and we were life long friends. Roy died in North Carolina a few years ago. Roy knew when he was going to die and did not want his wife to see him die. He drove to a remote area and parked and died. His son found him and knew why he did it. Roy was in the Navy during World War II on the USS Tuscaloosa. His ship was chased all over the North Sea by a German pocket battle ship and Roy was hit in the chest by a fairly large round. He lost several ribs as a result. My ship pulled into Boston once and I was in a bar and looked up and saw Roy Schmarkey walk in. We had a couple of drinks and went to the rest room. I was so glad to see Roy that I hit the wall in front of the urinal with my fist and the entire wall went down, leaving the rest room exposed to the general public. The bartender motioned for me to come over to the bar and I walked over and then turned and ran. I ended up going one direction and Roy a different direction and I did not see him again until after World War II.

William Hoggle lived near Bryce Insane Asylum. His

Father was a male nurse at Bryce. His Mother was a cleanliness freak. When we went in Bill's house we had to take our shoes off and prove our feet were clean. His Mother was always cleaning. She even took the kitchen chairs to the back yard and cleaned them in a large pot of lye water every week or two. She was a nice lady but she hated dirt. Bill was a natural born mechanic and he was on a program during high school that permitted him to go to school in the morning and work as a mechanic at Tuscaloosa Motor Company in the afternoon. Bill was an excellent driver and one of the few drivers I considered good enough to feel comfortable sleeping while he drove. Bill had a small brother named after John Wayne. I trusted Bill totally in any kind of transaction.

Bill Miller lived with his Mother and two of his bachelor uncles in a tent near the Warrior River. Bill's Mother talked to herself and no matter when you went to town you usually saw her on the sidewalk with a shopping bag in her hand walking along talking to herself. She had what appeared to be a tumor in her stomach. Bill was ashamed of his Mother and would walk past her and turn his head the other way as though he had not seen her. I would always stop and chat with her. Everyone called her Aunt Lizzie. Bill would walk on half way down the block and wait while I talked to her. Aunt Lizzie was a little confused but she was really a grand old lady and I enjoyed talking to her. She would finally tell me to go on before Bill got mad. Aunt Lizzie always wore old clothes and Bill wore $200 suits, which would cost a thousand dollars today. Bill had an old radio that had about 50 knobs to tune it with. It was a pain to change stations but it had the best sound I ever heard. You could hear it two miles away on the river but never got any louder as you got closer to it. The tone was beautiful. Bill could usually be found poking around in the trash dump, which was maybe a hundred yards from their tent. Bill got in the National Guard and trained most of the war but finally went to new Guinea. He shot himself in the knee to get home and drew disability pay the rest of his life. Bill died recently. Most of the people I cared most about are dead now.

L.B. Hughes was a horse fanatic and worked at a stable when he was not in school. L.B. and I agreed to get in the Navy on the buddy system where they guaranteed you would stay together. They turned me down because of fallen arches and took L.B.. L.B. was on the Arizona at Pearl Harbor and his body is still somewhere on the Arizona as it was never recovered. If the Navy had taken me at that time I suppose I would be on the Arizona with him now. Many people have forgiven the Japanese. I never have and I never will and no one can tell me the yellow sneaks will ever be any different than they were at Pearl Harbor and during World War II. People do not change for a certain occasion and then change back. They are as treacherous as they ever were.

Roy Schmarkey is dead and L.B. Hughes is dead. Bill Miller died in 1993 according to Bill Hoggle.. Bill Hoggle is alive and well and rather young looking. Bill lives in Northport and runs a junked car lot, buying junk cars and selling parts and crushing and bailing the remains and selling it as scrap metal. Bill and I write one another occasionally. He was the one who told me about Roy's death. Bill attended our 50th Tuscaloosa High School reunion a couple of years ago and said there are less than twenty of us left. I know of two who have died since then.

The Black Warrior River became my home away from home. My friends and I knew the Warrior and its banks like the backs of our hands. I did all my home work during class and when I got out of school in the afternoon I always walked to the river, usually with Roy. We would stop by and get Bill Miller. Bill Hoggle and L.B. were usually working on week days. It was 3 or 4 miles to the river but we thought very little about a walk less than five miles. If we got tired walking we would run awhile. We would check Lock 10 and Lock 11 and sometimes go to Lock 12. We usually had a boat of some kind. After the river had been unusually high we would go up and down looking for boats that had broken loose and tow them home and sell them for a dollar or two.

We got the idea of a motor boat for us and started searching and found a boat that had once had a large motor in it. It was on the bank and had large cracks in the bottom. We sold scrap metal and raised some money and bought it for five dollars. We packed it with oakum and sunk it in the river and let it swell. We sold some more scrap metal and bought a four cylinder Chevrolet engine for it. We raised money for parts and Bill Hoggle rebuilt it. We got the drive shaft and transmission with it. A machinist at the Chevrolet dealer said he would make us a propeller if we got the metal. We were on the river and found a heavy piece of metal. It was an inspection plate on a tug that pushed barges up and down the river. We mounted the engine and ran the drive shaft through the back of the boat and went over the side and under the boat and mounted the propeller. We put a muffler on the engine and cranked it up. We were in business and had one of the fastest boats on the river. We had less than twenty dollars invested in it.

The Black Warrior River. What good times it provided! It was no wonder we always headed there after school and spent most of the week end there. Sometimes we would put our bicycles in the boat and go across the river and ride around on that side. The main problem with that was the woods between the river and the road. I had a very old bicycle with high pressure tires filled with a fluid called "never leak" that someone had given me. It was really worth less than a dollar. Roy had a fine bicycle with balloon tires that his Father gave him. Bill Miller did not have a bicycle and Bill Hoggle had an old one that was in pretty good shape.

We went across the river once to steal some sugar cane and had cut a bunch of it when a man in overalls walked up with a shotgun in his hand. He said he was going to shoot us. James Fincher was with us that day. His Father owned a jewelry store. James had a package of cigarettes and begged the man to take them and let him go but the man said he was going to count to three and then kill us. We took off running and he fired two or three shots but we never knew if he shot in the air or shot at us. We were moving on. James Fincher never went with us again but we found other sugar cane patches and watermelon patches.

We were not just poor, we were dirt poor, the kind of poor that creates an empty feeling in your stomach, the kind of poor that lets you just weigh 122 pounds when you are six feet tall. It was not quite as bad when Dad was there but he soon lost his job and moved on. This time Mother refused to go to Smackover and told him to go his way and not come back. We were living at 1919 7th Street when he left. Not long after he left the creditors started closing in and finally the furniture store said they were sending a truck to get all the furniture. My Mother decided to fire up the wood cook stove and keep it hot so they could not take it. They loaded everything but the cook stove and it was glowing red hot. We were happy we would have a stove but a few minutes later they came back in an open pick up truck. Two men came in with two by fours in their hands. They reached over and knocked the stove pipe off and ran the two by fours under the stove, picked it up and walked out with it. It was still glowing red when they drove off with it.

We had no stove, no beds, no tables, no anything. The house was stripped bare. Herman left and came back with some orange boxes and took down a door and made a table. He got a couple of burlap bags and told me to come with him. We went down to the railroad switch yard and picked up coal along the track. When we had it all, Herman got on top of a coal car and kicked coal off. He said it was piled too high and might fall off and hit someone. When we got home Herman rigged up something so Mother could cook in the fireplace. We went outside and got pine straw and put it down and put quilts and blankets over it. We made some pretty good beds. We got an eviction notice there but stayed as long as we could.

This was when Mother got a job with Mr. Kincaid making slip covers and upholstering. She rented a room from Mrs. Kincaid and we moved there. Herman left us as he was married by this time and had one child. There was not enough room for the three of us in the one room so Mrs. Kincaid said I could use the tower. The house was the old Van de Graf home, built before the Civil War and there was a circular staircase leading up to a small room at the top. This room was almost fully used by the railing for the staircase but there was room to wedge a cot in it. The entire walls were windows and all the glass was broken out. The attic of the two story house had thousands of bats living in it and when they came out many of them flew through my room. I would wake up at times and find bats that had missed a window and fell on my bed. They were really nasty looking little creatures but they would leave you alone if you left them alone. In the winters that it snowed, snow would blow in and pile up on my bed. It was also tough when there was a blowing rain. But it was home and it was mine and school was just a block away and I could hear the first bell and get up and wash and get there in plenty of time. There was no breakfast meal at our house.

Tuscaloosa High School was located on the corner of 13th Street and two blocks from Greensboro Avenue at that time. We lived at 1217 Greensboro Avenue, which is now the site of a motel. The high school was a two story brick structure, with wood floors that were oiled. Everyone was assigned a home room in alphabetical order of last name so I knew the students with names starting with A, B and C better than the other students. This put Willis Bidgood and John Burnum, the brainiest students in the school, in my home room.

There were two algebra teachers, Ruby Gulleye and Grandma Gray. Ruby used a system of helping one another and students that understood it just drilled the ones that did not. She also believed in doing the homework in class in case you got stuck. She would tell us that as soon as everyone understands everything and everyone has their homework finished we will talk about the big ball game coming up. Her students really understood algebra. Grandma Gray's method was to go to the blackboard and work problem after problem that few of the students understood and then give them a pile of homework right before the class was over. Her motto was, "If you don't get it this year, you will get it next year." Cecil Jackson tried to flatter all his teachers to get better grades and he told Grandma Gray one day that she sure looked lovely. She is said to have looked at Cecil and say, "Cecil, I am as ugly as home made sin and you know it and if you don't get it this year you will get it next year." I do not think the students felt Ruby was a pushover, they just felt she was a good teacher and helped them understand something they were really afraid of.

Karl Bruder was the art teacher and art was a two year course. If you took it one year you were required to take it the next year. For some unknown and stupid reason I signed up for art and it developed I was totally devoid of artistic ability. I could not draw a straight line with a ruler and I was sloppy and had no perspective. Karl worked hard with me and at the end of the year he told me I had an F but he would make me a deal — if I would not take art next year he would give me a passing grade this year. I told him it was a required two year course and he said, "Trust me, I have pull with the front office." I think I was the only one at Tuscaloosa High ever allowed to take art one year and get credit for it.

The football coach and Mr. Ebersole taught wood working. The coach had two fingers missing on one hand and that worried me about wood working but he told me he had been hunting and somehow jammed the end of the shotgun in the ground and got mud in it. When he fired, the barrel peeled back and cut the fingers off. I had a hard time in wood working as I did not have money to buy wood. I would have to watch the construction sites and when I spotted something unlocked go back and get it. This meant I was always working on small projects. I had found a block of wood once and put it in the lathe to make a rolling pin. The wood was not very good and it flipped out of the lathe and hit me on the nose. Blood was running everywhere and Mr. Ebersole grabbed my arm and pulled me to the back door. I felt impressed he was concerned and apparently going to take me to the hospital until he opened the door and pushed me outside and slammed and locked the door. I was a block from home and went home and washed my face and put a wet cloth on my nose and went back to school. I asked Mr. Ebersole what happened to him and he said he just did not want blood all over the floor. Real concern, you know.

Sue McLeod was my favorite teacher. She taught Boy's Social Problems and we learned how to cook, wash dishes, set tables, decorate, talk to girls and anything else Sue decided we needed to know. We were required to have a white coat and I had no way to get one. Sue asked me if my Mother sewed and I told her she did and she just happened to have the right amount of material and a pattern. She was sweet to all of us. She was a member of the Business and Professional Women's Club and she made a deal for us to do some work at their club house out in the woods in return for spending a week-end there, and we could each invite a date. Sue personally visited the parents of our dates and assured them she would not sleep the entire week end and keep an eye on us. The girls would be on one side of the hall and the boys on the other side. Well, we made several trips up there cleaning up brush and painting and that sort of thing. Noah Smalley had a Model A Ford with a rumble seat and about ten of us got in it and on it. One time we were on a country road making a curve to the right and the left front wheel just rolled off and went straight toward a side road the WPA was working on. There was a man with a flag in his hand and he kept waving it at that wheel like that was going to stop it. We had so much weight on the back of the car that the hub did not hit the ground. We got a nut off of each of the other wheels and picked up the front end and put the wheel back on.

The week end was a fiasco. The girls were all flirts and there was not one among them that would put out but they sure made Sue think they would and she was really unhappy with us. She finally believed us and forgave us. I did not have any idea I would be using the knowledge I got in that class to cook for 40 boys in a CCC camp a year later. I wrote Sue and told her about it and she sent me some recipes and gave me some tips.

There were many fine teachers in Tuscaloosa High School

and I loved them all. I got a job in one of President Roosevelt's programs sweeping and mopping the cafeteria the first period after lunch and that helped at home a little. I stole a bar of candy one day and that still bothers me, even though I later sent the school a five dollar bill without saying what it was for.

My grades made me eligible for the Honor Society but Mr. Dowling, the superintendent of education, called me in his office and asked me if I could get some new clothes for the ceremony and a suit with black tie for the banquet and I told him I could not. He said he hoped I would understand that he was going to be forced to leave my name off the list. I told him I hoped he understood I did not care if he took a flying leap with his list. That is why I was not a member of the honor society. It has really never bothered me. This is covered in more detail elsewhere.

Our graduation was in May of 1940 at Denny Stadium. We were fortunate in Tuscaloosa to have access to University of Alabama property. Our speaker told us we were the hope of the future and people were waiting on us with open arms. The truth was that the economy was so bad there were already people with a doctoral who were willing to work longer and harder for less than we were and they could not find jobs either. There were no jobs.

Chapter Six

The Civilian Conservation Corps

I had exhausted the job possibilities and was in a blue funk when someone told me about President Roosevelt's Civilian Conservation Corps. I checked it out and found that they were accepting enrollees and I enrolled. In less time than it takes to say Lucky Strike Hit Parade, I was on the way to Fort McClellan in Anniston, Alabama aboard a bus.

I saw several other boys aboard the bus and hazarded a guess they were also enrollees in the CCC. I was right. When we arrived at the bus station in Anniston a loud and tough looking Army Sergeant yelled for the CCC goof-ups to "fall in over here." We fell in and were told to get in the back of a large truck with a canvas top and "to bust our asses doing it." We were driven to Fort McClellan and then to what we later learned to be the "boondocks." Once we were in the boondocks we were told to fall in again and were marched completely across the camp to a supply warehouse. We were told to strip naked and once we were naked we went to a counter and were asked our sizes for pants, shirts, shoes, etc. If we failed to respond fast enough they made up our minds for us. Each item was thrown at our heads, including heavy army shoes. We got one of each and were told we had better keep it clean as we would receive no more until we got to our CCC camp. We were also told we could ship our civilian clothes home if we had the money and could discard them if we did not. All of us had to discard.

We were given a bag to put our extra underwear in (they gave us three sets of that.) We were then given a mattress, a pillow, a blanket and a mattress cover and told to fall in. We were double timed back to the boondocks and assigned to a tent with a wooden floor and rotting canvas. We were told to make

Left: Bartow Browning. Right: Tom Bowerman digging a ditch at Stevens Pass.

up our beds and then told to fall in again. We were double timed all the way across the camp again, this time to a mess hall. We were fed and then told to fall in and double timed back to the boondocks. By this time it was after eleven PM and we were told we had better get to sleep as we would be up at four AM.

It was hard to get to sleep after all the excitement, regardless of how tired we were and most of us talked until two AM. At four AM we woke up with an Army sergeant yelling at the top of his voice to get out of bed, 'your asses belong to me." It was much later that we learned we were not loved by the Army as our pay was $30 per month and a recruit in the Army earned $21 per month. It made no difference that $22 of our $30 went to our parents and we received $8.00.

We were told that we were going to be sent to a CCC camp in the state of Washington, named Camp Icicle. There would be 200 of us and 190 would be new enrollees from Alabama and 10 would be from camps in Mississippi and Tennessee. What they were saying was that the good jobs were taken.

Our job at Fort McClellan would be to help get the troop train ready. I was assigned to help prepare the kitchen car. They were taking a mail car and converting it to a kitchen. The main job was to install a stove that would not set the car on fire. I was assigned to the mud unit. Four of us were to take tubs to this giant mudhole and fill them with mud and take them to the kitchen car. I do not know how much mud they used to build that stove unit but it was a lot of it. We were cautioned to be careful as the uniform we had on was the only one we would have until we got to Camp Icicle.

    I was as careful as I could be but hauling mud is not your typical white collar job. On the second day I was leaning out as far as I could to scoop up mud with a large tin can when my fellow hauler told me to reach out a little further and gave a little push to show me what he meant. I went belly down in the mud hole and came up totally saturated with that red mud. I was tempted to give him a dose of the same mud but the fact that I weighed 122 pounds and that old country boy weighed around 200 changed my mind. The sergeant in charge of the stove told me not to rub it, just let it dry. I followed his advice and a lot of it flaked off when it got dry but the stain was there to stay.

    All good things must come to an end and the train was finally ready. We kept our cup and mess kit and knife, fork and spoon and everything else was put in our bags, tagged and loaded in the baggage car. We were assigned to cars and to a seat and the five day trip began. We were all twenty years old or younger and none of us had ever been away from home and we were being sent from the Southeast to the Northwest. It was to be a two year experience I would never forget.

    When they called us for our first meal we grabbed our cups and mess kits and made a wild dash to be the first in line. The problem was that we were sent through the kitchen to the other end of the train and then the line was turned around to go back through the kitchen to be served. This way, we were headed back to our seats to eat. The last in line was the first served. The next time they called us everyone tried to be last and they served the first in line first and had them walk around the serving line and head back to the seats. This was pretty smart on their part since you never knew which end of the line would be served first and you may as well just be orderly about it. After you ate you had to go back to the kitchen car where they had three large barrels of water. You dipped your cup, mess kit and "silver" in the first barrel, filled with soapy water and then in two more with rinse water. This was supposed to be sanitary but from the food floating around in all the barrels it looked like a far cry from it.

There were three boys assigned to each double seat section and two had to sleep in the lower berth and one in the upper berth. There were a lot of arguments about who could have the upper by themselves but it was finally resolved by rotating. The trip was supposed to take five days but we were told it was almost certain that it would take six days so each of us would get the upper berth two nights. It turned out that it did take six nights and we arrived on the morning of the seventh day.

Almost no one had any money and we were without cigarettes or any other item that may have made life a little more bearable. Most of us did enjoy the scenery and when we stopped at a station there seemed to always be girls there to talk to. Most of them thought we were in the Army and we did nothing to discourage them. We even got names and addresses and promised to write to them. We did not realize at the time how hard it was going to be to get three cents for a stamp. Our eight dollars a month and room and board sounded big. There never seemed to be enough water on the train and by the time we were half way there the uniforms were so badly soiled from the cinders and soot from the coal burning engine that I was no longer the dirtiest one on the train.

All good things must end. It had seemed like it never would when the train was winding its way through the Rockies and we could see mountain peaks above us and rivers in deeply cut canyons far below us, but it did and on the morning of the seventh day we steamed into the beautiful little town of

Buck Lee and me. Camp Icicle

Leavenworth, Washington. There were hundreds of people on hand to meet us and we immediately gained a good impression of Leavenworth. Later we learned that the people of Leavenworth had heard a rumor that 200 Blacks were coming in from the South and they were there to protest us instead of make us welcome. Someone did have the presence of mind to make a welcome speech and then we got our bags and climbed aboard trucks and started the three mile trip to Camp Icicle. It was beautiful country with apple orchards, a creek (crick as they called it) and the mountains rising all around us.

It took only a few minutes to get to Camp Icicle. There was a wooden arch with Camp Icicle burned into the wood in large letters. There was a flag pole just inside the arch, with a circle of white painted rocks around it. The Headquarters building was to our right as we went in. The front contained a counter and behind that were a couple of desks. There was an alcove on the right beyond that, serving as the office of the Company Commander. On the left there was a short hall and then an alcove off of the hall that had two cots for the Company Clerk and the Supply Sergeant. A door at the end of the hall led into the supply room and beyond the supply room was a recreational hall with a canteen at one end.

Beyond the Company Headquarters was the office of the Project Superintendent for the Forestry Service and then vehicle storage and maintenance buildings and a blacksmith shop. Across the street from the Company Headquarters there were two barracks, then a boiler room, two more barracks and a laundry. The mess hall was behind the barracks and beyond that was the officers club and quarters. It is hard to believe how beautiful the camp was, nestled against a mountain and almost surrounded by mountains. Most of the water was in the form of melted snow and a small stream winding its way down the mountain. I had never seen a place as beautiful before and have not seen one more beautiful since. I fell in love with Camp Icicle. I had enrolled for six months and was eligible to stay as long as two years and I knew that first day that I would be in Washington two years.

We were assigned to barracks and to a specific bunk and then went to the supply room. The Supply Sergeant was named Minton, he was from Tennessee, he was mean as hell and he was an Indian. You walked up to the counter and he looked at you and decided what size you wore and started throwing it on the counter. You checked to see that you had everything, signed for it and got the hell out of his way or he would pick up your junk and throw it through the door. If you wore a size 14 shirt and he gave you a size 16 or if you wore 28-32 pants and he gave you

36-30, my advice would be to wear it and not complain until the Company Commander noticed it and took you to the supply room to exchange it. If the Company Commander said nothing you would be well advised to say the same thing.

The clothes they gave us were outdated Army clothes. The pants looked like the fuzzy Army blankets and even the shoes had fuzz on them. We had one boy who knew how to put lighter fluid on the shoes and burn the fuzz off and then shine them to a high finish. He charged a quarter and he got rich. There was not much to do about the pants other than try to save enough money for a pint of whiskey for Minton and then he would issue you nice looking pants that fit. The shirts looked all right. We had the fuzzy pants for winter and khakis for the summer.

The next day we went back to the supply room and were issued spike bottomed boots for fire fighting. We were then allowed to go to the canteen and sign for up to four coupon books. A coupon book had twenty five cent coupons good for trade at the canteen. The canteen steward would also give you seventy five cents in cash for a coupon book but we were sworn not to tell the Company Commander as what he was doing was giving you seventy five cents and putting the other twenty five cents in his pocket and it was not legal. Anyway, we bought tobacco and then went to a field to put on our spiked boots and get fire fighting training. I eased out my new can of Prince Albert and rolled a cigarette and someone yelled that I had tobacco. I quickly hid the papers and said I was sorry but I had no more papers. They started tearing the tissue that was in the boot boxes and I foolishly let someone have the can. The next time I saw it, it was not only empty but someone had already taken a knife and scratched letters out on the back of the can so it read "Pa covered Ma .... " etc. I learned two quick lessons. One was to buy a sack of RJR instead of a can of Prince Albert and the other was to get a buddy to spread the rumor that you were a nut and peed on your tobacco to keep it moist.

The fire fighting training was just in time as we were called out to fight a tremendous forest fire the next day. I had never seen anything like that, either. We had about two hours training but were put on the line like we were professionals. We gave a good account of ourselves, too. We had all been in the woods and had seen and used most of the equipment. We knew how to use an axe, a saw, a rake, etc. The boys at Camp Icicle before us were from New Jersey and most had never been off the pavement. I was so tired after two days without sleep that I found a hay stack and crawled in out of sight and went to sleep. The wind started and they had to pull back and if one of the boys had not seen me get in the hay stack that might have been the end of me.

Our very first fire burned five days before we got it under control. It was good to get back to camp. They fed us a hot meal and let us sleep eight hours before they got us up. It was time to make selections for permanent jobs. There were not more than four of us with high school educations and most of the boys had third grade or less. William Hanks had already clinched the best job in Camp - Company Clerk. Charles Henry Brucke (I later married his sister) was selected by Minton as assistant supply sergeant. Another boy was assistant to the educational advisor. The other top jobs were filled with Minton and others that had come from existing companies in Tennessee and Mississippi. That left me as the only high school graduate without a special assignment and they had read my resume and noticed I knew how to cook. There would be two side camps several miles from the main camp and I was selected as cook for the Stevens Pass side camp, 36 miles up in the mountains. Stevens pass was the top of a mountain pass and there were peaks above it. The CCC was going to build a ski lodge and ski run there. The other side camp was at Chatter Creek, which I never visited.

One thing you could always count on in the CCC and that is that nothing would ever be easy for you. The 40 of us selected to move to Stevens Pass had to load portable buildings on trucks. There was a mess hall, a bath room and two barracks buildings. Some of the roof sections weighed over three hundred pounds and we loaded everything manually. We set out for

Stevens Pass with the trucks loaded with the buildings, one dump truck and one stake body truck. When we arrived we started clearing the area and then started setting up the buildings. We set up a barracks that afternoon and slept in it that night. It only took about three or four days to get everything up and working, including the flag pole and the generator. Our foremen worked for the Forestry Service but had special skills, primarily carpenters, rock masons and ski experts. Our rock mason was a world ski champion from Norway. We were to learn later that he could pick up rocks that three of us could not handle.

Stevens Pass was as beautiful as Camp Icicle in its own way. There were chipmunks everywhere and they would come up and eat out of your hand. There was all kinds of wild life in the area, including bears. We did not try feeding them but one did keep breaking in our cooler. We had a shed behind the mess hall that was completely screened in. It had heavy burlap all the way over it, held out about three or four inches from the top and the screened sides. A water pipe with holes in it ran across the top and water continuously dripped on the burlap and ran down it on each side. This was supposed to make it cool from evaporation of the water and it worked. A bear kept tearing the screen open and getting meat. The chief foreman decided to sit up and wait for it one night and the bear came as usual. The foreman had a forty-five caliber pistol and killed the bear. I thought he was extremely lucky not to get killed or badly injured.

There was also an assistant cook and two Kitchen Police. Each cook and one kitchen police (KP) would work three days and then the other two would work three days. This meant that Bartow Browning (my KP) and I were off from work three full days at a time. We could sleep, climb mountains, or do whatever we wanted to do. There was a bar and dance hall at the top of Stevens Pass, across the highway from the camp. The owner planned to enlarge the building and asked Bartow and I to work for him. The main thing he needed right away was some rocks hauled in to fill in behind the present building. He told me to take the dump truck down the mountain and start hauling in rocks. I told him I did not know how to drive a truck and he told me I had long legs and would do just fine. He showed me the gears and said to just remember to go down the mountain in the same gear I would have to use to come up. I had no idea what he was talking about and he said he would send his father with me the first trip. I started down that steep mountain and before I knew it the truck was going much too fast and the brakes were doing no good. The old man kept yelling to shift it down so I threw in the clutch and pulled it out of high. It started really rolling then and I could not get it in a lower gear. The truck did not have a synchro mesh transmission and you were supposed to double clutch it but I did not even know what that meant. Somehow I managed to slam it in low gear and we almost hit the windshield. There was a horse shoe curve coming up and a drop off of several hundred feet on the outside of the curve. We managed to scream around that curve and the truck started slowing down. I made it to our turn off where we were to load rocks. It was a one lane road and another truck was coming out. I tried to pull over and the truck slid over the edge of the road. We were at a sixty degree angle and I could look through the passenger window and see nothing but space for several hundred feet. The old man clawed himself across me and went out my window and up on the road. He said he was going and tell his son I was crazy. I told him to tell his son to get down there.

    When the boss got there he looked at the truck and asked me how the hell I kept from going over. He said he wanted me to get in the truck and start the engine and put it in low gear and gun it and turn the wheels to the left. I told him I thought it would go over the side of the mountain so he tied a rope around my waist and said if anything like that happened he would pull me out. I got in and started it up and felt it sliding so I gunned it and it slid along the road for awhile and finally when I thought it was going over the back wheels caught on something and it went back on the road. I looked down and the rope was laying on the floor board. I asked the boss how the rope got inside and he said he had thrown it in when I got in as he did not want me sending for him every time I got in a little trouble. He got in his truck and left. When I got back and unloaded the rocks I went over to the camp and got Slim Hicks, one of our truck drivers, to teach me how to double clutch.

There was always plenty to do at Stevens Pass. About a dozen of the 40 boys had either a guitar or mandolin or fiddle and there was some real talent. Ezra Lee (Buck) was a great guitar player and pretty fair singer. Travis Lay was the best fiddle player I have ever heard. He could play anything he had heard once and could play it in the traditional position or behind his back or just about any position. He also sang. The gang could get together a group of almost any size and play about any type music you wanted to hear.

The Rangers would set up check points on the highway and we used to watch them stop cars and check the hunters. One guy had really slaughtered his deer and had it in the trunk. The rangers laid it all out and there were five legs. They asked the hunter to explain it and he said "This crazy deer really had five legs and it was running on the front three with the back two in the air." He was ticketed and would get a chance to try that one on a judge. They casually asked another hunter, "Where did you put your Blue Grouse?" and without thinking, he said they were under the back seat. They were, five of them, and a $5 fine for each Blue Grouse in those days was a fabulous fine. Most of the hunters were honest and had their deer fastened to a front fender and no out of season game.

We could pick blue berries and sell them for something like fifty cents per gallon but it took several hours to pick a gallon of blue berries. Some people made blue berry pickers, a box like contraption with wires extending out. The berries could be scooped with it much faster but it was illegal due to the damage it did to the blue berry bushes. I picked several gallons of blue berries and sold them but it just took too long and the pay was too low.

We had one crew working on the ski run and one crew building the ski lodge. The lodge was going to be fabulous with a tremendous fireplace at one end. The fireplace and chimney were being built by a rock mason and several of the boys. The boys were supposed to mix the mortar and carry the rocks to the rock mason. Some of the rocks were so large it took three boys to carry it. They would set it down and the rock mason would pick it up like it was a giant marshmallow. I was watching one day and three boys could not pick up a rock. The rock mason came down and pushed them out of the way with one arm and squatted, grunted a couple of times, and walked up the ramp with it like it was something he carried around all the time. The fireplace turned out great and you could burn huge logs in it.

It began to turn cold and I would get up in the mornings and grab my clothes and run for the kitchen, build a fire in the cook stove and dress as it warmed up. One morning I grabbed my clothes and ran out naked into almost three feet of snow. We never saw the ground again that winter. As it happened, all of the boys were working inside the ski lodge at that time. I guess everyone assumed we would be doing nothing but inside work. We were short on wood for the barrack stoves and I was off duty one day so the foreman asked me if I would take a truck and trailer into Leavenworth and get a load of press-to-logs. These logs were manufactured from sawdust and oil under pressure and one of them weighed 15 or 20 pounds. I went to Leavenworth and they showed me a box car and told me the entire load was for Stevens Pass and to take whatever I could haul. I backed up to the freight car and loaded the trailer about six feet high with press-to-logs. I started back and got past the first hair pin turn and the truck would not go any further, even in the lowest gear. I was over loaded. I had to back that truck down the mountain (one hell of a job) and turn around and go back and unload more than half of the load. I still barely made it.

The cook also had the job of turning the generator off at night, waiting for the engine to cool, and covering the generator with a tarpaulin. The next morning the cook had to uncover the generator and start it up. One morning it was so cold and the snow was blowing so hard I just reached under the tarpaulin and started the generator and made a mental note to come out after breakfast and take the tarpaulin off. Right!! I forgot. That afternoon the lights were getting super bright and then getting real dim. They finally went out completely and when they did, I thought "Tarpaulin!" I was right. It got so hot under that tarp that the engine burned up. That meant no lights and no power tools at the lodge construction until the generator was fixed. The mechanic that came to fix it estimated a week or ten days or longer if he had problems finding parts. I was the most unpopular person in the camp and was called many names I had not heard before and many that I had. It was more than two weeks before it was restored to service.

When I arrived at Stevens Pass I weighed 122 pounds and was six feet tall. I ate everything I wanted and frequently added a pint of milk to six raw eggs and beat it and drank it. I also worked across the highway and climbed mountains and went on 15 or 20 mile hikes. At the end of six months I weighed 214 pounds and there was not an ounce of fat on me. I had grown up. People even talked to me differently than they did when I first got to the camp. I even heard respect now and then.

No matter how good you are you can almost always find someone a little better. One day the truck came back from main camp and there was a boy named Basil Brown with the driver. The foreman told me Basil would be the new head cook and I would be the assistant cook. I objected and he said, "Look, you guys settle it and let me know which is which." I looked at Basil and he weighed about 175 and was about six foot two inches tall. He said he was from Arizona. I said, "Want to go outside and settle this once and for all?" and he said, "Yep." So we went outside and I bruised my knuckles on his jaw and he proceeded to just literally stomp hell out of me. I got up and looked at him and said, "Lets go inside where it ain't so bloody, boss." So he was head cook and got $45.00 per month instead of $30.00 and I dropped down from a $45.00 a month Leader to a $36.00 a month assistant leader.

The foremen were mostly Norwegian and they loved

strong coffee and were always complaining about my coffee. We put a big coffee pot on the wood stove and put coffee in the bottom and when it came to a boil we set it on a cooler part of the stove and poured a little cold water in to cause the grounds to settle to the bottom. I made three pots of coffee with one pound of ground coffee. One morning I decided to teach this one foreman a lesson and dumped in two pounds of coffee. There were about two or three cups when it finished. The foreman came in and I poured him a cup. He took a big slug and looked real surprised and said, "Now, that's coffee!" He drank it all. Some people. We got paid every month in silver dollars. We would sweat it all month waiting for that pay so we could get tobacco or even a coke. We were always broke from the fifth of the month to the end of the month. The bar and dance hall across the highway had slot machines ranging from five cents to a silver dollar machine. Several times, two or three of us would pool every silver dollar we had and go over to break their bank. We would stand there and pull that stupid handle till every dollar was gone and then say something like, "Oh well, easy come, easy go." One month we played every dollar we had without a single hit.

One morning the foreman announced that the ski run crew would resume work on the ski run and the lodge crew would cut firewood for the lodge. Everyone looked at him and someone finally said, "It is snowing and they don't work in the snow where I come from." The foreman replied that he was not where he came from and in Washington you did work in the snow. He responded that he would just go back where he came from and then nearly everyone chimed in. The upshot was that twenty five boys were not going to work, including me, and he told us to get out of his camp and told the head cook not to feed us anymore. We gathered up the few personal things we had and started a 36 mile hike down a snow and ice covered mountain to the main camp. We were frozen stiff when we got there.

The Company Commander called each boy in and tried to talk him into going back to work. Each one refused. When he got to me, he asked my job and I told him I was a cook. He said,

"You do not have to work in the snow." I told him I knew it but I was not going to cook for anyone who had to work in the snow. He told me to listen closely as he was going to say something one time and said something like this, "Tom, you are one of four people here who have a high school education. You are supposed to be smarter than these kids with an average education of 3rd grade. If you leave today you have to hitch hike three thousand miles home and when you get there you will receive a bad conduct discharge that will follow you the rest of your life. That discharge is an alert to everyone that comes in contact with you that you do not have the guts to do a job. Now you can stay here in main camp and get the dirtiest jobs we can find for you or you can tuck your sniveling tail between your legs and get the hell out of here. You have 15 seconds to give me an answer and there are no second chances. What the hell are you going to do?" I looked at him and said, "I am going to do the dirtiest damn jobs you can find and do them better than anyone else you got can do them." I have never regretted that answer.

The other twenty four were taken to the mess hall by the Company Commander. The Company Commander told them he was required by regulations to give each of them $5.00 in "cash or kind." He told the mess sergeant to give each boy a gunny sack with five dollars worth of dried beans in it. The boys all left camp with a gunny sack of beans on their shoulders. Several had a guitar on the other shoulder. If I had heard the saying, "There but for the grace of God go I", I would have thought it as I saw them straggle out of camp. I loved those boys but I know I made the right decision. My days at Stevens Pass were over. There were some hard days to come.

The Company Commander lost no time in finding me a dirty job. He sent for me the next morning and Joe Guiberson, Project Superintendent for the Forestry Service was there. He introduced me to Joe and told me Joe would assign my work. Joe took me a couple of hundred yards past headquarters and pointed at a snow bank and said he wanted that barracks set up right over there. I did not see a barracks and asked him where it was. He said it was under about four feet of snow. I got a snow shovel and started shoveling snow and worked at it all day. I had almost half of it uncovered and thought I was making good progress. The next morning it was all covered with snow again. I started shoveling and by dark I had more than half of it uncovered. The next morning I started at daylight. It was all covered with snow again. That day I got it all uncovered. I started at daylight again the next day and had it all uncovered a couple of hours before dark. I used the extra time I had left to stand some of it on its side. The next day it did not take as long to dig it out of the new snow and I had time to get some ground supports ready.

    The next morning I found the floor sections and they must have weighed two hundred pounds per section. I got a two by four and managed to move one over and get it up on the ground supports. It was heavy and I was in a lot of pain but I was determined to do it somehow. I learned a lot about leverage. The following day was Sunday and we were off but I started at daylight and got all the floor sections up and bolted together. Monday, I checked the wall sections and they did not weigh much more than a hundred pounds per section. I had to put a wall section on the floor and get a two by four ready. I would stand the section up and nail a two by four to it, line up the bolt holes and work the bolts in and tighten them up. I kept repeating this and the next day I had the walls up and all bolted together. I was ready to start the hard part, putting on the roof sections.

    I found the roof sections weighed around 300 pounds each and there was one of me. I spent a full day just looking and planning. I got some heavy wood and ran it from the top of the wall to the ground. I managed to get a roof section moved over in front of the timbers I had nailed in. I got a two by four and got it started on the timbers and it was not too bad getting the roof section up on the timbers. The hard job was going to be moving it to the top of the roof. I moved one side up three or four inches and drove nails behind it to keep it from slipping back, then did the same on the other side. I kept inching it up two or three inches, one side at a time. Eventually I got a roof section in place and bolted it.

I continued a section at a time and finally got the roof on. The rest was easy, hanging doors and putting in the windows. It was not as level as it was supposed to be and I got some jacks and jacked it up where it was low and adjusted the floor supports. I finally had an assembled barracks. I asked Mr. Guiberson to check it and he pointed out a low spot. I fixed it and again asked him to check it. He said it was fine and I asked him what he wanted me to do next. He said he had changed his mind and did not need the barracks and I should take it down and put it back where it was. The next day I started taking it apart and eventually put it back where it was and shoveled snow over it and cleaned up the area.

The next day I went to Mr. Guiberson for an assignment and he assigned me to Blacky's crew. Blacky (a White man) had a reputation for being rough to work for. It was well deserved. We left Camp Icicle after breakfast in the back of an open truck with snow coming down as hard as I ever saw it. Our crew was building Mountain Home road, up and across a mountain. You could not see the road for snow and every few feet the truck would start sliding off the road (if one was there) and we had to get out and push the truck back on the road. It was lunch time when we got to the work site and Blacky said we would work thirty minutes and eat lunch. We were trimming limbs off trees that had been cut down in the summer, and then sawing the tree into logs and splitting them for firewood. We got some work done in the thirty minutes because Blacky was on us continually. We then ate lunch and Blacky said we would work another thirty minutes. We did the same thing as before lunch and then Blacky counted all the tools and we started back to Camp Icicle.

We continued day after day. Some days we would work one hour, some days two hours, and if we were lucky getting there we would work as long as three hours. One day I was told to saw a tree into logs, working with another boy, using a cross cut saw. When we finished we started at the top splitting it into firewood and got all the logs split, using malls and wedges. We were at the stump and playfully I sunk a wedge all the way into the stump. When we were ready to go, Blacky counted all the tools and went over and sat on a stump and lit his pipe. He sat there saying nothing until someone asked him what we were waiting on. He said," wedge missing," and just sat there. Everyone kept looking at me and I finally went over and said, "Mr Glanert the wedge is in that stump over there. He said, "Get it." Several of the boys jumped off the truck and a couple of them grabbed a saw. He told them to get back on the truck, that smarty pants would do it. That was me. I asked about someone taking the other end of the saw and he told me to take them both. It is extremely tough for one man to handle a cross cut saw but I did it and cut the top off that stump and then got the wedge out and took it to Blacky.

  The crew was cold and miserable and I learned a lot of things on the way back to camp. The next day we were back on Mountain Home and I was a model worker. We finished cutting and burned all the brush and then went to work on the road. I was assigned as a front end man for a bulldozer. A front end man is the guy that digs out rocks by hand that the bulldozer cannot handle. It is a hard job. You dig around the lower side of that rock until it is exposed and then move it out of the way. It is back breaking work. On days now and then that were so bad Blacky could not get us to Mountain Home and back he would take us to the Ranger Station and we would lovingly clean tools and then dip them into hot melted wax. Blacky loved tools more than any man I ever knew.

  I was called in by Joe Guiberson one day and taken off Blacky's crew and assigned to a crew building a ski jump in Leavenworth. I was assigned to help make the ski lift, which was nothing more than an engine at the bottom and a pulley at the top, with a looped rope between them. The skiers just held on to the rope and were pulled to the top. The hard part was that there were logs for the rope to drag on and we had to cut birch trees and skin all the bark off with axes and cut the logs to the right length. It was snowing so hard we could hardly see one another. Our hats would pile up with snow. I had already reached the point that I would rather work in the snow than inside. I could stand as much cold as anyone, I thought.

Although we had a boiler, the hot water was just for the mess hall and the laundry. The barracks had no hot water. We had picked up five or six boys from Washington state after the boys from Stevens Pass left. One of them challenged me to a cold water duel, in which we turned the showers on full blast and each of us stood directly under a shower naked and the first to get out lost. The water was really ice cold and I gradually turned blue. I think I stood there an hour and forty five minutes before a friend talked me into quitting. I dried off and grabbed a blanket. The other boy stayed about ten or fifteen minutes longer and then told someone to pitch him a bar of soap as he may as well take a real shower while he was there.

The Company Commander called me in one day and said he wanted me to run the camp laundry. The laundry was the most lucrative job in camp. You had to wash all the blankets and uniforms as part of your job but if anyone wanted civilian clothes washed and pressed they had to pay you for it. The laundry attendant always had money. I took the job and started immediately. There was a huge washer and you threw in a full load and added soap. When it finished you ran them through a wringer and then took them to the attic and hung them on wire lines. They would dry in a little more than an hour because it was so hot there. While the clothes were washing you had to run outside and put wood in a small boiler that made steam for the presser. Then you ran back in and pressed awhile. If the steam began to get discolored you had to run out and open a drain valve for a couple of minutes. Then you went to the attic and brought clothes down and took more wet ones up to hang to dry. It was constantly running from a warm room to outside in the snow and back inside and then upstairs to the 125 degree temperature in the attic. I was making some money but I got sick doing it and had to stay in bed about two weeks. When I got ready to go back to work I was told to see the Company Commander.

The Company Commander told me he had to give the laundry job to someone else. I was disappointed but told him I understood. Minton, our first Supply Sergeant, had left after six months and Charles Brucke became Supply Sergeant. The Company Commander said then that Brucke was leaving and I was the new Supply Sergeant. I had been reduced to an enrollee when I quit cooking and the Supply Sergeant job was a full Leader position. I took the job on the spot and worked with Charles until he left. Charles told me there were many shortages, such as several hundred sheets, a lot of blankets, pillow cases, mattresses, etc. I signed for everything as the Company Commander was responsible anyway. I did a complete inventory and made a list of the shortages. I had to go to Olympia, Washington once a month for supplies and to turn in worn out items. I started taking someone with me and while they were turning in worn out sheets and blankets I would go in the warehouse and take stuff to the other side and put it on the ramp. When we left we would circle the building and one of us would grab the stuff on the ramp and throw it in the truck. The stacks of sheets and blankets and similar items had a red stripe painted down the side. We just refolded it all and turned them in the next trip. Soon I had surpluses instead of shortages and could call other camps and arrange to swap items we had a surplus of for items we were short. And before long we were not short anything.

There were a lot of personal activities at the camp that I have not mentioned. There was a dance every Saturday night in the recreational hall. Many of the boys had girl friends in town and a lot of girls and their parents came without dates. Square dancing was very popular in that part of Washington and you would see dancers as young as five or six years old and many well into their seventies if not older. The camp was a popular place. One of my friends, Zories Adron Trotter, married a Washington girl. There was also ice skating on the crick. Many of us borrowed skates. I never could roller skate but ice skating was very easy to learn. One of the boys fell while ice skating and after the fall Ezra Lee was the only one he ever recognized. Ezra (Buck) and he were from the same area in Alabama and when this boy came to he knew Buck immediately but never did recognize any of the rest of us. He would follow Buck around like a little puppy and if he lost sight of him he would get very disturbed and we would have to find Buck for him. Buck would hold his hand awhile and he would calm down. Buck tried to always be there when he woke up in the morning. They never did send the boy to a doctor, but based on my experience he was as well off.

    Speaking of my experience, I had to see the doctor three times. I mentioned one time when I got sick while running the laundry. The first time was when we first got to Icicle, not long after the forest fire. We decided to do some boxing. I still weighed 122 pounds and there was no one close to my size who would box. Heaton, who was selected as the camp blacksmith, weighed 260 non-fat pounds and there was no one his size. Heaton asked me to just spar with him and said he would not hurt me. I took him up on it and we put on the gloves. He started making me look like a fool and when I saw a chance I hit him as hard as I could in the chin. He had just stuck his tongue out at me and when I hit him he bit his tongue real hard and it bled. He had told me at the beginning to hit him any time I could and he would not get mad. He did get mad and swung as hard as he could and hit me on the side of the head. He knocked me across four bunks and it was several hours before I came to. I thought I was all right but when I got up the next morning I was drinking a coke and the bottle kept slipping out of my mouth. When I tried to smile I smiled on the left side but the right side of my lips would not move. I went to the doctor, who was really a vet, and he took me to a doctor in Leavenworth. He said I had Bell's Palsy from a cut nerve in my right temple and the nerve grew back at the rate of about one eighth of an inch per month and I would eventually be all right. It was a weird feeling and lasted about eight months as I remember.

Several of us chased a boy into the attic of a barracks and we thought it would be funny to take turns guarding him and make him miss lunch. It was my turn and it got very quiet up there and I was afraid he had found a way out and started staring up through the opening to see if I could see him. He threw a fishing pole at me and the sharp end hit me in the eye. I went to the doctor and he put salve in it and a bandage over it, like he did with cows, I guess. It kept getting worse and worse and I finally got him to take me to the doctor in Leavenworth. He looked at it and told our vet to get me to a hospital. The ambulance driver took me to the Marine Corps Hospital in Seattle. The doctors there checked my eye and said I was lucky it did not have to be removed as the salve and bandage were the two worst things that could have been done to it. I still have it, but there is now a cataract and I have no vision in that eye. Doctors hesitate to remove the cataract due to the scar tissue.

We had twenty-five boys come in from a camp in Pennsylvania for some type of training. They wanted to go to Wenatchee one Saturday night but that required a leader to be in the truck and I was assigned to go with them. We spent several hours in Wenatchee and started back to the camp. The truck driver decided to stop by the dance in Leavenworth. He met a girl he knew and had a few drinks and refused to take the boys to camp. I decided I would drive the truck back, although I was not authorized to drive with people in the back of the truck. Everything went fine until we went through the gate and I started to swing to the right to take the truck to the garage. The boy in front with me yelled to go left and let the boys out at the flagpole. I flipped back to the left real quick and the truck turned over on its left side. I was afraid some of the boys were hurt and scrambled up and out through the passenger window. All the boys had landed on the grass around the flagpole and no one was hurt. They flipped the truck back on its wheels and I asked them not to mention the wreck. All of them looked at me and said, "What wreck?" I checked the truck and there were no dents and the only damage was that a swing out turn signal was broken and there was a small scratch where the bed of the truck landed on a rock. I took the truck to the garage and removed a turn indicator from a dead-lined truck and put it on my truck. I got some green paint and touched up the scratch. No one could tell it had been wrecked. The following Monday the Company Commander called me in and asked me what happened to my truck. I told him the truck driver got sick and I had to drive it from Leavenworth and had turned it over when I got back to camp. He had seen some glass on the ground near the flagpole and had checked all the trucks and discovered the fresh paint on my truck. I had to pay for the turn indicator but he did not charge me with any action.

I did not drink while I was in the CCC. I never had a desire to drink during those days. Life was too short and there was too much to do to waste it on drinking. I knew I wanted to be somebody and make something out of my life. I had no idea what I wanted to do, just that I wanted to do something.

I have skipped over many events at Camp Icicle. For one thing, I worked several other jobs that I did not list, such as plumber, electrician, assistant educational advisor and truck driver. We taught a lot of boys how to read and write, plus other subjects they were interested in, like history and geography. It was a thrill to see young men who could neither read or write be able to sit down and write their parents a letter and read the reply.

Finally, a decision was made to close Camp Icicle and the boys were offered the opportunity to transfer to other camps or go home. Most went home but I decided to go to Camp Cowiche in Yakima, Washington. Before I could go, Camp Icicle had to be closed. All the boys left except William Hanks, who was company clerk and me, the supply sergeant. It was our job to finalize the records and the property. Hanks worked on records and I worked on property. When I had two truck loads of property ready to take to Olympia we would go in the two trucks and leave one truck there and return together in one truck. We finally had everything turned in except the ambulance and the records. Bill Hanks was a tall, quiet, capable person and worked long hours keeping his work up to date. Some of the boys began taunting him because he did not drink or curse or run around. This began to bug Bill and one day he ran out and got in a truck and went to Leavenworth. Bill bought a pint of whiskey and drank the entire pint. He then returned to camp and drove around and around the flag pole, faster and faster, until the truck finally turned over. They took Bill out of the truck and put him on his bed. He did not come out of it for two days. When they put Bill on the bed they had one arm under his body. When he came out of it he was unable to use that arm for several days but finally managed to use it. When Bill got out of the CCC he went into the Army Air Corps as a cadet and finished all training. Someone noticed he favored that arm during final tests and he was washed out as a pilot and served as a flight officer during World War II. A seemingly minor thing can affect you the rest of your life.

I had saved mostly steak and eggs for us to eat. The cook stove in the mess hall was a tremendous thing. I had an attic full of the old World War I rain slickers and they were mostly melted blobs but they burned like crazy. We would reach up in the attic and get an arm load of those old slickers and go to the mess hall and build a quick and hot fire. I would throw a couple of steaks on the grill and a little later add a dozen eggs. We lived in style.

Bill Hanks had a battery radio and the batteries were about gone so we would listen to it awhile and turn it off. We were listening when the announcement was made that Pearl Harbor had been bombed by the Japanese. The batteries burned out completely and all we had was our imagination. Our imagination led us to believe that Camp Icicle would be the next target. We really sweat it out that night but we lived through any attack that may have been made or planned (Smile). A few days later we loaded the camp records in the ambulance and took them to Olympia. Bill and I shook hands and he went home and I went to Camp Cowiche after being rejected by the Army, Marines and Navy because I had flat feet.

Camp Icicle was closed by the CCC but during World War II it was used to house prostitutes with venereal diseases while they were treated. It was later donated to the Catholic Church and now serves as a retreat. Even more recently I was told that the Church was selling Camp Icicle to someone in the private sector. I still write to the city manager in Leavenworth, as I have a deep affection for the area.

Camp Cowiche was vastly different from Camp Icicle. The CCC camps were set up with administration under control of the Army and the work performed under control of another government agency. The work performed by enrollees at Camp Icicle had been under the jurisdiction of the Forestry Service. The work at Camp Cowiche was under the Bureau of Reclamation and our work had nothing to do with forestry. Primarily, we were building canals used to move water to locations needing irrigation. Another vast difference was that Camp Icicle was beautiful and Camp Cowiche was a far cry from beauty. It was neat and orderly and clean but definitely not beautiful.

The Company Commander had lost a large number of boys, most of whom had enlisted in the Army or Navy the day after Pearl Harbor was bombed. He showed me a list of openings at Leader level and told me to take my choice. I strolled around the camp and looked at the different areas and went back and told him I would take the job as parts keeper. It was isolated from the rest of the camp and had a private office and all I had to learn was accounting. My job was to control all vehicle parts, issue them against authorized work orders and maintain accounting records. It looked like a snap to me and really it was.

I had not been on the job long when a gentleman named George Washington Wilson came in from the district office of the Bureau of Reclamation and introduced himself as the auditor. George told me he was officially there to audit the parts records and personally there to help any boy with any problem he had, official or personal. George became a life long friend whom I maintained correspondence with for 50 years, right up to his death in 1991. There was never a greater person and no person other than my Mother had as much influence on my life as George. George would complete his audit in a day and we would spend most of two more days chatting. George taught me to audit and had me make the audit while he observed. Many years later, when I took Auditing at the University of Alabama I made a score of 115 out of a possible 100 but that will be covered later.

George Wilson encouraged me to always do twice what a job actually required. He said that most people did the minimum required plus maybe ten percent more in an effort to obtain better ratings or monetary rewards. He said that doing double what was required was satisfaction in itself and any awards would be even more enjoyable as you would know they were truly earned and not just given to you by a liberal boss. He considered his extra effort was in helping youngsters believe in themselves. I took what George said seriously and went to the Company Commander and told him I could handle the parts keeper job in half a day and take on one of the vacancies he had in the other half. He said he needed a truck driver and I started driving half the day. I only had one problem driving. We hauled a lot of steel rods used in canal construction and they were very, very long. I made a turn on to a side road one day and knocked a power pole down with the trailer load of steel. Other than that it was uneventful.

The day came when Camp Cowiche was closed and George and I closed out my records and I was sent to Camp DuPont, near Fort Lewis, Washington. I really hated to lose my contacts with George but he said he would soon be relocating in Colorado anyway.

Camp Dupont was even less attractive than Camp Cowiche. It was under the Army and Soil Conservation Service. Before we left Camp Cowiche I had altered the records of a friend and myself to reflect that we were full time truck drivers. When we arrived at Camp DuPont we were automatically assigned as truck drivers. Both of us were assigned to assist the Army at Fort Lewis. They had just built a lot of new officer's quarters there and some days we drove dump trucks and hauled asphalt for the driveways. Other days we drove flat bed trucks and hauled sod from a sod farm to the lawns of the new quarters.

Only one or two old friends remained from the days of Camp Icicle and it was not as much fun as it had been but I continued to follow the advice of George Wilson and tried to do twice what I had to. I would go to the motor pool and wash and clean up all the trucks, even though it was not my job. What I did was noticed and I was well liked by the Commander.

My two years maximum time ran out and the CCC camps were being closed rapidly anyway so I finally said good bye to Camp DuPont and headed home. There were no longer enough enrollees leaving to use troop trains and I rode commercial for a change. I had built a large chest while I was in Camp Icicle. It weighed more than fifty pounds. The Company Commander gave me an old typewriter with a very wide carriage and I dumped it and a few clothes and pictures in that chest.

The trip home was uneventful until I got off the train in Atlanta, Georgia and discovered I had to go the rest of the way on a bus. The bus station was across town from the railroad station and I had no money so I had to put that hundred pound chest on my shoulder and walk to the bus station. It was a good thing I was in excellent physical and mental condition or that chest would have been dumped along the way. I made it though and checked the chest despite protests from the bus company that it was over sized.

It was about 225 miles from Atlanta to Tuscaloosa (still is, I guess). The trip went fine and when we got to Tuscaloosa I had only seven or eight blocks to go with the chest. What a relief to get that thing home. The next day I made the rounds of Army, Marine and Navy recruiting offices but was rejected by all because of flat feet. I heard that a contractor was looking for a truck driver and went to see him and was hired two minutes later. He had a contract to haul mail between the post office and train and bus stations, plus a couple of sub post offices in the area. I started driving the same day. Once or twice a week I would check all the recruiting offices and be rejected again.

I had no idea where some of the small towns were located and often put North bound mail on a South bound train, but I am sure that is still prevalent in the postal service so what was the harm. I was more interested in killing Japanese and started hitting the recruiting offices every day as one of them had told me he thought the restriction on flat feet would be removed. I was amazed one day when I walked in the Naval Recruiting Office and took a physical and the doctor did not look at my feet and said I was accepted. I was asked when I wanted to leave and I told them to give me half an hour to say good bye to my Mother. He made me wait two days.

I quit my job (I found him another driver) and said my good byes to my friends and my Mother. Little did I realize it would be more than four years before I would see my Mother and Sister again.

Chapter Seven

The US Navy and World War II

If I had to summarize my feelings at the beginning of World War II, I would probably say, "I am immortal and will never age." Somewhere along the line, I had to admit the immortality may be a figment of my imagination. Fortunately, I was right to feel I will never age. I am now in my 70's but in my heart, I am the same 20 year old I always have been. Everything I say here is based on memory. I have made every attempt to be completely honest, even when it makes me look bad. I was no angel during World War II, as you will soon see. I do have an excellent memory and I feel I have depicted events as they happened.

The Navy Recruiting Office in Tuscaloosa, Alabama processed several of us and took us to Birmingham where we became part of a larger group. A navy petty officer took us to the train station and handed me a large envelope filled with train tickets and meal tickets. We were on the way and I was already in charge. I assumed I would be at least a Chief Petty Officer by the end of the year.

My enthusiasm soon wore off while trying to keep up with those new sailors, most of whom had already developed sea legs and kept looking for a tattoo parlor every time the train stopped for more than half an hour. It was even worse when we went to the diner and I was the one who had to tell the waiter we were using meal tickets instead of cash. We were recognized on our second trip to the diner and it is amazing how a five foot six waiter can stare over the heads of a bunch of six foot non-tippers. To make things worse, we rode coach all the way. There were no pullman's for America's finest that trip.

**Tom Bowerman,
Gunners Mate Second Class**

I managed to get my motley crew to San Diego and into a waiting bus, but no commendation was forthcoming. In fact, they were rather rude when I explained what a good job I had done and one swabby in charge made a comment that, "If I want any crud out of you I will scrape it off your teeth." I had collected a few gems in the CCC and popped back, "Your sister is not so picky. She loved me when we got up this morning." He got very polite and asked me for my name and number and wrote it down in a little book. I knew I had impressed him.

Our bus pulled in to the San Diego Naval Training Center and we were immediately taken to the supply room and issued uniforms, under wear, socks, shoes, handkerchiefs, a mattress, a hammock, sea bag, ditty bag, a Blue Jacket's Manual and a coupon book. We dressed and threw our civilian clothes away. We were then shown how to pack everything in the sea bag and lash the hammock around the sea bag. We were then shown how to march with the hammock and sea bag on one shoulder. And we were shown how to dump it all out and do it all over again. We were then shown how to keep doing it until everyone got it right. Finally we were taken to a barracks and introduced to our company commander. I was fortunate as the company commander was the one who had written my name down in his little book. He told me, "My sister and I asked for you in this company."

Gene Tunney was over all Navy training and he had selected football players from colleges all over the country and given them Chief Petty Officer status, no matter how dumb they were. Most of them were really smart kids but they expected you to do things like chin yourself 20 times with one arm just because they could. They never hit you, they made you do it to yourself. Overall, the training was excellent.

Our Company Commander told us that until recently boot camp had been sixteen weeks but was now condensed into four weeks. He said that our coupon books were designed for sixteen weeks but the Navy, in its infinite wisdom, had not printed new ones yet. The main problem was that we had sixteen hair cut

Muster on the S.S. Charles M. Hall

coupons and would have to use them in four weeks. We had to get our hair cut four times per week. The Blue Jacket Manual was in the coupon book and he took our coupons for it and then marched us to the barber shop. I had a real nice barber and he asked me if I wanted to keep my sideburns. I said that I sure did and he told me to hold my hands right here and put them right in my hands. The hair cut took one minute but the Navy did not want the civilian barbers to take advantage of us. There was a sign "Customer must remain in chair six minutes", so we chatted five minutes.

There were four companies in our battalion. The Battalion Commander was a Warrant Officer and he was about five foot six inches and weighed around two hundred and fifty pounds. He was a real contrast to the Company Commanders. He always rode a bicycle and frequently rode along side of us when we marched, calling cadence and yelling that every man in the battalion was out of step but him. He decided to impress us and gave a nice speech in which he said he was a great judge of men. He said he could look at a man and determine what he could do best. He looked at me and said, "This man will make a perfect right guide for the battalion." I hated to disappoint him but I never could walk a straight line and the concrete drill field was painted with weird wavy lines and I was having trouble in the middle of my company, much less at the head of the battalion. He would not listen to me and I got the job. I led those poor devils a merry chase, wobbling as I went. The battalion commander was furious and began yelling commands like, "Battalion right, guide toward that damn telephone pole, march!", and "Battalion left, guide toward that damn fire plug, march!"

He refused to give up on me as that would indicate he was not a perfect judge of men. The drill field was extremely hot and the sun was blistering. I reported that my neck was blistered badly two or three times and was told to shut up. It finally got so bad they had to let a doctor look at it. It was scabbed over and re-burned and scabbed again. The doctor had to take a knife and cut it off. He gave me a permit to tuck that Navy collar under my cap. That was all the battalion commander needed. He gave another speech and said that I had mastered the job of right guide and he had never seen a better one after I got the hang of it but he could not have his right guide marching with that collar under his cap and was forced to select a new one. He let the company commander of my company make the selection to give him the experience.

We marched and scrubbed decks and washed clothes and scrubbed decks and got hair cuts and scrubbed decks and read the Blue Jacket Manual and scrubbed decks and exercised and scrubbed decks. The company commander left us one day with instructions to scrub the deck "clean enough to eat off of." When he came back he asked one boot if the deck was clean enough to eat off of and he assured him it was. He stepped outside and came back in with a large plate of beans and dumped them on the deck. He handed him a spoon and told him to eat. The guy just sits down and eats the beans and asked for seconds. The

The S.S. Esso Providence

commander looked at the deck and ran his fingers through the juice from the beans and yelled that the deck was filthy and we had to scrub it all over again. One thing that finally soaked in was that you could make cute remarks but only at a cost. You might be ten times smarter than the person in charge but the person in charge was still the person in charge. I recognized that and learned to live with it with no problem. However, it was also true that if the person in charge was corrupt, he was still the person in charge. I did not ever learn to live with that and that has given me many serious problems throughout my life.

I became very good friends in boot camp with Grover Cleveland Redding from Schulenburg, Texas. Grover was the All American good guy. You could not find anything about him to dislike so you had to like him. We were very close. We went to San Diego together on our first liberty in boot camp. We looked the town over good and drank a few beers. Neither of us had drank before and we got a little silly. We were walking along the sidewalk and I told Grover I had to pee. He looked all around and said, "There aren't any cars coming, just a guy on a motorcycle, go ahead." I walked up to a lamp pole and went ahead. The guy on a motorcycle was a policeman and he came over and said, "Only dogs are allowed to do that", so I started barking and Grover joined in. The policeman laughed and looked at both of us real close, shook his head and said, "One of you dogs get the other one back to the training center." Grover walked off and whistled and said, "Good boy, come on now." We found the bus and went back to the center. They checked us as we got off the bus and told Grover and I to wait. They found a couple more drunks and took all of us to a large area that had a pole with a lot of ropes (okay, lines) tied to it. They put the end of a line in our left hand and a bucket of water in our right hand and made us walk round and round the pole. We had to keep the line tight and not spill any water for 30 minutes. If someone spilled any water their time started over. Grover and I smelled worse than we were and finished in thirty minutes.

We were given a lot of tests and told that our assignments would depend on our test scores, with the best assignments available to those with the highest scores. Grover and I had very high scores. They had more than a thousand of us in a large auditorium and announced the first assignment and said there were twenty openings and the score required was one hundred sixty. Those with 160 or higher who wanted the assignment were told to stand up. Grover whispered, "Don't volunteer. The best assignment will be saved until last." There were only fifteen that wanted the assignment so they lowered the score to 159, 158, etc until they had twenty. The next one was another good school and they started it the same way and then dropped the score until they met the quota. They finally had to start the bidding with a lower score and if they got too many, they went up and if not enough they went down. Grover kept saying to just wait and the real assignments would come up.

Finally, there were only fifteen or twenty of us left and they had us all come to the front. The swabby running the show said, "Well, all that you dummies qualify for is The Armed Guard, and you got it." I asked what the Armed Guard was and he said, "You are gunners on merchant ships and you are going to the San Diego Destroyer Base for gunnery training; have fun dummy." We could have had submarine duty, high tech training schools or anything we wanted and we were going aboard ships not even run by the Navy, and in some cases not even run by the United States. I looked at Grover and told him I was going to kill him. He grinned and told me I was going to love the Armed Guard. He was right.

I am the fair skinned, easy to blister type of person. I can and have blistered with blisters containing fluid by the pint. San Diego was not a fun place for me. Everyone in the battalion had been talking about nothing except where they wanted to go and where they were going. Grover and I went to temporary quarters in Balboa Park in San Diego. Gunnery training was normally eight weeks but it had been reduced to three weeks recently. Grover said we could stand on our heads for three weeks. We needed to hang by our tails as we were housed in a zoo. I gave Grover a hard time but I really did not care where I went if I had a chance to kill a few Japanese. I was just afraid it would be the other way around on a merchant ship.

The only gun they had available to train us with was a four inch fifty shell gun. We had to learn the name of every part on the gun and were given manuals that had some pages in it clear enough to read. We took turns pointing (vertical movement) and training (horizontal movement) and putting in dummy rounds until we were sick of it. One day we were taken down to the dock where the gun was mounted and the head swabby said each of us would name all the parts of the gun as our final test. The first one missed a part and was told to put his billfold on the dock. He was then pushed into the water. This got my attention as I could not swim. They claimed that you might not know how to swim when you got in the Navy but you would know when you got out. I have no body flotation at all and it is impossible for me to swim. I nearly drowned in boot camp. They had finally told me I had to get from one end of the pool to the other and I just held my breath and walked on the bottom. Now he was pushing people in the bay. I started studying that manual and edging to the back of the group. When my turn came I reeled off every name of every part, right down to the Whelen Interruptive screw plug rotating shaft retaining pin locking nut (I was never able to forget).

When that part was over we had to go aboard a ship for actual firing practice. The ship was a very old Destroyer and the gun was a three inch 23.5. I soon learned two things. One was that I was very susceptible to sea sickness. The other was that the shorter the barrel the sharper the shock. The three inch 23.5 was actually what was known as a mule gun as it was designed to be disassembled and packed on mules for transport across land. It was a very, very old gun. I found I was also susceptible to nose bleed as my nose bled every time my crew fired it. It was just like being hit in the face with a boxing glove traveling at full speed. The gunnery officer reported that I flinched when the gun was fired but I do not call wiping the blood off your face flinching and told him so. I was not the only one who got nose bleeds and his comment was taken off my record.

The crew of the destroyer had a ball with us. The cook got in on the act by cooking the greasiest pork chops he could find. I did not get sick but three times in one day and Grover said I did good. When the destroyer returned us to the dock we were full fledged sailors and half assed gunners.

We were shipped to the Armed Guard Center on Treasure Island in San Francisco to wait for an assignment to a ship. Treasure Island was a great place but not if you were assigned to the Armed Guard Center. It was one heck of a place to be. We were in a large building with no duty to perform other than to wait for a ship. We were not allowed to sit down and were not allowed to stand still. We had to keep moving and look like we had duties we were performing. Idleness is the hardest work in the world, or maybe I should say looking busy when you are not is the hardest work in the world. We would find some papers and walk up and down the hall like we were on the way to deliver them to someone. Grover and I finally gave up and sat down in the hall with our backs against the wall. That lasted two minutes when a Boatswain's Mate first class (I will refer to him as Johnson - not his real name) rode up on a bicycle and said we were to follow him. We went to the other end of the hall with him and he opened a closet door and reached in and got two shovels. We were happy we were going to do some digging but it was not to be. We were instructed to hold the shovels on our shoulders like they were rifles and march up and down the hall calling cadence until he told us to stop. Every few minutes Johnson would bring us one or two more members of Johnson's Shovel Brigade.

The shovel brigade continued the rest of the week we were there. The only consolation was that Johnson was a Boatswain's Mate and the armed guard did not use them on board ship. We were on his shovel brigade every day. Finally, a Lieutenant Junior Grade called 28 of us together and told us we were boarding the SS Charles M. Hall, a Henry Kaiser Liberty ship, and that he was our gunnery officer. We were so happy we were getting away from Johnson at long last and patting ourselves on the back when he introduced Johnson and said he would be in charge of the gun crew. It developed that there was a shortage of gunners mates and they were using Johnson as he had gunnery training a few years before.

THE S.S.CHARLES M. HALL

The Charles M. Hall was new and this was the maiden voyage for her. They were already loading the holds when we boarded. It only took another day or two to finish. They then loaded a deck cargo of lumber and several light airplanes. Everything was ready to go and we were ready to leave when a barge pulled along side and they had a 75 ton crash boat to load on the port side. They loaded it over protests of the captain and suddenly we had a serious list to port. The captain was furious. The SS Charles M. Hall had a five inch 51 bag gun on the stern and a three inch 50 anti aircraft gun on the bow. There were also four 20 MM anti-aircraft cannons and we had a few small hand guns like the British Thompson and Lewis machine guns. We were miserably under gunned. Johnson had never seen a bag gun before and we had to learn how to use it. There was a tub of water under the gun and you pushed the projectile in and dipped a brush on the end of a long rod into the water and then rammed the projectile home. You then put a silk bag of powder behind the projectile while the gun captain put a primer in the breech and closed and locked it. The pointer controlled the vertical movement and the trainer controlled the horizontal movement. When the gun captain said ready and the gun was on target the pointer fired.

Johnson developed into a greater monster than we thought he would be and was only happy when he had made someone else unhappy. We were always in trouble with him and he loved every minute of it. He would accept money or cigarettes to get you out of trouble. He was a royal pain in the rear. Our first stop was Palmyra Island to deliver the crash boat. We had been told the Japanese may have taken the island and to be cautious. We pulled up close to the island and there was no sign of activity. We did not understand how we could get so close without being challenged. The captain finally sounded the whistle on the ship. It was like a volcano then with planes taking off and small boats headed our way. An Army crew arrived and a Second Lieutenant came aboard and rigged up our five ton boom. The Captain told him his crew would set the crash boat over but the Second Lieutenant insisted the Army would do it. The Captain quit arguing and went back to the bridge to watch. The crash boat was lifted a couple of feet and the five ton boom broke and a rope tore off one finger of the Second Lieutenant's right hand. The Captain continued to watch in silence. After awhile an Army delegation asked the Captain to set the boat over the side. The merchant Boatswain had his crew replace the broken boom and then rigged up a combination of larger booms and set the boat in the water.

We left Palmyra and went to Apia, Samoa, known as American Samoa. There was a natural harbor and we pulled up to the docks and tied up. They set the aircraft off first and we wondered what they would do as there was no way they could get them through the palm trees and then before we knew where they were, they were gone through the palm trees. There was a lot of excitement around hold number one, which was the hold they unloaded first. The top half of each hold was for Apia and the bottom half was for British Samoa. They unloaded the top half of hold one and then set everything in the bottom half off the ship and had a long discussion and after a long time started unloading beer from hold one. They then reloaded the bottom half of hold one.

We were told to wear shoes at all times as many Samoan's had a disease called Elephantisis and it was contagious. It caused one leg to swell several times the size of the other leg. The Samoan's were all over the ship. It had to be sterilized after we left port. We were allowed to go ashore in denims but there was very little to do there. I met a marine from Tuscaloosa and promised to call his father when I got back to the states and let him know his son was there and doing ok. I had a new friend named Horace Century Redman (not his real name), a full blooded Cherokee Indian, who insisted on being called Speedy. Speedy and I went ashore and walked around. There was little to see or do but Speedy spotted four upright 2 by 4's with a water pipe on top and a shower head on the end of it. He asked what it was for and it was a public shower where nearly everyone showered. We hung around and quite a few people came and hung their garment on a nail and took a shower. Speedy gave each one his assessment of their anatomy. Some really great looking girls came up and giggled and showered and Speedy compared them for their benefit. They finally started taunting Speedy and he took a shower. Then a Samoan Marine motioned for us to leave. Speedy ignored him and got a little nick on the butt from a bayonet and we left.

Speedy was a thorn in the side of the gunnery officer. He

always did what he wanted to and seldom did anything he was told to do. The gunnery officer had given us a lecture on survival at sea in case our ship was sunk. He mentioned that a paddle could be carved into a spear for spearing fish. Several weeks later someone checking the life rafts discovered every paddle had been carved into a spear. The gunnery officer headed straight for Speedy and he admitted it, yea bragged about it. He said it would be hot out there and he thought it would be best to go ahead and make the spears and we would be ready to spear fish right away. He also had a plan to burn the raft to cook the fish. The gunnery officer was also upset with Speedy because he had taken his only pair of shoes and cut the fronts open and made sandals. Every time Speedy looked around he had done something the gunnery officer was chewing him out about. He finally confined Speedy to his quarters and put a guard at the door to keep him in. Speedy stripped and rubbed himself with hair oil and managed to get through the port hole. The problem was that there was just a very narrow ledge and he could not reach the deck above and could not get back through the port hole. He hung on to the port hole for a couple of hours before he was found and then they had to lower a line to pull him on deck. It was almost enough to phase even Speedy but not quite. The gunnery officer had Speedy stand at attention, naked as he was. Speedy, determined to be agreeable, brought everything erect.

The gunnery officer told us we were not to associate with Speedy, not to talk to him or anything, just ignore him. Boatswain Johnson was to enforce it. I have always had this thing about the underdog and openly associated with Speedy. We became even closer friends and Speedy told me things no one else knew. He was not really Horace Century Redman; his brother was Horace Century Redman. Speedy had been in the Army Air Corps under his real name and had begun dating Jayne, the daughter of his First Sergeant. The First Sergeant had ordered him to quit dating his daughter and Speedy asked her to marry him, just for the hell of it. They got married and Jayne told Speedy her father had been having sex with her since she was six years old. Speedy beat the

Sergeant almost to death and got a dishonorable discharge from the Army Air Corps. When World War II started he enlisted in the Navy under his brother's name. I was the only one who knew other than his wife, her family, and his brother. Speedy was responsible for a nickname I had throughout my Navy career. We met some girls one night and Speedy introduced me as "Scardick." The girls kept asking where I got the name and Speedy finally told them the sad story. He told them our ship had been bombed by the Japanese and I was hit by scrapnel and had a 13 inch scar in a very private place. After that, I was always Scardick.

Johnson threw a lot of garbage jobs my way because I refused to ostracize Speedy but he threw a lot of garbage assignments to everyone so it did not make much difference. Speedy and I began to taunt Johnson openly and before long everyone in the crew had joined in. Johnson did not have a friend aboard the ship and even the gunnery officer could not stand him. Everyone knew he was taking money from the crew in return for not having to perform your duties or to get favored jobs and watch assignments.

We crossed the equator and naturally Johnson was the only one who had been across it before and we were all polywogs, lower than a whale's belly. Johnson clipped our hair and shaved our head and that made us old shells or something. My hair never did grow back on top. I had a bushy bright red beard and no hair on my head. The Lieutenant said I was the ugliest sailor on the ship if not in the fleet.

We arrived at British Samoa and there was no harbor so we anchored and the cargo was unloaded on barges. There was again much excitement around hold one and the cargo in that hold was quickly unloaded. They then unbolted the top of a large tank below hold one, but it was empty. We learned that British Samoa had been trying to get beer shipped in but the ships always went to American Samoa first and they always found their beer. They had arranged to have beer hidden in a tank below hold one but someone had told American Samoa about it. They were frustrated.

There was not much to do in British Samoa either unless you liked to walk and swim. Speedy and I went ashore and looked around. It was a beautiful island. We found a small stream of clear, beautiful water and since it was only a couple of feet deep I decided to go wading. I stepped in and kept going and going and going. I thought it was all over but somehow got back to the surface and thrashed around and got to the bank and just held on to the bank for dear life until Speedy held out a limb for me to grab. He pulled me to a place where I could crawl out. The bottom was coral and that little stream was more than sixty feet deep. It was so clear that the bottom looked less than two feet away.

They loaded the ship with copra, some kind of coconut product, and it was a disaster. The copra was loaded with copra bugs and they came out of the holds and were all over the ship. When you got up for duty your pillow case would be covered with dead copra bugs where your head and face had crushed them. Most of us took our hammocks and moved on deck. We delivered the copra to one island and picked up another cargo and took it to another island. We were in the Pacific many, many months before we started home and during this entire time no mail ever caught up with us. We were sending out mail but never received any.

Our main responsibility was to watch for submarines, ships and aircraft. We were divided into two crews and stood watch four hours and were then off four hours. During the times an hour before sunset and sunrise both crews stood watch. Each crew was already on duty during either the sunrise or sunset period in most cases, so you were on watch 12 hours per day plus two hours at either sunrise or sunset. In addition, we cleaned all guns daily and painted gun decks and other Naval equipment. This was 14 hours watch plus usually 4 hours of cleaning and painting. One meal usually took an hour of your off duty time. This was a nineteen hour day. You had to get up and wear special goggles to accustom your eyes prior to one shift change per day. That left four and a half hours per day to sleep. I am a creature of habit and still sleep four and one half hours per day.

We went to Tocopilla, Chili to pick up a load of nitrate to take back to the United States. Chili was still neutral at that time. Their police force was almost like an army and they were very nice to us and saluted us when we met on the streets. Chili was very famous for silver products and had beautiful jewelry for reasonable prices. They were also famous for their bars and houses of ill repute. Our merchant crew was making a lot of money and we were making fifty dollars per month. The merchant crew went to a bar and told the owner the ship would be there one week and they wanted to buy his bar and his girls for the week, with the bar closed to all outsiders for that week. They agreed on a price and the gun crew members were guests of the merchant crew. We had a real ball, with all the booze and female companionship we wanted at no charge.

The ship was at anchor and the holds were loaded from barges. The covers were not taken completely off but a few sections removed and the sections remaining were placed to form cracks that the nitrate could be dumped on and allowed to sift through. The reason for this is that you cannot burn nitrate even with a blow torch but you can place a piece of burning hemp in it and it will catch fire days later. They were afraid someone would do just that and the sifting would have disclosed the burning hemp. A nitrate fire can not be put out with fresh or sea water, but only with stagnant water. We were provided with one tank of stagnant water.

The loaders worked only with shovels. The merchant crew would move the boom over the barge and lower a large metal container and the workers would fill it with shovels and it would be raised and moved over the hatch and dumped. The workers fastened a heavy twelve inch wide board to the barge extending out several feet over the ocean. When they needed to go to the bathroom they would walk out to the very end of the board and squat and do their business. A rag had been tied to a line and the line was fastened to the board. They would pull up the rag and cleanse themselves and then throw the rag back in the ocean, ready for the next customer. Ground swells kept the barge moving around and up and down but it never seemed to bother them.

The ship was finally loaded and we headed to the Panama Canal. It was February but very hot where we were. When we got to Panama we docked on the Pacific side. We were given liberty and went out on the town. We had one gunner who weighed over two hundred and fifty pounds and he was the first one to get drunk. He passed out in a bar. We wanted to get him back to the ship but he was more than we could handle. Speedy said he had an idea and to wait on him. In a few minutes he was back and said he had a fork lift outside. We grabbed the gunners legs and drug him outside and dumped him on the fork lift. We got him to the ship and on the ship with no problem but on the way back the guy Speedy had stolen the fork lift from spotted us and we had to run for it.

The rest of the night was hazy but six of us, including Speedy, decided to stay in Panama. We planned to hide until the ship left and then head for the hills if there were any. We found a pile of lumber and slept on it. The next morning we discovered the lumber was railroad cross ties and we had black and white uniforms instead of white ones. We waited until about ten AM and decided to go make sure the ship had left at eight o'clock as scheduled. The ship was still there and we got all emotional over them waiting on us and went aboard. It developed the ship was staying another day and all of the crew got liberty another night except for us and we were restricted.

Our Gunnery Officer called the ship and said he was in the hospital and he needed for us to come get him so Speedy and I went to the hospital. The gunnery officer was in a bed and his entire mid section was bandaged. We were afraid he had been stabbed in the stomach but it turned out that it was his butt that was slashed open. He said that his bowels were loose and he was forced to use a toilet that was just porcelain with no seat on it. The commode broke and slashed his rear end open.

We went through the canal and headed North for home. It would be a long, long trip by the time we got there and still no mail from home. The ship had no foul weather gear as it had been anticipated we would stay in the Pacific. The Red Cross had brought several boxes of heavy jackets and coats aboard at Panama but Johnson shipped all of them to his home address and not one member of the crew got one. When we got far enough North to expect cold weather our captain followed the gulf stream and avoided cold weather a few more days. Finally we headed Northwest and left the gulf stream and it was below freezing in a matter of hours. We stood some rough watches. All of us had dumped our Navy coats months before and many of us stood watch in very low temperatures in shirt sleeves.

We got to New York during a blizzard and an ambulance took the gunnery officer to the hospital. Johnson was in charge and gave himself leave and left. We never saw him again. That left a Signalman Third Class in charge and he gave himself leave. There were now 26 of us left. Twenty five of us were apprentice seamen. The other one was a seaman second class, one notch above the apprentice seaman. He was a signalman striker and the rest of us were gunner strikers. The seaman second class was a Cajun, Pierre Bellaire (not his real name), and he said, "I, Pierre Bellaire, am in command and I say we need whiskey and mail. I appoint you three to commandeer a truck and get mail and I appoint you three to commandeer a truck and get whiskey. Everyone is to put forth money to pay for the whiskey. I will remain aboard and be lavished by my adoring subjects. I, Pierre Bellaire have spoken."

The two crews went on their appointed rounds and the whiskey crew returned with an average of two quarts of bourbon per man. We were at the half quart mark (on the average) when the mail crew returned and it was obvious they had imbibed en route. The fleet post office had sorted mail by name due to the amount of it and I had two mail bags of mail and packages. Most members of the crew had two or three bags of mail. We took Johnson's mail and everyone cheered as Speedy opened his bag and dumped it over the side. We then retired to our quarters with our mail and our bourbon and sat on the floor and began opening packages and reading mail. I had to make one trip outside with a package of fried chicken my Mother had mailed me the Christmas before, marked "RUSH."

We were laughing and drinking and reading mail when three officers came aboard to inspect our guns. They wanted to know who in the hell was in charge and Pierre staggered to his feet and gave a salute that knocked his cap off and said, "I, Pierre Bellaire, seaman second class, am in charge, sirs, have a drink." The officers stepped outside and then came back and said they would return in one hour and expected us to have ourselves, our quarters and our guns ready for inspection. They did return as they said they would and we were on the floor drinking and reading our mail. They talked about court martial and similar things and Pierre told them we were without mail for many, many months and we were now without leadership and we were going to read our mail and drink our whiskey and pass out and that tomorrow we would be sailors again. They had another huddle and came back and told Pierre they would see us the next day at 1000 hours. They did not come back the next day but we did sober up and clean the guns. We got our official visit in the afternoon in the form of a truck to take all of us to the Brooklyn Armed Guard Center. We were to be assigned to other ships.

The gunnery officer had been mailing in results of tests we took aboard the Charles M. Hall and all of us were Seaman First Class. I did not know it but I was a Gunner's Mate Third Class. We stayed in the Armed Guard Center a couple of weeks while paper work was processed. Speedy and I hung together and we were assigned to a tanker, the Esso Nashville. I still did not know I was a Gunners Mate Third Class and the gunnery officer did not know it. I was assigned as a Seaman First Class. I met a girl named Sally Grenner on my first liberty in Brooklyn and she was my girl friend during most of the war.

THE S.S.ESSO NASHVILLE

The gunnery officer on the Nashville was a complete idiot and tyrant. His idea of punishment was to have you wash his underwear and socks and I refused. I had done something he did not like and he threw me a pile of his underwear and told me to wash them and I threw them in his face and told him to court martial me. The ship left the next day for a trial run to Bay Town, Texas. Fuel oil was leaking into the drinking water tank and it was terrible. Seems like a water fountain in the Navy is called a scuttlebutt as well as I can remember and we had contests to see who could take a long drink of water and go the longest time without burping. The water ruined the coffee and tea also, as well as the food. We did not drink water the last few days and when we docked at Bay Town everyone ran off the ship with pitchers and jugs to get fresh water. The water in Bay Town was not terrific so people probably thought we were crazy.

They repaired the fresh water tank and we had no problem with the drinking water on the return trip. We passed a burning tanker eleven miles off the Florida coast on the return trip that had been shelled by a submarine and was sinking. Survivors had been picked up by the Coast Guard. We knew the submarine was in the area but we did not see it. The trip back to New York was uneventful except for the erratic behavior of the gunnery officer. He was a real nuisance.

We made one more trip, this time to Nova Scotia, Newfoundland and then on to England. Speedy and I went on liberty in England. We went in a pub and ordered two beers. We had been told the glasses were not always sterilized so we were drinking out of the bottle. A group of British sailors kept staring at our table and finally one came over and pointed at Speedy's glass, which was upside down, and asked him if he would turn it right side up. Speedy looked at him and just said no. A little later another sailor came over and said, "Look Mate, will you turn the glass up?" Speedy just said no. Finally, this huge British sailor comes over to the table and says to Speedy, "I'm sorry mate, but you probably are not aware that it is an old British custom that if you think you can whip any man in the house you turn your glass upside down. Now be a good lad and turn your glass over." Speedy got up and looked all around the room. He stood on the seat of his chair and looked again, slowly, and then looked one more time. He sat down and reached over and got my glass and turned it upside down and said, "I think I can whip any two of you limeys and my friend and I can whip any five of you, we just do not have enough glasses."

Speedy was hit by the time he finished and in less time than it takes to tell about it we were both beat up by about a dozen of them and thrown through the door. Speedy says, "I guess we showed them." Speedy was forever getting both of us in fights. When we were in New York we were sitting at the end of the bar nearest the window and he decided to go to the bathroom. He gets up on his chair and steps up on the bar and walked down the bar with glasses, drinks, bottles and money flying everywhere and jumped off the other end and went to the bathroom. People were so shocked they did not know what to say or do. By the time they had recovered he came back from the bathroom, climbed to the bar and walked back and jumped off at the window end. Someone asked why he did that and he said he did it because he wanted to. Three or four men asked him to step outside and he counted them and said "Get one more guy, my buddy is coming with me." Another one runs over and Speedy looked at them and asked if that was all of them. One guy said it was and Speedy opened the door and motioned them outside. When they got out he pushed me out and yelled, "My buddy does all the light stuff for me", and slammed the door. Those guys kicked the hell out of me and then went inside and ten minutes later they were laughing with Speedy about it and buying us drinks. I needed the drinks; I was hurting.

When we got back to New York the gunnery officer had to go to the port director to get us cleared from quarantine before we could go ashore. He said he would be back in four hours, which is about twice the time it usually takes, but we did not quibble about it. Twenty four hours passed and then forty eight hours went by and he had not returned. Some of us talked to the merchant marine captain and he said we would be in port about 36 more hours. The entire gun crew met and we decided that we would divide into two crews and one crew would take 12 hours liberty and then the other half would take 12 hours liberty and that would put us all back on board 12 hours before sailing time. We drew numbers and all those drawing a one went on liberty.

When we got back from liberty the gunnery officer was waiting and wrote our names down and confined us to our quarters. Later he had a meeting with the entire crew and said he had personal business to take care of in Maryland and did not get back when he thought he would but it gave us no right to leave the ship. He said a problem had developed on the ship that morning and the half of the crew that stayed on board would be given 20 hours liberty every day for the next seven days and the deserters would stay on board and keep his underwear clean and stand watch. The guys in the other half of the crew told him they had every intention of leaving and if he had returned a couple of hours later they would have been the ones missing. He refused to listen to them.

The other half went on liberty and he put all of us on watch and told us if we had to leave our station we would have to come immediately to his room and report where we would be and why. Ten minutes later I went to his room and told him I had loose bowels and would be in the bath room. The next member of the crew did the same thing and it continued until we were all in the bath room, where we stayed. He came in and told us to return to our stations and we did. Ten minutes later we started the same cycle. This continued through the day and night.

The mess went on for five or six days. We kept refusing to wash clothes. The gunnery officer left the ship and one member of the gun crew left and came back with a quart of whiskey and started drinking. He got pretty drunk and when we went to the gunners mess for coffee he came in. There was a long shelf with jars of pickles in mustard and he took a jar and broke it against the wall (okay, bulkhead). He thought it was such a pretty stain that he did three or four more. The merchant mess boy went for the gunnery officer and when he walked in the drunk gun crew member said, "There is that long, tall, ugly son of a you-know-what I have been looking for." He reached in his pocket and pulled out a long knife and told the gunnery officer he was going to kill him. The gunnery officer said, "These men are not going to let you hurt me." He then looked at us and told us to take care of the guy. We looked back and told him what that boy did was no concern of ours and if he wanted to kill a snake that was his business. The gunnery officer had a 38 revolver but was too chicken to draw it. Finally the boy charged him with the knife and I stuck my foot out and tripped him and then took the knife. The gunnery officer left the ship in a hurry. Several hours later a boat came along side and two shore patrol people came on board. They had a list of names and had us pack our stuff and lash our sea bags and hammocks and come with them.

They took us to the Brooklyn Armed Guard Center and we were given a bunk. The next morning they said they did not have the complete story and we were to come to the office every hour and sign in. We checked at four PM and were told we could go on liberty but to resume signing in the next morning. The one that had threatened the gunnery officer was not allowed to go. The next day we were told to just sign in every two hours and the day after that it was changed to twice a day. We met as a group and talked about what was going on and decided something had happened to the gunnery officer before he filed a report. It was decided that it would be best to get on another ship and I was elected to talk to Commander Coakley, the center commander. I made an appointment and asked him if we could be assigned to another ship as we wanted to get on with the war. He checked and said the gunnery officer had listed all names and indicated a serious charge would be filed against one man and he had to assume the rest of us were witnesses. I told him none of us had seen anything. He sent for the entire crew and each man said he had seen nothing. He selected one man at random as a witness and said the rest of us would be assigned to ships but no two of us would be aboard the same ship. I met the gunnery officer one time after that but never learned what happened.

THE S.S. CHARLES SUMNER

They were desperate for Gunners Mates and I was promoted to Gunners Mate Second Class and assigned to the S.S. Charles Sumner. We made trips to Great Britain. This ship was very slow as they were trying a new device. They had huge steel nets secured to the forward and after booms on each side of the ship. When we got to sea they lowered the nets in the water. They were designed to intercept torpedos. They reduced maximum speed from twelve knots to eight knots. We thought they were really ludicrous until they pulled them up and the merchant crew said a torpedo was hung in one of them. They had to get a special crew to remove it. I still really doubt they were worth the effort. We considered them to be a lot like the devices they always installed on the deck when we were in Great Britain. The British came aboard and installed small rockets with a box of wire next to them. We attached one end of the wire to the rocket and if planes dived at us we were supposed to fire the rockets and the wire was supposed to get tangled in the propellers of the plane. We fired one now and then just to watch the wire fly in the air but never fired one at a plane. I did not personally see the torpedo in the nets, but the merchant crew we had was a pretty honest group.

We took on cargo for Great Britain. We returned to England and docked in Liverpool. The gunnery officer got us cleared for liberty but we could not be paid until the next day. None of the gun crew had any money. The chief cook, a Black man, was a good friend or maybe we just had a good working relationship. I frequently gave him steel wool to use in cleaning the stove. Anyway, he asked if I wanted to go along as his guest as he had plenty of money. He said his girl friend had a daughter I could date. I just looked at him and he laughed and said they were white. I decided to tag along. We picked up the girls and started going from pub to pub and soon he was pushing his drink over to me every time he ordered a round. I began to get pretty looped. He went to the bar and bought five or six bottles of wine and had them put them in a cloth bag. We left and headed for the girls' house but I had a problem seeing and kept stumbling. The cook came back and got the wine and told me to come on. I suddenly went totally blind and yelled for them but they did not hear me and I ran into a wall. I got up and felt my way along and came to a door I could tell was a pub from the sound. I went in and felt my way around and found the bar. I decided a drink might clear my sight up and ordered a scotch. I drank it down and the bartender was asking for money. I remembered I did not have any and told him. He got very loud about it and soon several people were slapping me around. I could not even see who they were. I heard a voice say (imagine this in a thick cockney accent) " I say now, the Yank is getting the worst of it, don't you think?" Soon there were more voices telling the ones who were slapping me around to quit. It got louder and louder and I slid down to the end of the bar and found another drink.

    The police came and restored order and asked about me. My new friends paid for my drink and took me with them and put me to bed. I remember waking up several hours later and I was still blind. I got real sick and vomited and I knew I had my sight back as I could see I had vomited all over my hat. About six o'clock they woke me up and gave me a bottle of beer and told me to go back to sleep. Later on they woke me again and gave me a cup of tea and told me to get up and dress. I told them I had ruined my hat and they said they had already washed and dried it. I got up and dressed and they took me to breakfast with them. I was surprised at the small breakfast they got, just a small piece of liver and a piece of bread.

    They told me I was in an anti aircraft unit. They had not liked the treatment I was getting, not fair even for a Yank, eh what? They wrote directions for getting back to the ship and determined the cost and took up a collection. They were really nice to me and were very concerned. I started for the ship and found the first tram and made it okay to the place I was supposed to change. I made that okay but when I made the next change and got on the last tram I found I had over paid someone and did not have enough money. I got off and started walking down the tram tracks and eventually made it to the ship and went to bed.

In a little while someone woke me and said the gunnery officer wanted me at muster immediately. I told him to go to hell. He came right back and said the gunnery officer said I was to get up there immediately. I told him to tell the gunnery officer to go to hell. The next time my ribs were punched I told him to tell the son of a you-know-what to go to hell. The voice said, "This is the son of a you-know-what" and I said, "Go to hell son of a you-know-what." I was put on report, which meant he was going to tell Commander Coakley I had been a bad boy. The first offense before Commander Coakley was always a year in the Naval pen at Portsmouth. I was hurting too much to care. Castration would have been better than getting up.

I finally got out of bed the next day some time and apologized to the gunnery officer in front of the entire crew and he tore up the report. I knew I would not have done that if one of the men had done me that way and I admired him and made a public apology every day for a full week. He was a good man, interested only in what was best for his crew and the war effort and there was not a vindictive bone in his body. I have never had the qualities he did and I admired him very much.

THE S.S.LEWIS LUCKENBACH

Next I was assigned to the SS Lewis Luckenbach, a terrific German made freighter. The Luckenbach was not as new as the Liberty ships but it was ten times tougher. The merchant marine captain was a tough old bird and immensely proud of the Lewis Luckenbach. He would even be caught talking to the ship once in awhile. If we were assigned to a convoy he would find a way to get lost from it. Convoys were miserable with all the zig zagging and escorts running around and speed reduced to the speed of the slowest vessel.

Our rooms were terrific, with beautifully panelled walls and nice decks. Some of the gun crew found a way into the after hold and discovered we had a cargo of scotch whiskey labeled as communications equipment and also a shipment of candy in five pound boxes. They knew none of this was for enlisted men so they confiscated our share. They also found several crates of cigarettes in the old Lucky Strike green packages. They took our share and removed the panels in one of the quarters and stored the loot behind the panels.

The thefts did not go unnoticed when we got to England. The ship was searched from stem to stern and then a guard put on board to search us when we left the ship. The next day they gave up and the crew was free to start using the booty. They had a great time drinking scotch and eating chocolate candy. They never did get all the cigarettes out of the Luckenbach. Cigarettes were only fifty cents a carton at sea and most of us preferred to pay that and smoke the brands we wanted, like Camels for me.

The British always refused to give us the ballast we needed for the return trip and the ships usually rode much too high and were too rough in high seas. The Luckenbach was not as rough as the Liberty ships.

THE S.S.ESSO PROVIDENCE

My last ship was a Tanker, the S.S.Esso Providence. I decided I was going to start saving money. They told us we would be gone about three months so I tore up my partial pay card so there was no way I could draw any money during that three months. The problem with that was we were gone much longer than they said we would be.

We went up a large river to Carapito, Venezuela. There was nothing at the docks except valves and hoses. They started filling our tanks with oil. I met one of the workers and we became friends. He called someone and then told me he had permission to invite our entire gun crew to their club that night. I cleared it with the gunnery officer and they sent a small train down the narrow gage railroad to pick us up. The entire area was filled in swamp land. Their quarters and club were three or four miles from the river.

We had a really great time at their club and they invited us to visit them whenever we were there. Our crew was the first crew they had ever invited. We knew we were going to Montevideo, Uruguay and then come back so they gave the gunnery officer money to buy some whiskey for them. We visited them five or six times.

Montevideo was my favorite city in South America. On our way there my one remaining wisdom tooth started hurting. It was the worst pain I have ever suffered. We did not have a doctor so I got a bottle of APC tablets and chewed them day and night. When we got to Montevideo the gunnery officer took me with him to the port director's office and they called a dentist for me. I went to the dentist and he was an American dentist with twenty-five Uruguayan dentists working for him. He turned me over to one of them and he knew two words of English, namely "spit" and "hurt?" He gave me novocaine and said, "spit." and after a few minutes checked the tooth and said "hurt?" Naturally I screamed and he smiled and gave me more novocaine and repeated the dialogue. About the fourth time he used the "hurt" routine and I nodded my head, he smiled and held up the tooth. It was abscessed and they normally do not remove them until they have treated the abscess but that one was out of there.

I had told the gunnery officer to tell the six ship mates I buddied around with where I would be (a bar naturally) and I went there and got a quart of whiskey. My mouth was numb and the whiskey had no taste but I managed to drink the entire quart before they got there. They ordered another quart and the seven of us drank it. Another quart was ordered and we drank it. I was amazed that I did not feel the slightest bit drunk and decided the novocaine prevented you from getting drunk. I was clear headed and did not feel any effects of the alcohol. We decided to move on and I stood up and that was the last thing I knew until the next morning.

I woke up the next morning and some Uruguayan girl was standing by the bed yelling for money. I did not even know where I was. I looked around for my clothes and they were not in sight. I got up and searched the room with no luck. I asked the girl and she just wanted money. A man came in and I asked him about my clothes. He claimed I came in without them. I tried to borrow some clothes and he just repeated the girl's demand for money. I took a sheet off the bed and wrapped it around me and left the premises. The sign outside said "Good Girls" but one of the good girls was still running along behind me and yelling in Spanish or Portuguese.

I got to the docks and talked the guys there into taking me to the tanker without identification. I walked up the gangway in my sheet and the gunnery officer was laughing so hard he laid down on the deck whooping with laughter. I stepped on his stomach and dropped my sheet in his face and said, "Peasant!" and went to my room and to bed. I got up the same day and confronted my "buddies" and they brought me my clothes and billfold. They said they had drug me all over Montevideo and finally got me a girl. They put me in bed with her and took all my stuff to keep me from getting robbed. They forgot which house they had taken me to and came back to the ship. They had told the guys at the boat house to watch out for a naked sailor and bring him to the tanker.

I went to one of the places that made butterfly trays and one of the guys sketched the tanker and the club house in Carapito for them and I got them to make a huge butterfly tray for our friends in Carapito. We gave it to them on the next trip and they hung it on the wall. We loaded with oil and headed for La Libertad, Ecuador. The Straits of Magellan was fogged in and the captain was delighted as he had always wanted to go around Cape Horn. That has to be the roughest water in the world. We lost two of our rafts on the way around. We did make it though and then on to Ecuador. La Libertad was really nothing but a village with shacks on stilts and goats running around under them. There was a lively grass skirt business and we all bought some of them. When we got back to the docks a man in uniform demanded to see our purchases and levied duty on them several times the amount of the cost. We refused to pay and he said we could not leave. There was a little shack on the end of the dock and he went in it. We were just going to close the door and try to lock him in but during the fracas the shack went over the edge into the water. We got in the boat and went to the tanker. The ship had finished unloading and when we told the gunnery officer what happened he talked to the captain and we left La Libertad hurriedly.

We went to every country in South America except Paraguay. It was a real milk run except we were delivering oil. We were on the way to Montevideo again when apparently a submarine fired a torpedo at us and knocked our rudder off. We could not steer and we expected the sub to come up and finish the job but nothing happened. The Navy had a mine sweeper in the area and they came and patrolled around us. A tug came and tried to tow us but we were too heavy. Another tug came in and the two of them could not tow us. They managed to get us to Fortaleza, Brazil and the mine sweeper came with us. Esso sent another tanker and we transferred our oil to it. The two Navy tugs still could not tow us and we managed to get back to Fortaleza. We were given liberty and shared a boat with the Mine Sweeper. It took us to the beach and then we went to town in a truck.

We got back to the truck and a sailor from the mine sweeper was laying down on the seat on one side and there was no room to sit down. I woke him and asked him to sit up and he told me what to do to myself. I ignored him as long as I could. There was a Chief Petty Officer from the mine sweeper there and I asked him to control his man but he refused. The guy wanted to fight so I got out of the truck and drug him out and beat on him awhile. I thought that would shut him up but after we got on the boat he came and sat down beside me and made some really obscene comments about my Mother. I just stood up and grabbed his hair and pulled him up and hit him and knocked him in the ocean. I sat down and said nothing. When we got to the mine sweeper they asked where he was and I pointed and said, "back there." I found out later that he did not drown, unfortunately.

A commercial tug finally came from Newport News, Virginia and it was smaller than either of the Navy tugs. The Navy tugs had tried to tow us and when we were moving we would just drag them the way we were headed. The commercial tug tied on to the stern and told the captain to provide the power. When we started veering the wrong direction the tug would just pull the stern around to compensate. We had no problem at all and were soon in dry dock in Newport News.

We were sent to the Brooklyn Armed Guard Center to wait on another ship. Remember I told you I had torn up my partial pay card to save money during the three month trip and that we were gone much longer than that. These ship mates had been loaning and giving me money all that time and I owed them. None of them would accept payment so I talked them into a night on the town at my expense. There were twenty eight of us and I drew $1700. We went out to paint the town red. We went to a restaurant and ate and then went to a bar in Brooklyn. We went to Harlem and finally to Manhattan. None of us were feeling any pain. As a finale we rounded up twenty eight taxis with roof windows and formed a convoy back to the Brooklyn Armed Guard Center. It was a real parade. I spent the whole bankroll that one night. To top it off, the Ensign on duty at the center thought we were too boisterous and I told him he was cute when he was mad and kissed him on the cheek. He told the Master at Arms to put me on report. The Master at Arms drug me to the rear of the building and started laughing when we were out of sight. He told me to get lost, fast.

I did not want to skip around and write about Sally every time the ship went to Brooklyn. Sally was a special person in my life. I met Sally in the Coliseum Restaurant on 3rd Avenue the first time I went to Brooklyn. I spent practically every free minute with her when I was on liberty in Brooklyn. I do not know how to describe Sally or the feelings we had for one another. If I had to describe her I would just say she was a girl or maybe even the girl. She had far more than her rightful share of beauty. Even if she had been ugly it would not have mattered. Appearances were not a part of our relationship. She was Sally and I was Tom and that was all that seemed important. It was not even significant to me that she buddied around with other guys when I was at sea. I did not expect her to sit at home. When she wrote me she might just say "Hi" on a single sheet of paper and no more. It was enough. Once she just sent me an empty envelope.

When I got to Brooklyn I knew about where Sally would be and I always found her. If some guy was with her I would tell him to get lost and if he did not get lost I would hit him. If Sally saw me coming she would tell the guy to go away before I got there.

Sally always ran around with Florence Delgado. Speedy dated Florence more because she was with Sally than any other reason. Florence was nuts about Speedy but he really did not care for her much. I guess he dated her for my sake so the four of us could pal around together. We had some really great times and once in awhile some lousy times. The lousy times always started because Speedy would get fed up with Florence. Sex was never involved in our relationship.

Speedy and I went on liberty one night and he said he would like to have a night away from the girls, maybe just go somewhere and start a fight. I agreed and two or three minutes later we ran into Sally and Florence. I told them we were having a night for just boys and we turned and walked away. They followed us every place we went. We walked down and waited on a Staten Island Ferry to pull out and jumped on the ferry after it had pulled out and waved good-bye to the girls.

We went to the St George Bar on Staten Island and had a

few drinks and after an hour or so the girls walked in and sat down at the bar. The bartender told them un-escorted ladies had to sit at a table and they told him they were with us. The bartender asked us if this was true and Speedy said, "They look like a couple of you-know-whats to me and I never associate with you-know-whats." He made them move to a table and Speedy and I got up and left. They followed us out and Florence had a glass with her. She broke it and tried to stab Speedy and he hit her. We left and went to Harlem.

The next day we went on liberty again and found the girls in a booth in a bar. We sat down and Speedy said, "Yesterday was men's day and today is a new day. What do you girls want to do today?" They wanted to go to the St George Bar on Staten Island so that was where we went and the bartender kept staring at us all night. The girls never mentioned the day before and we didn't either.

After Speedy and I were separated I found Sally and Florence every time I was in Brooklyn but Florence said she never saw Speedy any more. On one trip she told me that another sailor said that Speedy went to England and walked in a pub with a sub machine gun and held it up. He was caught and sentenced to a long term in the Naval Prison at Portsmouth. I suppose you might say that there but for the grace of God go I because if I had stayed with Speedy I would have been with him all the way. On the other hand it is also possible I might have talked him out of it.

More on Sally Grenner:

Sally and I at one time talked about getting married when the war was over. We talked about it several nights and then she said something that sounded like she expected us to live in Brooklyn. I asked her and she said that was the only place she would ever live. I suggested Tuscaloosa and she just laughed. I got up and told her I guessed this was good-bye. She said she guessed I was right and I walked out and never heard from her again. I was never really in love with her. She was just a good guy.

I hope wherever Sally is that it has been a good life for her. I often think of the many times Sally and I drank until the bar closed at 4 AM and then sat in the doorway until it opened again at 8 AM. I think sometimes that if I went to Brooklyn and walked down 3rd Avenue between 4 AM and 8 AM I might find Sally sitting there. I hope not.

More on Louise Yorath:

I met Louise Yorath on my first trip to Great Britain. We went to Cardiff, South Wales. Louise was a tall, thin wonderful girl with stars in her eyes and Heaven in her smile. I guess I was captivated by her.

Louise and I had a total of three dates and they consisted primarily of sitting in a Pub and talking and then riding the bus to Whitchurch and seeing her home. She was required to be home

Louise Yorath

by 10:30. We were never sexually involved at all - not even close to it. We were double dating with a ship mate of mine named Keith and a girl named Frances. Keith was really quite foul mouthed and Louise did not like him at all.

Louise and I had a definite understanding we were going to get married. We tried to work it out after the war and my congressman, Ed DeGraffenried, worked very hard to get the red tape cut.

No one will ever know how much I loved Louise. She was a wonderful girl and I loved her with all my heart. She was so beautiful that I had a problem understanding what she saw in me when she obviously could have any man she wanted. I was not handsome or good looking and did not even have a job. Anyway, things never worked out for us, no matter how hard we tried and we finally gave up.

Later in life, (I was not involved) Louise had a baby and she was born a spastic. She lived for six and a half years and was still a baby when she died. Louise was a wonderful Mother to her. I never saw her. I mention this only so I can show what a wonderful person Louise was. She loved that baby with all her heart and soul and saw to it that the child always knew she was loved. The baby had a lot of problems but she received more love than most children ever know in a lifetime.

Many years later I received a phone call from a lady who said she was in Washington, D.C. and was Louise's traveling companion. I was at a loss at first and she told me she was Louise Yorath when I knew her. She said Louise was on a shopping trip. She wanted to verify my address so she could return the passage money I had sent her years before. Louise was not there but she asked that I call her back later. I wanted to call and I even dialled the number several times but always hung up before there was an answer. I finally got up the nerve to call and her traveling companion answered and said Louise had gone somewhere. A few days later I received an envelope with the passage money in it.

It was not to be. It is over. Only the memories of a tall,

thin and beautiful Welsh lass riding the bus from Cardiff to Whitchurch remain. However, fifty years after I last saw her, I wrote her at her old address and miracle of miracles, the people there knew of her and sent word for her to come get my letter. We corresponded awhile but that has ended. I am destined to leave this world without being loved.

More on Mabel Day:

Mabel Day is the only girl I ever knew for less than three days who impacted my life. I got a total of four days unofficial port director's leave during the more than four years I spent in the Navy. Our ship was in New York and was going to be there ten days and each half of the crew was given four days leave. It was not enough time to go home but Speedy was going to Cincinnati to visit his wife and invited me to go along with him. We got to Cincinnati and went to their house at 1616 Sutter Avenue. Speedy's father in law was there and when we walked in Speedy looked at him and told him he would be there three or four days and to get out and not to come back until he was gone. His father in law was gone in fifteen minutes. I knew the reason because Speedy told me his wife's father had started having sex with her when she was six years old. Jayne came in and Speedy asked her if she and her father had been doing it and she nodded her head that they had. He was very calm and made a remark like, "Nothing like a man finding his wife just like he left her - freshly sexed." A really beautiful natural blonde girl walked in and Speedy looked at her and said, "Your papa been doing you, too?" She told him her father knew better than to fool with her and he never had. The blonde looked at me and told me her name was Mabel in case I wondered and that she did not put out in case Speedy had told me she did.

Mabel had crooked teeth but the teeth really made her look cute. Not that she was not cute anyway, but they really added to her beauty. She and Jayne had a younger sister named Doris. Doris was about 13 and the first time I saw her she said,

"I am Doris and my father does not fool with me, I would kill him if he did." The family was well aware of what the father was doing to Jayne. Mabel told me that Jayne did not want to have sex with their father but she was the type person who did what her parents told her to do and had never had the strength to challenge him. She said her father tried to fool with her once and she bit him on the most sensitive part of his anatomy and told him if he ever tried again she would bite it off.

We had a lot of fun and when we left after three days there I had a semi-crush on Mabel and she seemed to like me, too. We wrote one another for a few months and one day I got a letter from her with pictures. She had her teeth straightened and although she was the same beautiful and dizzy blonde something seemed too different and our correspondence gradually died away.

More on Paul Gomez:

When I got back to the ship I let the other half of the crew go on port directors leave. I made watch assignments and checked to see that everyone got back. Paul Gomez (not his real name), from Pittsburgh, was older than most of us. He was in his thirties and most of us were in our early twenties. Paul had just returned from four days in Pittsburgh. I put him on watch in the aft gun tub. I really did not notice anything unusual about Paul. Some of the crew came in and told me Paul acted unusual and was drinking. He had told several of them good bye. I had given Paul a 38 revolver and it was loaded so I decided to stop by the other two posts and get their guns and then go back and get Paul's. By having the other two guns I could tell him I was going to clean all of them without making him suspicious.

When I got aft I did not see Paul and I climbed in the gun tub and found him laying on the deck. I was angry because I thought he had passed out on duty and I kicked him and told him to get up. He did not move and then I saw a small hole in his jacket. I checked and he had a pulse so I thought it might not be too bad. I turned him over and he had a hole in the back you could stick your fist in. I yelled for someone to call an ambulance and took off my shirt and undershirt. I stuffed the undershirt in the hole and tied the shirt around him, not knowing if that was bad or good. The ambulance was there quickly and hauled Paul off.

The Navy decided I may have been at fault in letting Paul have a gun when he was drinking and they had a hearing. It was messy awhile but the gun crew members testified it was very hard to tell Paul was drinking and the only way they knew was he had offered them a drink. I was exonerated. It developed that Paul got home and his wife was not there and he found some pictures made of her and another sailor in a hotel room. When she got home he handed her the pictures and left. He was deeply in love with her and told the doctor he would finish the job when he got a gun. The Navy brought his wife to Brooklyn and got her a room. She was still in love with Paul and Paul said he would not kill himself if they let him out of the Navy. They gave him an honorable discharge and several years later someone told me she and Paul were doing fine and still in love.

The war in Europe was winding down and gunners mates were in demand in the Pacific. There was a requirement in Guam for 400 of us and when I got off my last ship I was put on a troop train with approximately 400 gunners mates, heading for Bakersfield, California. The troop train was filthy and there was no drinking water or wash water. The engine was a coal burner and we were covered with soot and cinders. The seats were the most uncomfortable I had ever sat on and we were sore and aching. The train stopped in Chicago and there was a water hose laying there. We got off the train and drank and washed our faces. A train pulled in on the next track and did not have pullman cars but did have mattresses. It was loaded with Italian prisoners of war. We went aboard the train and got the mattresses and took them to our train. We kicked the seat backs off and spread out the mattresses. The conductor came in and opened his mouth. I pushed him against the wall and said, "Don't!", and he didn't.

Nothing was said and we were more comfortable than before.

We got to Bakersfield and it was the most miserable place I saw during the war. There were 40,000 Naval personnel there, most waiting for a new assignment. Permanent party personnel had authority and seaman second class were bossing first class gunners mates, chief cooks, and others with high ratings. I was a gunners mate second class and was assigned to mess cook duty and not even allowed to change from my dress uniform. There were four serving lines at the mess hall and it took so long to get through the line that it was time to get in line for the next meal when you finished eating. Seaman second class, with their little permanent party badges, had authority to pull you out of the line and assign you to mess cook duty. I had never seen anything like it. Frequently, when you lined up to get a liberty pass you were put on mess cook duty.

One day I walked as far away from the center of activity as possible and found a hill of red dirt. I went to the top and sat down and sat there all day and until noon the next day, trying not to think at all. My uniform was red with dust and dirt. I finally got up and went back to the hell hole. I quit speaking to anyone and quit shaving. No one even noticed. In a few more days they posted a notice with a list of the four hundred going to Guam. My name was not on it. I checked and there were 407 gunners mates and the seven with the most sea duty were being assigned shore duty. I was number one for shore duty. I was afraid it meant shore duty there and was prepared to fight to go to Guam. I was being sent to New Orleans.

When I arrived in New Orleans I was told there were no available quarters and I would be paid an allowance. They said I would be there a minimum of one year and could lease a room or apartment for a year if I wanted to. I knew the Navy better than that so I found an apartment and rented it for a week and talked the landlord into writing me a fake lease for one year. One week later I was called in and told I was being assigned to Galveston, Texas. I laid the lease on the desk and asked how I was supposed to handle that. They said they would pay me temporary duty for Galveston.

I arrived in Galveston and was assigned to work on a small island there. My job was to go aboard merchant ships and remove all small items of Navy property and tag the larger items, like guns, and get serial numbers. I then typed bills of lading and contractors removed and shipped the items. It took two hours work per day to stay current.

I shared a room in a local home with another sailor. The owner of the home was a close relative of a professional football quarterback. His sister, Bennie Andrus, was very attractive. I had another room in another house by myself and no one but me knew where it was. I also shared a house with six other sailors. We rented it complete with furniture, cooking utensils, towels, linens, etc. So I had three places to hide out and I planned on a lot of fun.

Galveston was a great place to be and such a contrast with the hell of Bakersfield. I loved it. I made a lot of friends. The Naval officers I was associated with were all mavericks, having been enlisted at one time. They just looked at whether we were getting the work done or not. It was not important what time we got there or how long we took for lunch or when we left, if we got all the work done.

One of the boys who shared the house with me had been in numerous battles in the Pacific and during one of those battles his turret had gone out. The gunnery officer kept screaming at him over the phone to get back in action and had finally told him he was coming down and shoot him if he did not get it going at once. He was working as hard as he could and when the gunnery officer did actually come to the turret he hit him in the head with a ball peen hammer and killed him. He had been tried and found not guilty of murder. He always had a ball peen hammer by the side of his bed and we walked on egg shells around him. No one wanted to upset him and if we voted on something about the house we always asked him to vote first and then it was unanimous. I do not really think he would have hurt any of us but what the heck.

Some nights I would stay at the house and some nights I would stay at the apartment. When I wanted to be secluded from the world I would stay at my unlisted room. It was a good life. I did miss sea duty but not badly enough to volunteer for it again. If I never got sea sick I might have but when I was aboard ship I was sea sick around half the time; maybe even more if you included the times I just had a vague discomfort.

One of the boys was living with a woman in her sixties. She bought him anything he wanted and gave him money all the time. He always had around a thousand dollars in his billfold and sent a lot of money to his wife. He said he would have plenty of money to start a business when the war was over.

The war did end and the VJ (Victory over Japan) celebration in Galveston was something to see.

The war ended after the atomic bombs were dropped over Japan. The VJ celebration was spectacular in Galveston. Kissing was the order of the day and we shy people had to be extremely careful to prevent the girls from taking advantage of us. Girls that would not normally give you the time of the day would run you down and lay one on you.

I thought it meant I would go home the next day, surely within a week. They told us about the point system where you got a point for each month of service and another point for each month of sea duty and the ones with the most points got out first. I came out near the top and it was not too long before I was on the way to a separation center in Memphis, Tennessee.

The guardhouse lawyer types stayed at the separation center longer, trying to get disability pensions. I just wanted out and told them I had suffered no disabilities. They found a shadow on my x-rays and kept me several extra days anyway, but finally said it was just a childhood tuberculosis scar and nothing significant. They finally let me go.

Fifteen of us went to a restaurant across from the bus station and had a beer while we were waiting on our bus. The waitress was a real cute girl but had an awful frown and we wanted to see her smile. Each of us gave a dollar tip and one of us handed it to her. She looked at it and put it in her pocket but her expression did not change. We talked about that and each one put in five dollars more and gave that to her. She looked at it and put it in her pocket but her expression did not change. I suggested we go all the way and each of us put in twenty dollars and I handed it to her and told her it was our final installment on the tip for the day. She gave us a smile that lit up the room. Boy, $390.00 to get a smile. Life was great and all should smile. Many of us found little to smile about when we got home.

I often think about the productive things I could have done with my free time during World War II if I had been a non-drinker. But then I also remember that I got it all out of my system then and have been a non drinker for more than 40 years, so maybe it was worth it.

Now I look at the list of World War II Armed Guards and see all the deceased indicators and it tears at my heart to think of those strong and vibrant young men growing old and in some cases infirm or deceased. The Armed Guard is something not ever likely to be seen again. Enemies now have all the high tech equipment enabling them to not only know exactly where the ships are, but of destroying them instantly with little chance of resistance. We are truly a dying breed, never to be seen again.

Chapter Eight

The US Army and Return to Civilian Life

I was disappointed when I got home. I do not know what I expected but it was different from what I found. I took a few days to get familiar with the changes made while I was gone. Alabama has alcoholic beverage laws by county and Tuscaloosa was a dry county. That meant you had to deal with a bootlegger or drive to Greene county to purchase beverages and hope you did not get caught on the way back. There was a place you could drink beer just across the Greene County line, called Midway. Cars were about impossible to find but William Hoggle sold me an old 1935 Dodge. William (Bill) Miller and I would drive over now and then and drink a beer or two.

Goofing off got old and I was ready to go to work. A different contractor had the post office contract so I did not have a right to my old job. I tried several places and I guess the results were best summed up by the one honest answer I got at Hardin's Bakery. The man looked at me and said, "We have too many veterans we are forced to rehire. Veterans think the world owes them something and are generally very poor workers. We have a few openings but are saving them for non-veterans. If you know any non-veterans looking for work, tell them to stop by and see us."

Eugene Barlow was a good friend from high school and he was out of the Navy and found the same treatment. He told me he had been reading his Blue Jacket's Manual and was going back in the Navy. Gene went to Midway on his motorcycle to drink a couple of beers and on the way back he was leaning on a curve and his head hit the fender of an Army truck going the other way and cut the entire top of his head off.

Champ Lewis had decided to stay in the Navy. He was on PT boats in World War II and a shell had gone through the radio room and missed his head by inches. He went to New London, Connecticut for submarine training and had a heart attack and died a week after he got there.

L.B. Hughes had died on the USS Arizona at Pearl Harbor. Roy Schmarkey had taken a shell in the chest and lost several ribs. He married a Boston girl and stayed in Boston. William Hoggle was married and working all the time. Bill Miller was too lazy to work and never paid for anything. Many old class mates were killed in World War II. The girls had all got married. I could not find a job and there was nothing to do. I quit drinking and there was less to do. I talked to the recruiting people and the Army recruiter told me there was a bill in process that would permit them to give equivalent rank and if I joined I would not have to take basic training and would be given staff sergeant status as soon as the President signed the bill. I decided to go for it.

I joined the Air Corps branch of the U.S. Army and was sent to Wichita Falls, Texas. It developed that it was a basic training camp and I would have to take basic training after all. It also developed that the President did sign the bill the recruiter told me about but it was not retroactive and therefore did not apply to me as I joined two days before he signed it into law. I always felt I got the shaft but several people have told me it is the breaks and I had nothing to complain about. The end result is that I was told I would receive 16 weeks of basic training.

I felt like I ought to know my way around the service by now so I started checking for problem areas and learned that company commanders were concerned about property as the service had cracked down and the commanders were responsible for all property, including the buildings in their companies. My company had many shortages and many damaged buildings. The commander was worried about it.

I went to the commander and told him I could take care of all his shortages and if he would put me in supply and carry me on the books as receiving basic training I would guarantee he would have no shortages at the end of my 16 weeks there. He agreed, and I did not receive a day of basic training. I was rated, however, as outstanding.

I found that the techniques I had used in the CCC worked in the Army. It was a matter of getting to know people and being willing to take a few chances. I had expected to be a staff sergeant and was a private instead so I could not see how I had much to lose. I did a complete inventory and found out what the shortages were and was surprised to find there were some significant overages. I did a lot of trading with other companies and made a real dent in the shortages in record time.

There were no shortages by the time basic training had been completed. I had even managed to get damages to buildings repaired. Everything was in good order. The commander had kept his end of the bargain by giving me credit for basic training, with excellent ratings. I looked forward to getting out of there and started checking the bulletin board frequently for shipping orders. My name finally appeared on the bulletin board but I was going nowhere. Based on my excellent marks in basic, I had been selected for advanced basic, a six week course. I was reassigned to another company and my commander had a talk with the new commander and soon I was making up shortages in another company while being given credit for advanced basic. I insisted on marginal ratings.

When I completed my basic training I was given a medical examination and the doctor found I had a hernia. Two days later I received surgery. The doctor gave me a spinal and adjusted a ceiling mirror so I could watch. It was very interesting. They took me to a bay and in an hour the feeling returned and I got up and shaved. The doctor came in and was really upset and made me go back to bed. He left and I got up and walked around the ward talking to other patients. Some of them had the same surgery I did and were still in bed after three weeks had passed. The nurse made me go back to bed but as soon as she left I was up again. The doctor came back and she talked to him. He came over and asked me if I was going to stay in bed and I told him I was not. He talked to the nurse and after he left she told me I was on K.P. duty and would serve breakfast to everyone in the ward the next morning. Most of those guys stayed in bed four weeks and I was working the next day.

I was selected to attend airborne radar school in Boca Raton, Florida and finally got out of Texas. I would get Observer wings but actually be an airborne radar operator in the Air Sea Rescue Service.

I was given a long recuperation leave that I really did not need. I had known Bennie Andrus pretty well in Galveston. I called her and talked to her about coming out for a visit and she said to come on out. I took off to Galveston. When I got there we talked awhile and decided we would have a week-long party and then get married. We invited a lot of people to help us celebrate. Bennie invited a sergeant from Fort Crockett and he had a cousin in Houston and got our approval to invite her. Don't ask me how marriage came up. We were not in love.

The cousin arrived from Houston and I will just call her Billie Jo. When Billie Jo walked in and I looked at her, I knew I was in for some trouble. She was actually around 35 years old but could easily pass for 16. She was a beautiful woman and I mean really beautiful. We sat around and talked awhile and Bennie decided she wanted to go bowling at Fort Crockett. I told her I did not bowl and Billie Jo said she didn't either. It was decided that Billie Jo and I would go to a family bar near the house and Bennie and the Sergeant would go bowl and join us at the bar.

Billie Jo and I went to the bar and had a couple of beers and then kissed. We were kissing again when Bennie and the Sergeant got there and Bennie was pretty miffed about it. I told her we were just killing time. We had a few more beers and went back to the house. Billy Jo was staying there and we talked about me coming to her room but decided we had better not. I got up early the next morning and Billie Jo was taking a shower. When she came out of the bathroom she told me she was going back to

Houston and asked me if I wanted to come with her. I packed a few things and we left.

When we got to Houston we checked in at the Rice Hotel and spent the day and the night there. The next morning we went to her house. She had two children. I stayed there about a week. Bennie called and it was just my luck that I answered the phone and she recognized my voice. She asked me if I was coming back to Galveston and I told her I probably would in a few days. The next day Billie Jo and I were talking and she said she needed to warn me about her former husband. She said he was still very jealous and had killed two of her boy friends. He had walked up to the last one and handed him a knife and then shot him and claimed self defense. I got up real early the next morning and went back to Galveston.

When I got back to Galveston Bennie asked me if I still wanted to get married and I told her it really made no difference to me and if she wanted to we would and if not, we wouldn't. She said she thought maybe I should just pack and leave so I packed and left.

Bennie was a really nice person and I regret what I did to her. Her first husband was an enlisted man in the Army and was selected for Officer's Candidate School. Bennie supported him all the way and when he graduated she bought him several uniforms. After a few days he told her she was fine for an enlisted man's wife but he deserved better for an Officer's Lady and he wanted a divorce. She gave it to him with no strings attached. Bennie was closely related to Slinging Sammy Baugh, a well known professional football quarterback. She later married a man who appreciated her and I was happy for her.

This could have been the beginning of a successful and rewarding career if I had the right attitude but I must admit my attitude was really bad. I don't know why I have always felt it was my job to save my immediate world from the local villains. I could have saved myself a lot of grief by just being one of the oppressed and letting it go at that. Circumstances have sometimes led me into a situation. That is what happened at Boca

Raton.

The school was twelve weeks in duration and before it even started, I was called to the Public Information Office (PIO). The PIO wanted a series of twelve articles written for the Fort Lauderdale, Florida newspaper and it was preferred they be written by a native Floridian. The PIO had checked and I was the only student in the course born in Florida. I was to give him an article every Monday morning covering the events of the previous week. We discussed content and I was told to write anything I wanted to and the PIO would edit it and remove anything contrary to regulations or local policy.

I gave the PIO my first article and he read it and said it was great and he was not going to edit a word of my stuff. Maybe I should have known he was referring to all future articles but I assumed he was referring to just that one single article. I continued to write on the assumption that he would remove anything offensive.

The Base Commander was Colonel R. Beam. The base, as I remember it, was long and fairly narrow and a bus service was required to get around the base. There were many bus stops, each with a roof and benches. Colonel Beam observed some men standing under one shelter and not sitting down and had the benches removed from all bus stops. He then saw some men standing in the sun instead of under a roof and had the roof of every bus stop removed. The Colonel then saw some men walking and discontinued the bus service. I reported this chain of events in my weekly articles, along with my personal opinion of Col Beam as a Commander.

The Officer in charge of the school was named Dan and was disliked by students and fellow officers as well. He was called Dangerous Dan by everyone, behind his back. I openly referred to him as Dangerous Dan. I reported many of his stupid and insipid remarks and gave my interpretation of them. I came down on him pretty heavy with my pen. In addition, I was reporting on the lack of quality of the food, referring to it as slop and several less flattering terms. I reported on the poor condition of the planes we were using for our training missions, and the fact that one Major refused to fly in them and frequently resulted in us going on training missions without an instructor. In short, if it was unflattering, I reported it in blunt and brutal language. I suppose I was at war with the Army Air Force.

I had seven articles published when Colonel Beam sent for me. He was very sarcastic, asking if the chair he told me to sit in was comfortable enough or if I preferred his chair. I got up to try his chair and he told me to sit down and shut up. I threw my cap on his desk and sat down. He then read aloud, very slowly, and with great emphasis, all seven articles I had written. I had not seen any of them after I gave them to the PIO, but I soon realized all were exactly as I had written them, with not a single word changed. I later learned that the PIO was leaving the Army for a job with the Associated Press and had decided to have some fun before he left. Unfortunately, the fun was as much at my expense as that of the Army.

When he finished, Colonel Beam looked at me and said, "Explain, please." I told him I had been instructed to write whatever I wanted to and the PIO would edit in accordance with policy. He said that would not cut it so I just told him it was all factual and if changes were needed, they should be changes in the attitude of him and his staff, not in how I perceived what they were doing. I told him that in my opinion, he and his staff were immature, inconsiderate and unconcerned.

Colonel Beam told me that he would reduce me from PFC to Private if I was worth the cost of the paper work. I told him to check into the cost and if it was not too bad I would pay for it. He told me to get the hell out of his office. I started out and he asked me if I had forgotten something. I went back and got my cap off his desk and he said that was not what he meant. I knew he meant I should salute him but I pretended ignorance and said, "Oh, the remaining five articles? I will continue to turn in one each week." He said to just get the hell out.

The PIO was leaving when I stopped by and told him what had happened and he said, "Good stuff for the next article, give him good coverage." He said he was sorry he got me into it. I continued to drop off an article a week in the PIO office but of course no more were printed.

The airborne training was particularly bad. We flew in C-47's and B-26 bombers. When we got in the air we had to crank a radar unit down below the plane. We then used the radar to plot a course and give the pilot headings. The planes were in terrible condition and we frequently listened to the ground crew telling the pilot what all the known defects were. Parts and mechanics were in short supply. In addition, pilots were required to fly four hours and make three landings every month to retain flight pay. It was not unusual for up to seven pilots to fly with us and for each one to shoot three landings. The training flight was half over by the time this was done. Training flights were supposed to be five hours but several times a Colonel would insist he only needed four hours to qualify and insist on cutting the flight short. The pilots were rusty and frequently missed the runway when shooting landings.

Our final examination was to navigate the plane from Boca Raton to Jacksonville, Florida, then to Havana, Cuba and back to Boca Raton. We were asked where we wanted to be assigned and I asked for McChord Field in the state of Washington. I was assigned to West Palm Beach, Florida, just a few miles away. I am certain Colonel Beam arranged that for me.

There was nothing to do at West Palm Beach as there were no Air Sea Rescue planes. All I did was sit all day and then go to town and drink beer. It was plain miserable. Someone finally recognized they did not need me there and I was asked where I wanted to be assigned. I had learned something by this time and put down Key West, Florida as first choice and McChord Field, Washington as last choice. Sure enough, I was assigned to McChord Field, Washington.

I had been writing Mae Brucke for four years and although I had never seen her, we felt we were candidates for marriage. I made the worst mistake of my life and asked Mae if she would marry me. Mae said she would and I was given a seventeen day delay in route to McChord Field. I packed and left for Birmingham, Alabama to get married.

Let me recap what I have mentioned before. One of my best friends at Camp Icicle in the Civilian Conservation Corps (CCC) was Charles Brucke. Charles was one of the five (out of 200) boys at the camp with a high school education and worked in the supply room. He was later made Supply Sergeant. Charles gave me his sister's address and I wrote her a letter about once a week while I was in the CCC. We became good friends. Mae was what I called a good buddy, just a plain old country girl and certainly not much to look at. I liked her a lot and she was always ready to cheer me up if I mentioned having a problem or if she detected I was down in the dumps.

I continued to write to Mae while I was in the Navy and then when I got in the Army, but I had never met her. When the Army Air Force decided to send me from West Palm Beach, Florida to McChord Field, Washington, Mae and I decided I would get a delay in route and meet her in Birmingham and we would get married. We had still never met and I guess we just drifted into it from having corresponded so many years. I still do not understand why we decided to do it. I never loved her.

I got off the train in Birmingham and Mae was waiting on me. I really knew the minute I saw her that I did not want to marry her. Mae was just not my type and she talked in a loud voice that irritated me. She was so excited and happy about it that I kept putting off telling her I did not want to marry her. We found a doctor and had blood tests and he back dated them so we could get a marriage license. I still kept thinking I would find a way to break it to her that I did not want to marry her. An old man watched us get the license and came over and asked if we needed a minister. We told him we did and in less than ten minutes we were in his home "around the corner" and married. I still could not believe we did it. We stayed in Birmingham that night and the next day we rode a bus to Jasper and went to her Mother's home.

Most of the Brucke family members were as nice as

Charles and Mae and it was a pleasure meeting them. I had 14 days delay in route but after two days in Jasper with Mae I told her that I had to go on to McChord Field, and left. I met a girl on the train who lived in Gary, Indiana and stopped in Gary and stayed with her a week. I then went on to McChord Field, arriving there a day or two early.

I arrived at McChord Field several days early and was assigned to an Air Sea Rescue unit. It surprised me that they had planes with APQ-13 RADAR Units. It would have been more in character for the Army to have had no radar at all. I was assigned to a crew after taking the flight examination. It seemed like it would be a good assignment at McChord if I was not worrying night and day about my marriage. I never have determined why I married Mae as I never loved her. It seems like something I just drifted into and that it just happened and I had no control over it. I keep rambling about it as I still wonder why I did it.

A Marine plane with 32 Marines aboard was reported missing and we were told we were going to search for it when the weather cleared. It was snowing so hard you could not see two feet ahead of you. The parents of one of the Marines were very wealthy and influenced their Congressman and Senator to use their influence to get us in the air without regard to the weather and flying conditions. Someone came to the barracks to take us to our plane and we had to hold hands to keep from getting lost in the snow. I turned around and went back in the barracks. I was not about to get in a plane with those flying conditions.

Our plane took off and the pilot got lost and landed in California. The Marine plane was not found until the snow melted the following spring. I was sent to the doctor and he disqualified me for flight duty because I had refused to fly. It did not matter that I was right and there was nothing that could be done. I was assigned to menial tasks and it was obvious there was no future for me. Fortunately, about this time there was a push to reduce personnel and it was announced that anyone below a certain rating, and married, could apply for and receive a hardship discharge. I applied and was soon on the way to Alabama again.

My Mother and I had a house very close to the courthouse in Tuscaloosa. I went to Jasper and got Mae and brought her home. I found a job at B.F. Goodrich, building truck tires. It was third shift work and very hard work at that. The tires we built were so heavy that when I first started I could not lift a tire to the overhead conveyor when I finished building it. The job was tough and then when I got home it was even tougher because I did not love Mae. The tire plant unionized and things got even worse. The Union agreed to piece work and standards were set and I was paid 32 cents per tire and making about eight per shift, which came out to $2.56 per day. Then my machine broke down and the foreman said that the Union contract specified I would sweep floors until the machine was fixed and be paid $1.00 per hour. I had made one tire when it broke down. I checked my time card the next night and I had not been paid for the seven hours I spent sweeping floors. The foreman said that the Union contract specified that my hourly pay would not begin until the mechanic arrived to fix my machine and he had not arrived when I left so I had no hourly pay coming. I quit the job when he told me that. He asked how much notice I was giving and I told him the same amount of notice they gave me when I swept floors seven hours free.

I went to the office the next morning for my final pay and they said it would be mailed in 30 to 60 days. I picked up a bench and told them they could write me a check right then or get the office torn apart with that bench. They wrote me a check. I started working with my Mother upholstering furniture the next day.

Mae got pregnant and things drug on. Mae decided she wanted to go to Jasper and have the baby there where she knew the doctors. She said it was time for the baby, even though she barely looked pregnant. We arrived in Jasper on Saturday and went to the clinic across the street from the hospital. The doctors were listening to an Alabama football game but checked Mae and laughed and told her to come back in five or six months. She insisted it was time so a doctor took us to the hospital and had her admitted and went back to the clinic. The baby was born between the front desk and her room.

The baby was perfect in every way and we named him Charles Henry Bowerman, after Mae's brother. The doctor billed us for delivery but I refused to pay as a nurse actually delivered the baby and the doctor had nothing to do with it. He did not push the matter. I went back to Tuscaloosa.

Mae and I never lived together again. I sought and received advice from just about everyone I knew on what to do. I finally decided it was best to get a divorce as soon as possible. The divorce is the only thing I ever did in my life that I am ashamed of. I cannot justify it as Mae was never unfaithful to me, she was a good woman, she had my child, she was a Christian. No matter how I try to rationalize I still understand I did her wrong. She loved me and I did not love her. She tried to do everything I asked to please me and I discarded her. I will go to hell for that.

I went to several lawyers and every one of them told me that at that time adultery or being in prison were the only two grounds for divorce. I found one lawyer who said he could do it and turned it over to him and in a few days we were divorced. Mae was awarded custody and child support and I paid her child support for twenty years.

Mae is still alive and still living in Jasper.

Chapter Nine

Charles Henry Bowerman, My First Son

Charles was born in Jasper and raised there. I did not visit as there were bad relationships with several members of the Brucke family and it appeared at the time to be the best approach. I know now that if I had it to do over again I would visit often. That is life; you do not always know the right thing to do until it is too late.

Charles was drafted in the Army and sent to North Carolina. His Company Commander called me several times about problems Charles was having adjusting to Army life. He called one day and said he was going to recommend a bad conduct discharge. I was able to talk him into recommending a discharge under honorable conditions so it would not reflect on Charles all his life. He agreed and I was told that Charles was discharged under honorable conditions.

Charles and his wife, Linda, visited me one time in Anniston and I enjoyed the visit very much. I am sorry I was not more supportive of Charles. I took the easy way out and let him down miserably.

When I step back and look critically at my support of Charles, I can find much to be critical of and nothing to be proud of. I have no admiration of myself in this aspect of my life. I failed miserably. God help me.

Charles had two daughters and a son. Sandi, the oldest daughter, called me for help several times and I always helped her when I could. She quit high school and married John Tidwell in Jasper. I gave them $500 to make a down payment on a mobile home. They have a daughter now, my first great grand child.

Charles Ray, my grandson (son of Charles) quit high

Left to right: Sandi, Terri, Charles Ray

school and got married. He and his wife have a son, born just a couple of weeks after Sandi's daughter. Terri, the other child of Charles, remained in school and she graduated in May, 1996. She was 18 May 19, 1996.

I do what I can for Charles and his children, but on retirement pay there is not too much I can do other than helping them financially at Christmas.

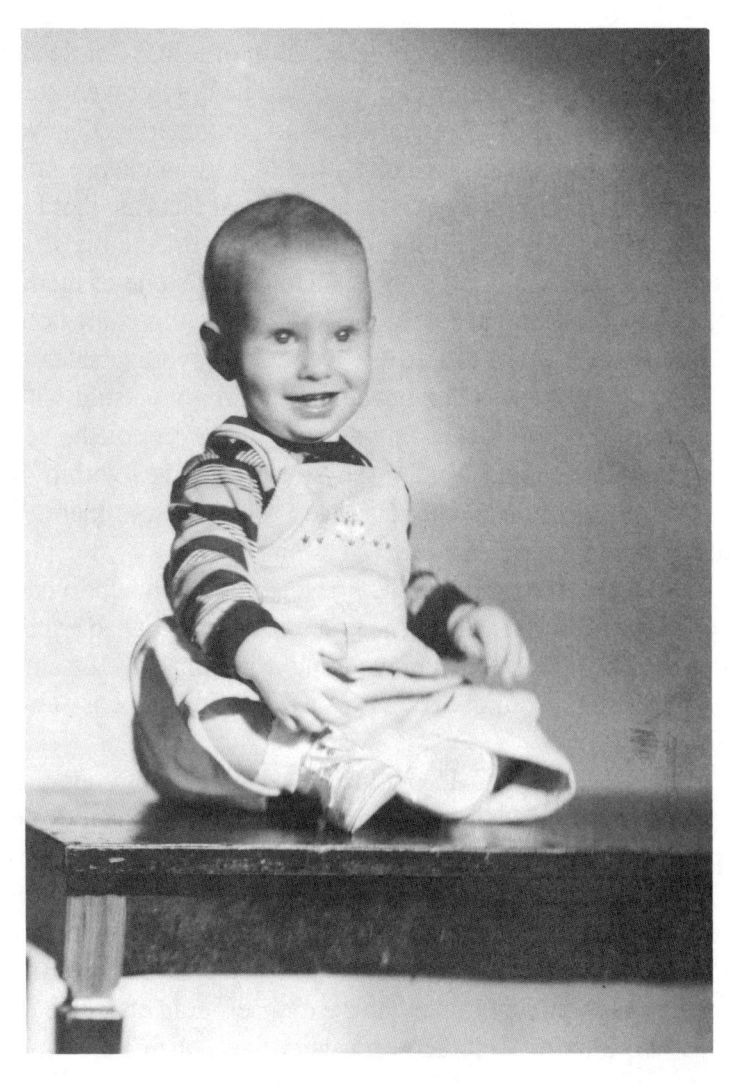

Charles Henry Bowerman

Chapter Ten

Life After Marriage

Divorcing Mae did not win me any friends in her family. Charles and I had been good friends a long time and Charles just told me it was between the two of us and he did not want to get involved. The rest of the family was not so generous. They all wanted to get involved. I guess I used this as an excuse not to visit my son. It was a poor excuse and the real facts are that I just did not visit. There are things you would do differently if you had the chance to do it all over again and this is one of them.

My Mother and I sold the house near the court house. Tuscaloosa had voted to legalize alcoholic beverage sales and the law at the time was that beverages could not be sold within one mile of a school unless it was within 400 feet of the court house. Several people wanted the house as it was within 400 feet of the court house and beverages could be sold there. We sold the house to the Carpenter's Union.

We bought a new house in Meadow Lawn subdivision. It was a two bedroom house. The first one we bought had a spring under the house and the man we bought it from gave us a new one on higher ground. It was a new house and cost about $6,000.00.

My Mother and I bought a 1941 Chevrolet coupe and got William Hoggle, who was working at the Studebaker dealership then, to repair everything he could find wrong with it. We then invited Bill Miller and his Mother (Aunt Lizzie) to go on a vacation to Colorado with us. Bill did not want his Mother to go but I told him he could go only if his Mother went. I asked Bill if he had enough money to pay their expenses and he said he did.

We left for Colorado and when we got to Fort Smith,

Arkansas the car kept jumping out of high gear and the speedometer quit working. I had to hold the gear shift and guess at the speed and miles the rest of the trip. We went to Colorado Springs, Colorado and the surrounding area. Bill had enough money for their expenses for one or two days and I had to pay for everything the rest of the trip. It was a nice trip, though and we really enjoyed it.

My Mother met a man named Archie Claypool and they decided to get married. The house was too small for all of us and I could not afford to move and pay my own expenses so I decided to get in the Air Force. The Air Force said I would have to prove I had no dependents so I got Mae to sign a document to the effect that she and our son were not dependent on me. The document meant I never had to pay her child support again but we had a verbal agreement that I would continue to pay and I did.

My Mother married Archie in Columbus, Mississippi and I left for the Air Force.

Chapter Eleven

The Army Air Force

I was told again that I would not have to go through basic training, due to prior military experience. I was again sent to a base and assigned to basic training. I decided to just go along with it and found I enjoyed it. Nothing to think about, just grunt and groan with the young kids. It wasn't too bad and half the time the drill instructor goofed off and gave the company to me.

There was the usual stuff, learning to make a bed, drilling, long hikes, drinking beer in the PX, telling jokes, fights, home sick kids, writing letters, working KP duty, standing watch, scrubbing floors, smoking cigarettes, doing without, being broke and wondering what the hell you were doing there.

It seemed like you were busy every minute, yet had all the time in the world to reflect on where you had been and to wonder where you were going in life. It had to end and it did and I was assigned to Ellington Air Force Base in Houston, Texas.

I arrived at Ellington Air Force Base and was assigned to an organization responsible for helping planes land in difficult situations. We had large trailers filled with tube technology electronic equipment. We had to pull the trailer to the end of a runway and level it with hydraulic jacks, calibrate it, and then bring planes in to the runway. We were supposed to be able to tell them when they were a few feet from the runway and a few inches above it. Sometimes it worked that way and sometimes it didn't.

The organization had forty eight enlisted personnel. Forty six were Master Sergeants, converted from former Army Air Corps officers, one was a Technical Sergeant, and myself - the lone PFC in the group. If you are wondering who cleaned the barracks, who scrubbed the floors, who emptied the trash, who went for coffee, who washed the truck and trailers, who did the dirty work, let me set your mind at ease - I did. I also worked in the control tower, giving clearance for taking off and landing and keeping records. That duty lasted until a plane came in one day and hit the runway and bounced in the air a hundred feet, hit the runway, bounced in the air fifty feet, hit the runway and spun and ran into the grass. I told the pilot, "Roger, I have you down at 11:03, 11:04 and 11:05." A few minutes later a bird Colonel came in the control tower and asked who the wise ass was. I asked if observing a plane playing leap frog with the runway made you a wise ass. A few hours later I was terminated from control tower duty and assigned to maintaining all back up power supplies and the control tower radio transmitter.

The duty was not too bad. I was soon dubbed Bowerman the Powerman. I was provided with my own 4 x 4 to travel around to all the units. The transmitter was several miles from the base so I had a pass to come and go as I wished. I could also get all the gasoline and diesel fuel I needed and used some of it for the power units.

It was my responsibility to check the lights on the very tall antenna and replace them as required. I had to notify the control tower when I was going to lower the antenna so they could switch to the reserve transmitter. I went out one day and some bulbs were burned out so I called the control tower and then hooked the winch cable to one of the antenna anchor cables and started lowering the antenna. The cable ran through a large metal eye on top of a huge slab of concrete. The concrete came out of the ground and the antenna crashed. The damage was many, many thousands of dollars and they invented a new rule that said two people had to be present when the antenna was lowered. Naturally they made the rule retroactive and threatened to take the cost out of my pay if I had to serve a hundred years to pay for it. Fortunately they got bogged down in their own red tape and dropped it.

I had a friend named Paul Carr who had played football

in high school in California. Paul managed to save up $200 and bought an old Hudson car. It took both of us to get it started but once it was started it ran pretty good. We would go out and run around Houston when we could afford gas for it. It guzzled a lot of gas and also consumed an amazing amount of oil. Paul had a visit one day from some people connected with the University of Houston. They were starting a football program and wanted Paul to play. He told them he was in the Air Force and he was supporting his Mother. They told him they could get him out of the Air Force and would bring his Mother to Houston and take care of her expenses. In little more than a week he was out of the Air Force, his Mother had an apartment in Houston and the old beat up Hudson had been replaced with a new car. That is when I learned there is no such thing as amateur college football. It is professional football at college level.

    I found a new friend and he had a really old beat up Dodge. The paint was long gone and the car was a real eyesore. We found what they called powder puff paint. You actually painted the car with a powder puff. I helped him paint it and it was real surprising how well it looked as compared to before. It did not pass for a factory paint job by any means but it was not bad looking at all. He got out of the service and drove his old car back to Michigan. He did not have any money and I called my Mother and arranged for him to stop in Tuscaloosa and get a night's sleep and a good supper and breakfast.

    It was obvious I was not going anywhere in the Air Force and my Mother and Archie were divorced. I decided to get out of the Air Force. I found that a hardship discharge was the only way and they did not want to release me. I filed for it, on the basis that I had to pay child support and my Mother needed me at home. My commander wrote a blistering recommendation for disapproval and stated that if I had to pay child support then my enlistment was fraudulent. The request had to go through five levels of command and each level sent back a copy of their recommendation for disapproval. I had discussed it with Ed DeGraffenreid, my congressman, in advance and he had arranged for someone at the next to last level to alert him when they released it. They did, and he went to the approval authority and asked them to approve it. They did approve it and routed it back through the chain of command, with each level adding a nasty comment. Then it disappeared and could not be found. I called Ed and he went to the top and gave them five days to have me out of the Air Force. The fifth day was on Sunday and I called Ed and told him I was still waiting. About noon I was called to the office and discharged. The only officer on duty with authority to sign was a female and a female had never signed a discharge for a male before. Mine was the first in the Air Force. That afternoon I headed for Tuscaloosa.

Chapter Twelve

The Formative Years

My Mother operated her own upholstery shop in Tuscaloosa from about 1943 to 1982 or 1983, roughly forty years. She upholstered and made slip covers for furniture, plus making pillows and cushions and covering bicycle seats. When business was slow she would take scrap material and make about a hundred bicycle seat covers. The bicycle shops in town bought them to cover ragged or torn bicycle seats. She also made the spring sets to go in cushions and sometimes she would sit down at the machine and make cushion units all day long. She was never idle, always busy, and she had more friends than anyone I knew. Total strangers would come in the shop and many would become friends for life. It was unusual as she was a very unemotional woman, never smiling or laughing and sometimes not talking much for days. People were still attracted to her and I think it was because they could sense she was a very compassionate person.

Anyway, I joined her in the upholstery business. I was never really great as an upholsterer. People were generally very satisfied with my work but I was never satisfied with it as I could see where it could be improved and that bothered me. Dealing with the public is not an easy thing and particularly where you are working on their furniture. They all wanted lower prices and perfect work. In many cases the furniture was just not worth recovering and I always tried to be honest and tell them if it was costing more than the furniture was worth. Sometimes the frame was not properly built to begin with and occasionally even damaged by termites. I found most people were insulted when you told them their furniture was of low quality and not worth repairing.

Many people also wanted to buy their own material and were confused when you told them the labor had to be more if they did that, because you were not making a profit on the material. Also, in many cases they bought very cheap and inferior material that was harder to work with than good quality material and even when you increased the labor you still lost money. Some shops in town charged double their cost for the material and could have afforded to do the labor free if they wanted to. We charged a reasonable markup per yard for material and our material was considerably lower in cost than most shops.

There was a lot of competition and some of the competitors did very good work and some did extremely poor work. John Sykes was the best in town but his prices were ridiculous and J.O. Woodyard was the cheapest in town but his work was ridiculous. I have seen Woodyard stop to smoke a cigarette and prop a foot up on a white satin sofa he had just finished and flip ashes on it. Of course it did not look much worse dirty than it did clean. Woodyard would run advertisements that said something like, "You have tried all the rest, now try the best." People would go for it and he always had his shop full of work. Unfortunately he was in poor health and sometimes did not work for weeks at a time.

I visited the Veterans Administration and they approved a program in which my Mother would pay me a salary for working and I would train as an upholsterer. The Veterans Administration would pay for necessary books and tools and a small payment each month to augment the salary. I bought a cushion stuffing machine, a cushion form machine, hammer, scissors and miscellaneous tools. We then had the best equipped shop in town and some of the other shops brought their cushion work to us. The appearance of our work was improved considerably.

No matter how you looked at it, upholstering used furniture was a dirty and dusty job. When you ripped the old material off, dust clouded the air and there was no way to avoid breathing it. The dust and dirt would get all over you and then the sweat would make it like a filthy mud. It made your eyes itch and burn and your nose run. There was not much way to not be allergic to it.

I was hauling most of the furniture in the trunk and passenger seat of the Chevrolet. I would open the trunk and put a chair in it, cover the chair with a quilt, lower the trunk lid onto the quilt and then put a sofa cross wise on the top of the trunk lid. If there was another chair I would turn it upside down and put it in the passenger side of the car, with the arms on the seat. I picked up a chair at a house one day and put it in the passenger side and drove back to the shop with it. I took it in the shop and put it on the work benches and ripped the dust cover off. A rat that was at least a foot long jumped out and ran. It took me an hour to find it and kill it. It made me shudder to think that rat came to the shop less than two feet from my face.

The only way you could be effective upholstering was to take a large hand full of tacks and stick them in your mouth. You could then pull the material with your left hand and put the magnetic end of the hammer in your mouth and flip a tack on it with your tongue. You then started the tack with the magnetic end and flipped the hammer and drove it in with the other end. Many days I would leave the shop with a mouth full of tacks and not know they were there until I started to eat supper. It was so automatic you forgot about it.

I eventually got totally disgusted with upholstering and went to the Veterans Administration and talked to them about going to the University of Alabama to get a degree in engineering. They said that since I had used six months of my entitlement in upholstery training they felt I should take an aptitude test. If I agreed to major in accordance with the results of the test they would approve the change. I agreed and took a battery of tests and they said it indicated my aptitude was in accounting. I agreed to major in accounting and enrolled at the University of Alabama in Tuscaloosa in the summer of 1952.

I continued to work at the upholstering shop all the time I was going to the University of Alabama. I got a lot of work at fraternities. Most of them had genuine leather furniture and the hand stitching had rotted out. I would sometimes go to a fraternity and sit on the floor and re-stitch leather for hours and hours. The pay was very good and usually one of the parents would pay the bill. I knew it was going to be a long and tough job getting my degree but I was determined I would see it through.

Chapter Thirteen

University of Alabama

Tuscaloosa High School had a college level and a commercial level and I had opted for the commercial level as I knew I would never be able to attend college. The University of Alabama decided that I had to take two courses that I would not get college credit for, because of that. One was English and one was advanced algebra. I started as a freshman during summer school in 1952. One semester was five weeks, six days a week and the other was six weeks, five days a week. I took English and Advanced Algebra the first semester. I made A's in both courses. I was not allowed to take Accounting courses in summer school so I took two elective courses the other semester, that first summer.

By the time the Fall semester started I felt like an old pro. I signed up for more courses than are allowed and had to get approval from the Dean. The Dean was Dr Bidgood, the father of Willis Bidgood. Dr Bidgood knew I had attended high school with Willis and never gave me any problem getting approval. I signed up for an overload every semester I went to Alabama. I wanted to get through before my Veteran Administration benefits ran out.

The freshman year was the only year I had any problems, and none of the problems I had were serious in nature. It was a matter of learning where everything was and how to get there within the time constraints. I worked my schedules out so I could take all courses before noon. I then worked at the upholstery shop from noon to about ten PM, studied from ten PM to three AM and slept from three AM to seven AM. During my Junior and Senior semesters I also graded papers for an Accounting professor and that frequently took four hours a day. I did that during my study time, so I started doing homework during class time.

I seemed to have a penchant for selecting courses taught by weird professors. It began with my first class in English. There were more than two hundred students in that course. It was taught by a lady who seemed more interested in seating arrangements than course content. I asked to be allowed to sit near the front because the guns in World War II did a lot of damage to my ears. She insisted on alphabetical order, starting at the left most seat and going to the back of the room and then the second seat, and to the back, etc. My seat was first column, rear seat on the left. I could not even see, much less hear. The second morning she announced there was a second class and anyone having a reason for transferring to the other class should stand and state their reason. I was the first one to stand and stated the reason as, "I do not like your looks or anything else about you." She stared at me and waved toward the door and I left.

I had an economics professor who was the most weird of all the weirdos I had. He announced at the first class that everyone who had been in one of his previous classes and failed should stand. About fifteen students stood and he told them to go select another course as he taught no one who had previously failed. He then asked all who had failed any course the previous two semesters to stand and another fifteen or so stood. He told them to get out of his class. He then asked all who had bought the prescribed text book to stand and another dozen or so stood. He told them he would teach no one dumb enough to buy that ridiculous book and asked them to leave. He then said that he only had two grades. He said you knew it or you did not know it. Those who knew it got an A and those who did not got an F. He asked all who had a problem with this to leave. He then said that he had never given more than one A in a single semester and that meant only one person would pass the course, maximum. More of the students left and there were then two of us left out of a class that had started with about sixty-five. There was a tall boy, about six foot eight inches, and me. He asked the tall boy why he stayed and he said he had been told this course would make him think and he had never done that before and wanted to have the experience. He asked me why I stayed and I told him I stayed because nothing he said ruled me out; that I survived the process of elimination. He told us to do anything we wanted to get comfortable and the tall boy promptly brought his knee up and knocked the top of the student desk off and picked it up and threw it across the room. We were told to get a 400 page notebook as we would write a text book during the course. I ended up with an A and the tall boy got an F.

I had another economics professor I considered normal all through the course and had no problems. I had an A average going into the final exam and the final exam was no problem at all. I knew the answers to all the questions. In our final class we received our final exams back and I made 100 on it and had an A for the course. The professor reviewed the questions and answers with us. There were five questions, but he went on discussing questions 6 through 10. After we finished I went to his office and handed him my exam back and told him I had a problem. He looked at the 100 written on the front and said he could not imagine why. I told him he had discussed 10 questions and I had only seen 5. He opened my exam booklet and checked it and said he had overlooked that. He said there were five questions on the board on my right and I must have missed seeing them. He scratched through the 100 and wrote 50 and then opened his grade book and made a change and told me I had a B instead of an A. I told him I was willing to take another test because I fully understood the course. He looked at me and said, "No, you are one of those kooks who think honesty is the best policy and it is high time you realize that is a bunch of crap. The B stands." I was shocked by his attitude as he was one of the few I had considered normal.

I made a horrible mistake. I took a course in debating in the speech department. I did not realize I would be the only one in the course who was not on the debating team traveling around the country with the instructor as part of the debating team. I did not realize the instructor was under pressure to assign fewer high grades. I soon learned I could spend hours preparing for an assignment and do a very good job and the instructor would say, "D". A member of her debating team would be very poorly prepared and get up and do a lousy job and the instructor would say "A". I got really tired of it. The course was drawing to a close and I had a D average. I had never received a D before. One day I was assigned a topic and got up and said that today I was going to talk about integrity. The instructor got wide eyed and told me she had not assigned integrity. I told her it was probably because she did not understand integrity, so I would teach her. She kept protesting and I kept talking. I said that I could research, study and prepare for an assignment and knock myself out doing it right and the instructor droned out a D when I sat down, whereas a member of the debating team could get up and if they accidentally belched the instructor would think they had finished and sing out an A. I said I was tired of it and I was not going to take it any more. I said that I would go to department heads and other university officials if that was what it took to get credit for the work I was doing. When I sat down the instructor sang out an A. I talked to her after class and she told me about the pressure. She said the department head wanted their grade structure in line with the rest of the university. I understood her problem and we agreed on a C for the course.

  One professor I had was one of the best report writing professors in the business and an outstanding professor. He had written several books and was highly regarded in the profession. One day he did not come to class. He never did come back. His wife was not teaching at the time but she was also terrific in report writing and the university talked her into taking over the class. She told us her husband just disappeared and she had no idea where he was. She was a very attractive woman. She walked around the room a great deal while she talked. She passed my desk one day and smiled and then came back and pulled her dress up and sat on my desk with her bare rear end flat on one of my hands. She kept talking and looking down at me smiling.

She did this several more times during the course. I decided both members of this couple might have problems and started keeping my hands off the desk.

The above are mere examples of strange professors I met at the university and is certainly not all inclusive. There were quite a few more, such as one who told dirty jokes and graded you as much on your ability to tell a good dirty joke as on anything else. He did have an interest in you knowing course content but enjoyed being called by his first name, being one of the boys, and telling dirty jokes.

I took Cost Accounting under one professor and he announced a few days after the course began that the remainder of the semester would be the completion of a case study. He gave us the problem and said we could spend as much or as little time per day as we chose and when we finished the study we would not have to come back to class that semester. I did the entire thing the first week end and turned it in on Monday. He was certain I had done it wrong and wanted me to check it. I told him it was right, so he said we would just see and went to his desk and started comparing it with his copy. He finally called me and said my procedure was correct and I just had a few minor interpolation errors. I told him that all of my interpolations were correct. He said they did not agree with his master copy and it was done by one of his best graduate assistants. I told him his graduate assistant had obviously made an error and he handed me the master copy and told me to prove it. It took ten minutes to find the error and I showed the errors to him. He said that well, he did not know about that, so I asked him to prove they were right. He finally sat down and got the text book and studied it and the master for half an hour. He then told me the graduate assistant must have used a different text book. I pointed out the text book was at least five years old and was the latest version and the one prescribed by the accounting department. He said he would accept my case study without changes and then corrected the master copy to agree with mine. I had a perfect score on all tests and my case study was used to correct the master copy. He gave me a B for the course and when I asked him why he simply said I had an A and talked myself out of it. He also once had my respect and talked himself out of it.

We had one accounting professor named Humble that everyone called Mumble because he mumbled and no one ever understood a word of what he was saying. He absolutely mumbled everything. I told him one day, "Hey man, if you can't say it, spit it out and we will read it." He was not the type to hold something like that against you and even started writing about twice as much on the board as he had been doing. I was about thirty one at the time and all the kids called me Pop. Several commented after the class that they had other professors they would like for me to talk to.

I knew two professors who were giving female students A grades for sex. I am sure there were several I did not know about. The girls trading sex for grades did not even attempt to understand or participate in the class and did not even attend regularly. They came often enough to make it look honest and that is about all. There was also one sorority where many of the girls sold sex for cash, including a drive-in back seat operation, but that strays from the point of strange professors.

I was selected to grade papers for one of the accounting professors. The university paid $130 per semester and it turned out to be a nightmare job. The professor was well into a nervous breakdown and in a fight with the university over his teaching methods. He taught a CPA review course and used a method of letting that class select a leader. He then put lectures on tape and they could listen to them or not. They could vote to have him make guest appearances. He decided to use the same strategy for a beginning accounting course. The class selected leaders and sat and listened to tapes while they drank cokes and ate candy. They did not understand a word he was saying. One student was married to a graduate student in accounting and her husband taught her. One student was close to genius level and just read the book. The other forty students had no idea of what the course was all about. I would pick up the homework and spend hours and hours writing explanations of correct answers. I was told to give them their first test and to grade them. Two students had excellent grades. The other forty averaged less than 10 out of a possible 100. The mid term test was worse and the final examination, which I administered, was a disaster. The professor refused to talk to the class and told me to meet with them and just ask each one what grade they wanted. The two students I mentioned had earned A's so they were no problem. Out of the other 40, 2 wanted an A, 2 wanted a B and 36 wanted an F if they could not get an I (Incomplete). The reasoning was that 4 were from Arts & Sciences and accounting was not important to them and the other 36 were accounting majors and knew it was important to understand beginning accounting. Dr Bidgood talked to me about the course and the professor and then placed the professor on a one year leave of absence. The professor asked me to help him clear out his office. This consisted of throwing everything in the office into trash cans (50 gallon drums). I told Dr Bidgood and he had someone remove all of it and place it in boxes and store it.

 I was selected for membership in Beta Alpha Psi and I think, Beta Gamma Sigma honorary accounting and commerce fraternities. I attended meetings when I could. I suppose they were nice honors and I appreciated it but had so little time. Compressing a four year course into two and a half years while working twelve hours a day consumes most of your time.

 I am sure a college degree is essential for doctors and scientists and perhaps engineers and attorneys. I am not so sure about accountants and some of the others. When I graduated as an accountant I still had no earthly idea how to set up books or do bookkeeping for someone. I think I would recommend that anyone interested in being an accountant work as a bookkeeper a couple of years before going to college.

 I had always thought that when you graduated from a university you were a real professional and could handle anything in your field that came up. I did not find this to be true. I really felt inadequate and I was on the Dean's List seven of my eight semesters. I observed other graduates and found many of them to be really incompetent. I felt the value of a college education was greatly over stated. I was really disappointed. Thirteen years later I would start and complete the work for a Master's Degree and find the same feelings. In my opinion, education does nothing but help prepare you to learn on the job. College should be totally revamped to become more meaningful, with some practical and helpful experience mixed in.

    I guess the bottom line is that I never decided for sure that college was a meaningful experience. I felt that I could have put forth ten percent of the effort and graduated without a problem. Maybe that is what it is all about; it is the first adult level of education and you get back what you put into it.

Chapter Fourteen

Graduation, Gen Accounting Office and Army Audit Agency

Graduation from the University of Alabama was a significant event in my life. The jobs as a professional auditor with The General Accounting Office and The US Army Audit Agency were also events I will never forget.

I graduated from the University of Alabama in February, 1955, two and one half years after enrolling. It was fifteen years after I graduated from high school. There were two years in the CCC and service in three branches of the armed forces, as well as a marriage and a divorce between high school and college.

My Father came in on the bus from Arkansas for my graduation. He had remarried, this time to a woman he said he knew when he was a very young man. He had a severe nose bleed and went to a hotel and was not able to attend my graduation. He told me that an FBI agent had visited him in Arkansas. I had applied for a job with the FBI and they were doing a check on me and had visited my Father. He said they knew about his drinking and my Brother's drinking. I told him they turned me down because of it. They are very particular about who they hire and felt that the life my relatives had lived would compromise me as an agent. Dad was very sad that his life had kept me from getting a job I wanted so much. I had made a hundred on their written test but had flunked the background test.

Dad left after the graduation. I told him I loved him very much. It was just a few days later that his wife called and said he was dead. He had another nose bleed on the way home and had got off the bus and had a doctor pack it. He packed it too tightly and that caused his death. No one ever knew who the doctor was. Dad's wife said he got up early and went out and sat in a rocking chair while she cooked breakfast. He was dead when she went for him. She had a funeral there and then I had Dad shipped to Tuscaloosa and buried there. There were only five or six people at the funeral. Dad is buried next to my brother, Herman.

I was becoming a little concerned. I was almost 33 years old when I graduated and was being told at most job interviews that I was maybe a little too old to fit in their plans. I was interviewed by one national accounting firm and the guy interviewing me laughed when I told him my age and said they did not hire the elderly. I told him I was not interested in a job with his firm, that I only wanted to compare what unprofessional firms such as his were paying with what the better firms were paying. He complained to the university that I had insulted him. I was asked about it and told them people like this guy could not be insulted, but it would be a good idea if it was possible.

I was offered a job by a carpet manufacturing company in Mississippi and by a large national company that made cooking oil but neither job appealed to me. Then a representative of the Federal Government's General Accounting Office interviewed me. I knew after five minutes discussion that I wanted to work for GAO and started trying to impress him. He looked at me and said, "Hell, man, do you want the job? Say yes and it is yours, you don't have to impress me." I said that I did want the job and he put an agreement on the table and told me to sign. It was that simple and I had my first professional job. I was hired by Milt Snider from the General Accounting Office in Atlanta, Georgia. He told me I would need enough money to live for about three weeks after I got to Atlanta as I would have to work two weeks and then get paid about a week after that. He said I could make it on $200 if I was careful and if I got into financial problems to let him know and he would help.

I arrived in Atlanta on the Sunday before a Monday reporting date. I tried three hotels before I found one with a rate I felt I could afford. I checked in and then located the building

General Accounting Office (GAO) was in so I would know where to go the next morning. It was hard to sleep that night, so I didn't. The next morning I reported to GAO and was sent to the office of the regional director. I expected to spend five minutes with him and then be turned over to someone else. I stayed in his office all day and all day the next day. He was interested in new employees and in assuring they got off on the right foot. He went over every course I took at the University with me and had questions about them. He was very interested in the fact that I had received an A in report writing. He gave me a large number of GAO reports and asked that I read them and make notes on what I considered their good points and their bad points. He then told me he was going to do something a little unusual. He was going to give me a private office and all the work papers from a large audit they had made and he wanted me to write a proposed audit report.

I got a private office and people started bringing in large boxes of working papers. The regional director, Mr Madison, took a few minutes showing me the codes they used and then told me I was on my own and had two weeks hassle free time to come up with something. There were so many working papers that I decided to use a process of elimination to reduce the volume to something workable. I dumped all the papers and sorted them and those I considered not significant I put back in the boxes.

The main significance of the audit was that someone made a decision the U.S.A. needed another chlorine plant to produce an ingredient needed in the manufacture of nerve gas. The plant was built at a cost of around $20,000,000 and it was decided it would be a Government Owned, Contractor Operated (GOCO) plant. A contract was issued for the operation of the plant. About this time a survey was finally made on the need for another chlorine plant and it was decided that the capability for making chlorine was already something like 2000 percent of the requirement and there was no need for the new chlorine plant in Muscle Shoals, Alabama. The contract for operation of the plant should have been terminated but was not. The contractor hired a full operational staff and paid them for a full year to report to the plant daily and sit and do nothing. The Contracting Officer then renewed the contract for a second year and the entire staff required to operate at full capacity was paid a second full year to report to work and sit and do nothing. The contract was then renewed for a third year. After the third year the plant was declared excess and was sold by the Government to Diamond Match Company for less than two million dollars. Diamond Match Company then sold the mercury in vats at the plant for $13,000,000, making a profit of almost $12,000,000. They then sold the plant for more than they paid for it.

There were copies of both informal and formal letters from the GOCO contractor to the government procurement officer thanking him specifically for extending the contract twice to permit the contractor time to relocate his key people. It was obvious the contracting officer knew there was no need for the plant and had paid several millions of dollars as a favor to the contractor. It was also obvious that the contracting officer could have saved millions by reducing the contract to a stand-by crew instead of a full operational level.

The audit was so significant that efforts to write the report had been unsuccessful. I sat down and wrote a report with the expectation it would meet the same fate as previous efforts. When I finished, I took the report to Mr Madison. He opened a desk drawer and pulled out several reports and asked me to read them. They were the previous efforts. He told me he had asked several supervisory auditors to write the report and then had written one himself and he had not been satisfied with any of them. He read my report at least three times. We then went to my office and he checked some of the work papers. We went back to his office and he called someone in and handed them my report. He asked him to coordinate it and give him any reasons they found not to issue it, but not to make changes. The next day my report was issued and sent to GAO headquarters for staffing and to be issued to the Congress.

In the meantime I had run low on money and had moved from the hotel to the YMCA, where I got a bed for one dollar a day, and low cost meals. I realized that the pay I would receive as a GS-5 auditor trainee ($3415.00 per year) would not support living in a hotel. A good room in a hotel was $5.00 per day. Atlanta was considered my home and I would not draw per diem until I left Atlanta.

I was finally assigned to an audit as a member of a five man audit team to make an audit in Nashville, Tennessee. This meant I would get $7.00 per day travel expense. Milton Snider was the team chief and we were to leave from the GAO building. I met them in the parking lot and we were all scheduled to go in Milt's car. We stood around the car looking at our luggage and four large boxes of working papers from the previous audit and five of us. Milt said we were just not going to fit and went to ask Mr Madison to approve a second car. He came back with Mr Madison. Mr Madison finally got all the luggage in the trunk and then had all five of us get in the car. He pushed three boxes of working papers in the back seat and one in the front seat and said there seemed to be plenty of room. We were miserably cramped and had not left the parking lot. Milt sat there awhile and got out and went back to Mr Madison's office. They both came back in a few minutes and Milt asked Mr Madison if he would like to make the trip cramped like that. Mr Madison said he would do it for GAO. Milt then asked, "And where would you put this year's working papers on the return trip?" Mr Madison thought about it and asked if any of us had a larger car, then finally approved a second car. Milt told me that GAO computed the dollar savings versus dollar expenses and Mr Madison tried to keep expenses as low as possible. He said Mr Madison's job was authorized at the GS-15 level and he refused to accept the promotion and was a GS-13, just to save GAO money.

When we got to Nashville we checked in at the hotel and got in the elevator. It was operated by a Black lady. There were at least twelve people in the elevator. Milt asked the operator, "Where is the best place for a man to get a little stuff in this town." There was utter silence in the elevator and then the operator told him, "That is not in my department. If you have wishes I suggest you contact the management for help." Milt got off at the fourth floor and I rode on up a couple more floors. The operator asked me if I heard that man and I said I did. She asked me if I didn't get on the elevator with him and I told her I never saw him before. I got off the elevator and found the stairs and walked back down. I soon learned that Milt always took the direct approach.

I was on two short audits where I got temporary duty travel pay and then I was assigned to an audit of General Services Administration in Atlanta. The audit had been going on almost two years and it looked like it would continue forever. It was hard to meet expenses when I was on an audit in Atlanta. The people in GSA were very unfriendly due to the length of the audit. The working conditions were unpleasant. The girls had been advised not to date us even if we were single. Very few of them would even speak to us.

Jim Blackburn and a couple more I had gone to school with at Alabama stopped by the GSA site one day and said they were on the way to an interview with Army Audit Agency in the Peachtree 7 Building. They would go to a three week audit school in Washington, D.C. and would start off at the GS-5 level and be promoted to GS-7 in six months. All their audits would be out of town. Mr Madison's policy was to require one full year at GS-5 level before promotion to GS-7. I asked my auditor in charge for leave and went to the interview at Army Audit Agency with Jim. I was offered a transfer provided GAO would release me.

I went back to GAO and talked to Mr Madison about a transfer. He said he had big plans for me but I would have to serve a full year as a GS-5. I asked if it was legal to promote me and he said I had entered in a trainee program designed for promotion in six months but he felt everyone should serve a year. I told him that I wanted to be released and he released me. I transferred to Army Audit Agency without a break in service. Milt came over a day or two later and was very upset with me for leaving GAO. He said Army Audit Agency (AAA) was not a professional organization and he was going to tell the director what he thought of him while he was there. About a week later Milt was back and I thought he had come to visit me but the director had made him an offer while he was telling him off and Milt had transferred to AAA.

The Atlanta office of AAA had five new auditor trainees and we went to a three week school at the Dodge Hotel in Washington, D.C. There were trainees in attendance from AAA regions all over the country. There were about fifty of us in all. The classes were held in large rooms in the Dodge Hotel. We received $7.00 per day to pay for our rooms and meals. There were other government employees staying at the hotel and several of them told me they were paying a dollar per day less for their rooms than the employees of Army Audit Agency. I asked the hotel manager about it and he said AAA had arranged to charge each of us an extra dollar per day to pay for the rooms used for our training classes. I asked him to give me an itemized bill showing the dollar charge as training class rooms and he agreed.

The training was excellent, with many speakers on many different subjects. The speaker on ethics was a Black man from California named Campbell. He made what should have been our dullest subject one of the most interesting. We had a coffee break after his first talk and he found our Atlanta group and asked if he could have coffee with us. He knew this was probably the first time any of us had ever been trained by a Black person and he was interested in our reaction. He was pleased that we felt his talk was the most interesting so far. He was originally from the South and was a Certified Public Accountant (CPA) and had an excellent practice in California. He was a regular speaker at all the AAA training classes and paid his own expenses and did not charge AAA. We came to know him well before the training was completed and I corresponded with him for several years. It was my first experience with an intelligent Black person that I knew was intelligent. I was raised to believe it was not possible for a Black person to be intelligent.

The training concluded and we boarded the train back to Atlanta. We were well pleased with the quality of the training and with AAA for having provided it. We were not pleased that AAA had made us pay for the class rooms without telling us they were doing it. I vowed to get my twenty one dollars back from AAA. I brought it up to the person who had been designated as training officer but got no satisfactory answer. I filed a claim with the agency that handled our travel pay. My claim was approved and AAA was ordered to pay every trainee. It did not make me popular with national AAA but had no local impact. In fact, I was told by our regional director that he admired me for doing it.

We were assigned to some minor audits in the Atlanta area but were soon called in and asked if any of us wanted to go to a new branch of AAA being opened in Birmingham. They were having trouble getting volunteers and since none of us had roots in Atlanta they felt we might volunteer to go. All of us decided to take them up on it and soon we were reporting to John Stroud in the Calder Building in Birmingham. I found a small motel willing to give me a special rate provided I stayed there all the time I was in Birmingham. They knew I would at times be on an audit for months out of town.

I did not have a car and decided it was time I got one. I bought a 1955 Ford in Birmingham and had many problems with it. They could never fix it so I went to Tuscaloosa one week-end and bought a 1955 Chevrolet. I had a problem with AAA though in that they would send three or four of us on an audit and just authorize one car. They always authorized the same person to provide the car and he had a very old car with terrible tires on it. We would have a flat tire every fifty to one hundred miles and have to wait around while he changed it. Then at the next town he would have the flat fixed and we would wait around again. We finally objected so loudly that they gave up and authorized each person to take their own car, for which they paid five cents per mile if you drove alone or seven cents if you had another auditor with you.

We audited the American Red Cross blood program. The Army paid the Red Cross the portion of the expense applicable to the Army portion of the blood program. We found that in many cases expenses unrelated to the Army or the blood program were being charged to the blood program and prorated to the Army. Our audit was extended to Red Cross blood programs all over Alabama and we made short visits to a dozen small towns. We discussed our findings with the Red Cross director in Birmingham, pointing out that his wife did not even work and was being paid a huge salary and all of it was being charged to the blood program. There were many, many expenses being charged to the blood program that had no relationship to it and overall the Army was paying about five or six times what it should pay. He just laughed at us and told us we could take our findings and stick them and when the dust settled Red Cross would be paid in full. He was correct because the national procurement officer chose to ignore our findings and paid Red Cross the full amount billed.

We were assigned to assist Tom Howard, an auditor in charge from the Atlanta AAA office in making an audit of Anniston Ordnance Depot. This was where I met my future wife. She was a supervisor in the Depot Property Branch. I was selected to audit Depot Property and went to Building 22 and saw her there and decided we would get married. I asked her for a date and told her on that first date that we were going to get married. The rest of that story is covered elsewhere.

Depot Property had a big job and a tough job providing not only house keeping supplies, construction materiel, etc to the entire depot but also parts required for rebuild of a wide range of major items by the Depot Maintenance Division. It was a wonder they did as well as they did but there were many minor things wrong and we made each one into a finding, usually making it sound like it was worse than it really was. My future wife had many of the findings in her area of responsibility.

If I had my auditing to do all over again I would give the minor findings to the responsible supervisor without making an official record of it. I learned much later that the Army Inspector General will also report the minor findings. In many cases they got it from our AAA reports and rehashed it, just causing much more administrative work for units already bogged down with routine work. In some cases, reporting corrective action on audit report findings further prevents them from getting routine work accomplished. They also had audits from General Accounting Office and from their local Internal Review Office.

The depot was also responsible for national supply and had missions to receive, store and ship general supplies. Their customers were scattered all over the world. They also had branch offices of five Army Stock Funds. We did not discover the stock funds until our audit was almost over. Harry Barr and I made the stock fund audits and discovered the stock fund financial records were all out of balance and that imbalances were being maintained on spread sheets and prorated at month end to balance the records.

The audit of Anniston Ordnance Depot lasted five months. The depot was happy to see us leave. Frances Caton and I were engaged before I left (details later) and I had talked to the chief of the Internal Review Office and had a promise of a job starting the day we were married.

My next audit was at Fort Rucker in Ozark, Alabama and also lasted five months. J. Thornton from Atlanta was our auditor in charge. J. was just a GS-11. His drinking problems had kept him from being promoted. He had several GS-11's, a couple of GS-9's and John Cotten and myself on his team. John and I were the only two of the trainees assigned to this audit and we were GS-7's now.

We checked in at the Mills Hotel in Ozark. They had a weekly rate of $15.00. John and I were both scratching bug bites the next morning and decided to find a better place to stay. The only place in town other than the Mills Hotel was The Candlelight Inn and a room was $12.00 per day. Our per diem rate was now $9.00 per day to cover room and meals. John and I got a double room with two beds for $18.00 per day. The room rent took our entire per diem, with nothing left for meals. We decided it was worth it as neither of us enjoyed scratching.

We were assigned to an old Bachelor Officer Quarters building at Fort Rucker. It was unheated and we were told personnel were not available to fire the boiler and we would have to do it ourselves. I was assigned that as an added duty. I built a fire and checked it several times per day for a couple of days, getting dirty in the process. I got tired of it and went out to the boiler room and shut off the water and built a roaring fire. Soon the radiators were dancing and it was very hot and all the windows were open. J. Thornton notified Fort officials and someone came and checked it and ordered us to clear the building as the boiler was likely to explode. The fort assigned someone to fire the boiler.

There was one GS-11 named Clatie. He had transferred in grade from Internal Revenue Service to Army Audit Agency. Clatie spent half his time worrying about his hair and the other half worrying about how to get more gas mileage and save more money. He had a really thick head of hair and I could not understand why he worried about it so much. He carried a mirror and was forever looking at his hair. John and I found someone with identical hair and talked them into cutting off some of it for us. Clatie kept his comb in his coat pocket and one day when he had his coat off we got his comb out and hung a wad of that hair in it. Later in the day he whipped his comb out and ran it through his hair a couple of times and when he looked at the comb we thought he was going to pass out. He got real white and kept staring. John passed by and looked at it and told him no wonder his hair was starting to look thinner. I followed up with a similar comment and Clatie took leave and went to Birmingham to see a hair specialist. Clatie was a real cheap skate and had a device to increase gas mileage. About all it did was increase the air and decrease the gas and when you used it you took a real chance of seriously damaging your engine. The car was very hard to start with the device on it. You had to remove the carburetor, put the device on and then put the carburetor back on. You had to be

Frances J. Bowerman

Wedding: Tom & Frances in center, Franklin on Left, Eleanor on right.

ready for the highway as it would not keep the engine running in town. It took a long time to do but Clatie would put it on his car, remove it when he got home, install it before he left, and remove it when he got to Fort Rucker. He went home every week-end. John and I were the only ones that stayed there seven days a week.

John Stroud, the Birmingham branch chief, stuttered very badly. At times it would take him almost a minute to say a word. John and I were called in once for a branch meeting and were sitting around the office. We kept hearing someone talking and peeped in Mr Stroud's office. He had a tape recorder and was recording. When he got to a bad word for him he would turn the tape off and try to get it back on just as the word came out right. Much, much later he played the tape back and it sounded really cool, compared to his normal.

Ruth Savage was one of the office girls who typed, mimeographed reports and did general office work. John and I always cornered Ruth when we got to the office as she would tell us who was in trouble, who was brown nosing, who was getting promoted, who was screwing who, and much, much more.

Milt Snider came down to check on us and insisted on all of us going to a local dance. We went in Harry Barr's car. Milt came running by yelling for us to come on. We ran with him and jumped in the car just as a crowd of people came out and started picking up rocks and throwing them at us. We asked Milt what had happened and he said he asked this young girl to dance and while they were dancing he asked her if she wanted to do sex. She said she would have to ask her boy friend and next thing he knew two or three kids were coming at him with knives in their hands.

One of the GS-11's was a CPA but was either awfully dumb or senile. He was in charge of an audit of transportation for a couple of days. He was asked by a fort official what the purpose of the audit was and after rambling around for awhile he said the purpose was to write a report. He was sitting on a waste basket while he talked and was smoking a cigarette. He was flipping ashes between his legs and the paper in the can caught on fire. We had to lift him off the can as he seemed to be pretending the fire did not exist. J. Thornton put me in charge of the audit the next day. This same guy complained to Milt that he was a GS-9 and Milt asked him if he wanted his grade changed. He said he did and Milt had him sign a form letter. A couple of weeks later he received notice of change to lower grade, per his request, to GS-7. He called Milt and Milt just told him that he had asked for a change and he was not worth more so he thought he meant less.

This was the same guy John and I played a dirty trick on. We sat near him and I said "12" and John laughed hysterically. John said "33" and I rolled on the floor laughing. I said "48" and John laughed and said "29" and I laughed. We kept it up and finally this guy said "45" and started laughing. Neither of us cracked a smile and then went on with our funny numbers game. The guy tried three or four more times and we would look at him and shake our heads. Finally he asked why we did not laugh and John told him that number was not funny. He tried three or four more times with the same reaction from us. Finally he repeated the number John had just used and pointed at us and laughed. We looked at each other and said nothing. He told us we had just used that number and laughed. John told him repeats were not funny. Then John immediately used it again and we rolled in the floor laughing. He started yelling that it was a repeat and John told him of course it was but it was a repeat once removed and eligible for funny. He then tried that and yelled it was a repeat twice removed. I told him John had already used a repeat twice removed. We almost had him in tears before he quit and left.

John and I became very close friends. We found the GS-11's and GS-9's were incompetent. J. Thornton found the same thing and set up two teams with John in charge of one and me in charge of the other. We made a comprehensive audit of Fort Rucker, with many significant findings, plus the minor garbage we were expected to include in the report. When the audit was finished, J. Thornton released everyone but me and I helped him write the final report and discuss it with the Commanding General of Fort Rucker.

I was finally released and that ended my career with AAA. I went to Anniston on leave to get married and my records were transferred to the depot Civilian Personnel Office. I was to be a GS-7 auditor in the Internal Review Office after the honeymoon.

Chapter Fifteen

Courting Caton

I was working for Army Audit Agency and assigned to work for Tom "Bulldog" Howard on an audit of what was at that time called Anniston Ordnance Depot, or AOD. I was a GS-5 at the time of the audit, an Auditor Trainee. My trainee status should not be construed to mean I did not know everything, as I was sure I did. The team generally recognized that the people at the depot knew very little and we would have to give them the guidance they needed and help them climb a little bit toward our level of expertise. Well, we were not really that bad but we were cocky and very sure that our recommendations would help the depot. The correct answer of course is that the people at the depot knew immeasurably more about the operation of a depot than any of us would ever know. What we would really find was a few minor errors made under the pressure of operation and people doing things differently than we would prefer, but producing equal or better results.

The above should make it easier to understand my frame of mind when I met Frances Johnson Caton. Frances was slaving away at a tough GS-5 supervisory supply job in Depot Property at Anniston Ordnance Depot when I met her. I knew the instant I met her that we were going to get married so I asked her for a date. She said yes and it was all settled from that point. I asked her to marry me on that first date, or rather I just told her we were going to get married. Her response was a laugh. She just did not understand that it was all set.

I decided I would not push the proposal for awhile as she seemed so amused when I mentioned it. We just mainly had a good time. We went to movies, we went to the club at the depot, we parked, we did everything but sex. Sex before marriage was not very common in those days. Neither of us were blessed with money so the things we could do were limited to available funds, or maybe I should say unavailable funds.

Frances would still go out with someone else now and then but I had no interest in dating anyone else. She went out with a man named Walter Barney one night and Albert Lingle and I went to the AOD club and tied one on. This was my last drinking party. I had twenty one drinks that night before we decided to flow back to town. I had the 1955 Chevrolet and it had the old power glide transmission. Lingle made a comment that my car would not pull the steam off a biscuit. We were stopped at the exit from the depot road to highway 202 when he said it. There was no traffic in sight so I put the transmission in neutral and floor boarded it and when it was fully revved up I knocked it out of neutral into drive. We burned rubber for half a mile and by that time the highway patrol lights were flashing behind us. I pulled over on the shoulder of the road, determined to keep my mouth shut. I just answered yes sir and no sir to the questions. Lingle was making a real ass of himself in the meantime but I kept quiet. A highway patrolman drove my car in to town. Lingle kept telling him he was exceeding the speed limit and he had no more rights than a private citizen and he was making a citizen's arrest, etc. The patrolman had said he was going to drive Lingle to the Purefoy Inn and take me to the county jail. He stopped a mile from town and said he thought we had a flat on the right front and asked Lingle to check. Lingle got out and the patrolman leaned over and slammed the door and yelled, "Walk the rest of the way, you smart assed SOB." We went on to the court house.

The Highway Patrol told me I had been pretty decent and they did not think I was drunk and were not going to make a sobriety test. They said they were just charging me with reckless driving for burning rubber. I was locked up until I could make bail. Lingle came by and found out he had to have bail money and the signature of a judge. He decided the only one with money was Sherwood Sorrell. Sherwood was an alcoholic but always had money. Lingle had seen Jewel McAlpin carry Sherwood out of the club while we were there and decided she took him home with her. He went to her home and woke her at two o'clock in the morning wanting to speak to Sherwood and she unloaded on him. Jewel was six foot five inches tall. She did tell him she had left Sherwood at the Purefoy Inn so Lingle goes to the Purefoy and wakes Sherwood at about 2:30 AM. He told him what he needed and why and Sherwood told him to get what he wanted out of his billfold and get out. Lingle then got the name and address of the judge and woke him at three AM and told him he had an emergency, that my Father had died and he had to get me out of jail and to the funeral by ten AM. The judge signed and then Lingle had to get someone else out of bed to accept the money and sign a release. He had me out of jail by 4:30 AM. They told me I could not move my car before 8:00 AM and I went back and got it. I did not have to go to work as it was Sunday. I did not even have to go to court but had to pay a fine of about $27.00. I decided I would never drink any more other than an occasional beer and I have kept that vow.

I think that was when Frances knew I was serious when I told her we were going to get married. She had been married to an alcoholic named Welch Caton for quite a few years (Jan 1938 to Mar 1950) and had thought she would probably not marry again. Since they were married twelve years and never had any children she was certain she could not have children.

Frances and I were engaged from the day I met her as far as I am concerned but she thought we were engaged when she said she would marry me and that was in October of 1955, or close to it. We (she) decided we would get married April 14, 1956.

James McKamee was Chief of Internal Review at AOD at the time we became engaged and committed a job for me in April, 1956. I was to keep working for Army Audit Agency until April and then transfer to the depot. It seemed like a good plan. I did not particularly like McKamee but I decided beggars could not be choosers. McKamee, as Chief of Internal Review, was a

GS-11, which meant I could not go above GS-9 in Internal Review unless he left and I got his job.

I spent most of our engagement at Fort Rucker in Ozark, Alabama, but managed to visit Anniston a couple of times. I called as often as I could afford it, probably more often. If John Cotten had not been such a good friend the wait would have been unbearable. John was also engaged and had a job waiting in Huntsville, Alabama when the audit of Fort Rucker was finished. We had similar problems and were both making phone calls. John was from Mississippi and had graduated from Mississippi State.

I called Frances one night and she was not home so I took a long shot and called her at the Officer's Club at AOD. It turned out to be not such a long shot after all as she was there and obviously partying. We came very close to breaking up over that but managed to work our way through it.

April 14th had to come sooner or later and it finally did roll around. We went from engaged to married that day.

The Johnson Clan

I liked all of the Johnson family. They were always like members of my own family and made me feel like I was a member of theirs.

Alvie and Nellie were her Father and Mother. Alvie was always sick and I never knew him very well. Nellie, or Nanny as we called her, was always my buddy and took my side in any argument. It was too far to go to Tuscaloosa so when Frances and I had an argument I went home to Nanny. Nanny would get on Frances about not treating me right and that would make Frances mad. Most of our arguments were about finances as we always had financial problems. Alvie and Nellie are both dead now.

Maudie Mae Browning was the oldest child of Alvie and Nellie and lived in Saks. We were married at her house. She was married to Sid Browning and I liked Maudie Mae and Sid both.

They had two children that lived, Donald and Charlotte. Don was a city policeman, a highway patrolman, an air conditioning/refrigeration repairman and finally opened his own business. Charlotte worked at several different office jobs. Sid and Maudie Mae are both dead now.

William D. (W.D.) was the oldest son. He was a postman for many years. He was almost always neatly dressed, usually wearing a suit. He was married to Vera and I liked both of them. Both W.D. and Vera are dead now.

Marshal Hendrix Johnson was the next oldest. Marshall worked for years at the Anniston Star and wrote editorials frequently. Something happened to Marshall during World War II and he did not hold a steady job after the war. He lived in a garage behind Franklin's house at the time Frances and I married. Marshall is dead now.

Franklin Stephen Johnson was Frances' twin brother and he warned me sternly that he knew all about these guys making mistakes and ending up in bed with their wife's twin and he wanted me to watch it. Franklin was a really terrific guy, with all the dry wit you would ever need. I loved him like a brother. Franklin was married to Charles White. Franklin and Charlie have five children, Lynne, Steve, Anita, Rita and Elizabeth. Both Franklin and Charlie are dead now.

Eleanor Hinds was younger than Franklin and Frances. She was divorced and had three children. Her children were Marsha Nell, Michael Stewart and David Mark. Her ex-husband, Jimmy Hinds, sometimes paid child support and visited the children very infrequently. Eleanor was (and is) a good Mother to her children. She is still alive.

Margaret Ann Gracie was married to Stephen Gracie and lives in Panama City, Florida. She and Steve have three children, Stephen, Jo Ann and David Graham. Steve was a pipe fitter in construction work. He has retired and both are still living. Ann is the youngest of the family.

We went to Panama City on our honeymoon. We drove to Ozark the day of our wedding and spent the night at the Candle-

Left to right: Barry, Terry, Tommy

light Motel where John Cotten and I had stayed for five months during the audit of Fort Rucker. The next morning we went on to Panama City and stayed at the Escape Motel. We also visited Ann and Steve while we were there.

We had two basic problems at the very beginning. One was that we did not have much money. We were in a world of hurt financially. The other was mainly frequency of sex. It was not frequent enough for me and too frequent for her. She told me during the honeymoon that if I expected her to love me like she loved Welch, to forget it as that was a once in a lifetime love. At least I knew where I stood. Money and sex continued to be our only problems during our marriage (39 years as of the time I am writing this.) Every argument or problem stemmed from one or the other. It also may have been a serious mistake to marry someone who had sex with another man for 12 years.

We returned to Anniston after a week in Florida. We had rented an apartment in Terrace Homes, adjacent to the depot. We bought most of our furniture from Haverty Furniture Co in Anniston. I bought some items, such as the Television set, from Farris Faulkner in Tuscaloosa. We had a pretty nice apartment.

I reported to the depot and was shocked to find that McKamee had left for a job in Huntsville and a man named John Stanton was the new Chief of Internal Review. John told me he did not like McKamee and did not want anyone McKamee had hired and he preferred I find a job somewhere else as he was not committed to take me. I made a deal with him that I would be hired and any time after thirty days that he decided he did not want me, I would quit. John said that was fair enough and he expected me to live up to my end of the deal. One week later John told me I could forget the thirty day deal, he was one hundred percent satisfied with both me and the work I was doing. That eased the pressure a lot.

Our marriage will continue in other chapters in the book. I have thought Frances was right for me since the day we met. I have never really had a comfortable feeling that this went both ways. I have always felt she continued to love Welch Caton.

Left to right: Rita, Anita and Steve Johnson, Tommy Bowerman, Lynne Johnson, Marsha, Mike and Steve Hinds.

Life goes on. It is not easy to compete with memories of a dead man. I quit trying. I could never help wondering why a woman would continue to love an abusive bum like Welch Caton when he beat her like he did. I never hit Frances and would never have dreamed of abusing her either physically, emotionally or mentally. But I knew she continued to love him.

Chapter Sixteen

Tommy

Frances reminded me frequently that she could not have children and she was sorry as she knew how much I loved children. The first child was born eight months and 25 days after we were married.

We never had sex before we married, so our first child was truly five days early. He was probably conceived at the Candlelight Motel in Ozark, Al.

Frances was getting nauseated in the mornings and concerned about her health so she went to the doctor and the doctor told her she was pregnant. We were happy about it but Frances was thirty eight years old and we were concerned about it also. She had the usual weird desires, such as wanting ice cream in the middle of the night. One night she wanted a room divider and stayed up half the night designing the way it should look. I had to build it the next day.

I had quit smoking so Franklin went to the hospital with me and smoked for me. The baby was born after about two packs of cigarettes and we named him Thomas Roy Bowerman, Jr. He had long, thick curly black hair and was beautiful enough to be a girl. In fact, everyone who saw him until he was six months old thought he was a girl. He was one beautiful baby. We were so proud we could pop.

Frances went back to work and we had to get someone to come in and keep Tommy while we were at work. We hated to leave him in the mornings and rushed home in the afternoons. I think we were really convinced we were not smart enough to raise a baby and were scared to death we were going to lose him.

He was too tough and healthy though and survived our amateur efforts. He had a real personality of his own and he blessed our lives.

Tommy did not hang on to our undivided attention long. His first brother arrived when he was just thirteen months old. We did not love him any less but there was another one to love. Nineteen months after his first brother was born, a second brother came along. Frances was forty one when the last one was born.

Tommy was always a really lovable child. He displayed his affection for you and craved it in return. He was a camera hog, really loving to be photographed and crazy about the movie camera. We made thousands of pictures and hundreds and hundreds of feet of movie film.

His childhood was interwoven with the childhood of his two brothers as when you saw one of them you saw all three of them. They were never apart. They were very close. When one had a birthday he got the big present but all three got presents. A lot of his childhood was spent with Eleanor and Franklin's children as we visited a lot and they always came to his birthday parties. Christmas time also brought them close together.

Tommy was seldom sick but when he did run a temperature or get the sniffles we ran poor Dr Judge crazy. Our children were always healthy but it did not take much for us to set up a twenty four hour per day watch over them. I guess we really thought they would never make it.

We bought a house in Delray Subdivision on highway 78 for $12,500 and had a chain link fence put around the back yard. I built a sand box and put up a swing set and the boys seemed happy there. We were there when Tommy started to school and we let him ride the school bus. We were proud of him when he got on that bus the first time and scared to death and pacing up and down when the bus pulled in that afternoon and he got off. I never got accustomed to that child riding in anything when I was not in control. Frances quit work for awhile and then went back. Eventually she quit for good and I was relieved that she was taking care of them instead of someone else.

We had a Black lady named Rosemary for awhile and she was conscientious and loved the children, but it was not the same.

Tommy had a normal childhood and was always a good son and still is. We never really had to worry about him doing something wrong or getting in trouble.

We had next door neighbors that were really great, Mr and Mrs Thurman King. But the King's soldtheir house and life got unbearable and we put the house up for sale. We were unable to sell it but we found a real estate company willing to take it in on trade and bought a house on Bramble Road in Golden Springs. The boys grew into teenagers on Bramble Road.

Tommy never really gave us any problems. He probably did things we did not know about but was never on drugs and did not drink. He and his brothers and a neighborhood friend made some phone calls once and got caught. They just dialled numbers at random but when they found a woman it really upset they kept calling her over and over and scared her half to death. Her son managed to trace the calls and caught them and was going to prosecute them but relented and agreed not to prosecute if they would apologize and promise never to do it again to anyone. They were lucky to get out of it without a police record.

Tommy went through the bicycle and motor bike stage and finally got his driver's license. The driver's license has to be the most frightening experience of every parent. We lived through it and so did Tommy, but not before totalling one car.

Tommy was shooting baskets in our driveway one day and came down wrong and broke his foot. A bone popped through and blood was spurting everywhere. He told Terry to go get a towel. He put the towel across his foot so the blood did not show and then told Terry that he could go get Mom now. He was more concerned over her than he was over his foot. The paramedics came out and got him and he knew all of them and was telling them what to do and how to do it. He never got excited under pressure.

We bought a tent and then a pop up camper and then a

small trailer and then a twenty five foot travel trailer. We camped out, went fishing, went on vacations to places like Colorado, pulling that enormous box of a trailer and we all survived somehow. We also went deeper in debt going from tent to enormous trailer. The large trailer required a large station wagon with special trailer package options to pull the thing. More money down the drain.

Tommy married Susan Butler, daughter of John and Eva Butler. We love her and consider her more the daughter we never had than daughter in law. Tommy and Susan have two children, Thomas Roy Bowerman, III and Tiffany Bowerman. They are great kids, as we always knew they would be. They live in Talladega, Alabama, about twenty miles from us.

Tommy worked as a sales clerk at Britts Department Store, as a paramedic and now as a Detective on the Talladega Police Department. He loves to hunt, especially deer. He bowls regularly and is active in other areas as well. Tommy is what most parents hope their child will be and we have never been disappointed in him. We love him too much to express. He and Susan bought a larger house recently and added a swimming pool in 1993. Susan's Father, John Butler, died from cancer.

Chapter Seventeen

Terry

Terry was born February 13, 1958, just 13 months and 4 days after Tommy was born. Frances was thirty nine when Terry was born, and she had a rough time with him. Terry's oxygen supply was diminished prior to birth and he shed some skin as a result. His head was not shaped perfectly and we were concerned about him. Doctor Judge laughed at us and told us he was a beautiful baby and perfect in every respect. He said we would have to use bean bags to force Terry to lie on the side of his head we wanted him to and that while we were holding him we should rub his head and shape it the way we wanted it. We did that and it was not long before he was a great looking boy.

Terry was much different from Tommy. Tommy loved to keep his bottle as long as we would let him. Terry threw his bottles as hard as he could when they were empty. He wanted no part of an empty bottle.

Terry was jealous of Tommy and wanted to do everything Tommy did. Tommy had walked and taken a couple of falls and crawled awhile longer and then walked again. Terry crawled until he was nine months old and on his nine month birthday he stood up and walked and never crawled again.

We had moved to Bramble Road in Golden Springs by the time Terry was old enough to go to school and he started school in Golden Springs Elementary School. I think it always bugged him that Tommy was one grade ahead of him, but he did fine in school.

Despite his rough start, Terry turned out to be a fine looking boy. He was popular with other children and always a leader.

Terry was the average teenager. He did fine in school, but could have done much better if he had wanted to. Terry always found out what the minimum requirement for passing was and he quit when he got to that point. If there were ten questions on a test and he knew he had the right answers for the first seven, he would not answer the other three if seven was enough for passing. If he had to write a five hundred word book review he was likely to stop at the end of the sentence that gave him the number of words he had to have. He told me several times that anything above minimum was just giving it to them and he just wanted what he had to do to pass and no more as he did not want to give them anything.

Terry was a competitor. He did not want to participate in team sports because when he won something he wanted it to be him winning, not some team. He went for golf, tennis, wrestling and anything that proved he won instead of some team he was just a part of. He won more times than he lost.

Terry was playing some type of ball on our driveway and stepped on a rock and broke his ankle. He had to have a pin put in and had to stay in bed a long time. He was so miserable in bed that Frances and I felt we were the injured before it was all over. He had a cast and I know it was tough but boy he sure made it tougher.

Terry married a girl named Susy but the marriage did not last long and they got a divorce. Frances and I both loved Susy and she still came to visit us from Birmingham almost until Frances passed away.

Terry then married Joy and we saw him start settling down and acting domesticated for the first time. They bought a house and have a garden and dog and really seem to be happy. This marriage has all the signs that it will last.

Terry has been working out with weights since he left high school. He weighs around 225 pounds and has won hard body contests frequently. He seldom misses a day working out and it is the focus of his life. He says he will continue forever and I do not doubt it.

Terry had several minor jobs and finally got a job at Anniston Army Depot as a key punch operator. It was tough going but the job led to computer operator and then after a transfer to Fort McClellan he was selected for Programmer Trainee and went to Virginia for a year of programmer training and did great at it. He has been promoted until he is now a GS-12 responsible for the main frame at Fort McClellan. Joy had an excellent job in Birmingham and they are doing well and the future looks bright for them. Joy left her job and is in training to be a nurse. She was really helpful during Frances' illness. Joy recently graduated and passed her tests and is now in charge of Intensive Care on her shifts at Citizens Hospital in Talladega, Alabama.

Chapter Eighteen

Barry

Barry was born September 26, 1959, by Cesarian Section. Frances had gone on maternity leave and was supposed to be taking it easy but decided to mop the entire house before she did. We had to rush her to the hospital and the doctor recommended we not wait for normal child birth.

We decided also that now we knew what was causing these babies we would have the cords cut and we did. We knew that Barry was the last. He may have been last but he was certainly not least. We loved him as much as the first two. Three children were enough at our ages.

Barry never bothered learning the fine points of talking when he was a baby. If Tommy and Terry wanted something, all he had to know was "Me too." He mastered that in short order. All three of the boys enjoyed playing together. They had a few friends but the three of them were so close together in age that they were really pretty self sufficient.Barry followed them into Golden Springs Elementary School but since he was born the latter part of September he was really allowed to start school one year too soon. He had problems in the first grade and again in the second grade. We talked to the principal about it and followed her advice to let Barry repeat the second grade. I always felt bad about that, like maybe I robbed him of a year of his life. It did make a big difference though, as he never had a problem in school after repeating second grade.

Barry and I were always very close, or at least I thought so. I do not believe it was that I loved him more than his brothers. It was just that he always seemed to be ready to try things I liked to do or needed to do. When we moved to Springdale Avenue we knew we were going to be short one room and I decided to build another bedroom in the garage. Barry worked with me on it and we built the entire room. It was a lot of hard work and used a lot of his time but he never complained.

Barry was industrious and went to work while he was in high school. He worked at a drug store awhile and then went to work at a Hardee's fast food place. He quit taking an allowance when he got a job.

I guess I really began to panic when Barry got to be a teenager as it meant that the boys would soon be gone. I was so accustomed to having them around, helping them study, advising them, helping them with their problems, etc, that I could not bear the thought of them leaving. I guess I thought when they were children and I held them by the hand that I just assumed they would always be there and life would go on like that forever. I never realized they left the nest. The idea of them on their own and taking the knocks of life on their own seemed absurd.

Barry married Shelby Burgess and they have one child named Christopher Lynn Bowerman. They bought trailers and houses and I guess Barry and I built more decks than anyone else around. It seemed we were always building a deck next to a trailer or house somewhere. Even when he bought a trailer in Georgia, I went over and we built a deck there. The marriage broke up and Shelby got custody of Chris. Then Barry went to court and he got custody. Then they had a shared custody arrangement. Finally, pressure on the job got to the point that Barry could no longer stay with Hardee's and he had to take a job in Georgia. Shelby went back to court on the basis that they had agreed that Chris would stay in the Weaver school system and regained custody because Barry had moved to Georgia. Now she has remarried and moved to Georgia, so go figure. I never understood Shelby anyway. Barry divorced her because she was a Lesbian. Then her family pressured her into appearing normal and she started dating again and got pregnant. Then she had an abortion. The closest I can come to describing her sex life is that she is AC/DC.

Barry met Shannon Hiett and they had one son, Dustin

Chase, and a daughter, Cylie. They were living in Cleveland Tennessee until Frances passed away and then Barry, at my request, quit his job and moved in with me, including Shannon and the children.

Barry is a worker and if anything explains his life, it is work. He worked a long, long time as a manager at Hardee's and finally was selected as an area manager with five to seven stores assigned to him. Then he made the mistake of dating a girl at one of his stores and was demoted to manager of a single store.

Barry bought a house in Weaver and did a lot of work and spent a lot of money fixing it up. When he was an area manager he was paid mileage for using his car and had bought a second car for store use. He was unable to maintain payments on a current basis after he was demoted and the AMSouth Bank repossessed it. That bank jerked him around a lot and I went down once and told the President what I thought about it. It turned out he was a figure head with no more authority at the bank than I had and I pitied him so much I just left.

As mentioned above, Barry and the girl that he was demoted for dating have a son named Dustin Chase and a daughter named Cylie and were married in 1993. Barry is a fine boy and deserves the best. I did not mean to indicate that the young lady was at fault for causing his demotion.

If a cause of his problems can be identified, it is more likely to be due to marrying Shelby Burgess, who later decided she was a Lesbian. She admitted to a court appointed psychiatrist that she had a Lesbian affair while she was married to Barry and later, due to pressure from her family, started dating men again and became pregnant and had an abortion. It is hard to believe that a judge can award custody of a child to someone who admits they had a Lesbian affair and an abortion, but it happened.

Barry had a tough time finding a job after moving in with me. He tried a couple of jobs and they were miserable. Then he went to work for Rice Pest Control Company and is very much satisfied with his work. Shannon was working for a

Nursing Home in Heflin and doing very well. She left the nursing home and was out of work a short while but found a job as data entry clerk for Cooper Chevrolet in Anniston. The major problem they have right now is that the children have to get up too early to go to a baby sitter. This makes them irritable.

Frances never liked Shannon, but chances of her liking anyone who married her youngest were slim to none. I like Shannon. She is a hard worker and willing to do anything for you. She is a good mother. She has been here just over a year and is on a her fifth vacuum cleaner. She gives those carpets hell.

Chapter Nineteen

Anniston Army Depot

I mentioned already that I had arranged for a transfer to the Depot Internal Review Office when I was with Army Audit Agency and James McKamee was chief of the Depot Internal Review. When I reported in, McKamee had transferred to Huntsville and John Stanton was Chief of Internal Review. John told me he did not want me as he did not want anyone McKamee would hire as he had no use at all for McKamee. I promised him that if he would try me for just thirty days and he was not fully satisfied I would quit and he would not have to try to fire me. After a week, John told me to forget the thirty day deal as he was fully satisfied and glad to have me on his team.

Internal Review was the internal audit department of the depot. We had what we called appropriated funds and non-appropriated funds. The latter were organizations like the Officers' Club, Post Restaurant and flower funds. The former were not only financial accounts of the depot but also organizations like the Director of Supply and Maintenance and Depot Property. We reviewed both accountability and responsibility, planning, effectiveness, and just about anything we considered appropriate.

I found the Depot Executive Officer, a Lieutenant Colonel, was involved in some way in every activity I audited. He was usually not directly involved but was involved in some manner in everything. I began to watch for indications of his involvement in everything I audited. I was seldom disappointed in the search. I held an exit interview with the people responsible for procurement and the Executive Officer attended the interview and started making sarcastic comments about my audit. I asked him what his responsibility was and he refused to say, so I asked him to leave. He said I could not tell him what to do as he was the Executive Officer and I told him if he had no direct responsibility I wanted him to get out. He left but reported me to John Stanton, the Comptroller and the Commanding Officer. John went to bat for me and we held our ground. Ed Melton was Comptroller and wrote a memo to the Commander accusing the Executive Officer of suborning his auditors.

John Stanton had a year as a GS-11 and transferred to Huntsville and I was selected as temporary Chief of Internal Review and promoted to GS-09. The depot did this to stall until I got a year as GS-09 so they could select me as Chief and promote me to GS-11. I continued to watch the Executive Officer and learned he had a girl friend, a civilian employee at the depot. I observed she could come to work when she wanted and leave when she wanted and the depot time keepers were not allowed to say anything about it.

Regulations required that the Depot Commander or his designated representative visit each post, camp and station in the Third Army Area once per year. This amounted to a lot of travel and the Commander appointed the Executive Officer to do all the visiting. I began to compare the leave record of his girl friend with his travel and they matched perfectly. She was on sick leave or annual leave every time he made a trip, and always the same amount of time. I started calling some of the posts he was visiting and found he seldom arrived there. He filed travel orders and collected the travel money and made trip reports covering his supposed travel.

I went to the Commander, who disliked me very much, and told him what the Executive Officer was doing. He ordered me out of his office and told me I was a vicious damn liar and he had implicit trust in his Executive Officer. The Executive Officer came up for reassignment and left for California with his wife, enroute to a new station in Hawaii. His girl friend went on a date with a member of a team from General Accounting Office making a small audit at the depot. She gave him a book where she had recorded every trip they made, with where he was supposed to go, where they actually went, the name of the hotel they stayed at and the names they registered under. The GAO went to the Commander and asked that he have the Executive Officer brought back to the area. They intercepted him in California and brought him back to Fort McClellan. He was assigned there as Assistant Post Quartermaster while the audit was finished. He was given the choice of resigning for the good of the service or facing a court martial and he resigned and lost all benefits, including veteran status.

The Commander was asked if he had known what was going on and he told the General Accounting Office and Army Criminal Investigation Division that he had no idea at all. He was questioned further and finally he said that the Chief of his Internal Review Office had told him but he had just been totally unable to believe it. I showed them what my discussion with the Commander was based on and things looked dim for the commander for awhile. However, the Army takes care of its own and he was cleared of responsibility for not taking action.

Shortly after that I found the commander was traveling in his depot sedan and collecting mileage for driving his personal vehicle. I also found he was being overpaid on many trips. The depot Finance and Accounting Officer refused to take action so I prepared collection vouchers and took them to the commander. He wrote a check each time and finally asked what percentage of travel vouchers I was auditing. I told him I was auditing one percent across the board and one hundred percent of his. He took exception to the one hundred percent but told me to finish all of his and he would write one check for the total. The Finance and Accounting Officer flatly refused to do his job. I did it for him.

I made an audit of the Officers' Club and found a note where the Commander had asked for a price for a party and then had changed the price to a much lower price and sent the note back saying these were the prices he would be billed. I wrote a note to the Club Secretary asking if club members were allowed to set their own prices and stated it looked crooked to me. He took my note to the commander and I was called in and asked if I questioned his honesty. I told him there was no doubt about his honesty and I was just trying to ascertain the extent of his dishonesty. He was so angry he tried to come across the desk at me. He was only five feet six inches tall and could not get his knee up on the desk. I remarked that when he grew up he would probably be able to get across a desk and hurt someone. He was furious and ordered me out of his office. He called me in the next day and asked that I prepare a bill for the difference in the original prices and what he had paid. I did and he gave me a check for the club.

The audit of the club had twenty six major findings and each of the twenty six began with the phrase, "The Commanding Officer failed to properly perform his duties in that ... ." I was required to get the signature of the commander and forward the report to the Chief of Ordnance. The Comptroller refused to take the report to the commander and I took it myself. He read every word and asked if I expected him to sign it. I told him I expected him to but did not really think he had sufficient integrity to do so. He looked at me awhile and signed it and threw it at me. He then asked what I would have done if he had not signed it and I told him I would mail it anyway and explain he had refused to sign it. He said that if I ever did that, it would be the last report I mailed from his depot. I told him I may have been born poor white trash but I was born with integrity and would always do my job regardless of the personal impact on me.

Several weeks later the report was returned by the Chief of Ordnance and I was commended for the job I had done and the commander was commended for his integrity in signing a report in which he was cited twenty six times for failing to carry out his responsibilities. Signing that report was a large factor in him being promoted to Brigadier General.

I became eligible for GS-12 and all previous chief auditors had left the depot at this point. I went to the personnel office and asked them if the job would support a GS-12. They did a survey and said it would, and upgraded the job. The comptroller prepared the paper work to promote me to GS-12 and the commander refused to approve it unless I would agree to support him one hundred percent. I took the paper to his office and asked him what was the bitch. He said I must agree to support him one hundred percent before he would sign it. I told him I would always support whatever I considered to be in the best interest of the government and I was sure he had to be in agreement with that. He said he was not satisfied with my response and I told him I would support him as well as the comptroller and personnel officer supported him and both those jobs were higher than GS-12. He sighed and signed the paper and tossed it to me and said, "I don't like you but you are the only one on the entire depot I can trust to tell it like it is instead of what they think I want to hear, so I want to keep you here."

This particular commander had a report prepared for the Chief of Ordnance before he left. Every organization on the depot had to prepare a portion of the report and state how poorly they were operating when this commander arrived and how much improvement had been made under his command. I wrote a small paragraph stating that Internal Review had been operating very well before he got there and there had been no change. He would not accept that so I wrote a paragraph stating that life in Internal Review had been very routine before he came but with the problems he had created our life had become much more exciting. He would not accept that so I wrote one more stating that Internal Review was able to operate before he came, only if we obtained the best and most outstanding people, but we had become so proficient under his administration that we could now lose all our people and the depot could get half a dozen monkeys from the zoo and they would be able to perform our jobs as well as we did. He gave up and wrote the Internal Review section himself.

The commander finally left, as they all do eventually and we got a new commander. The new one had been in procurement and had been burned badly by auditors. He made it clear that he disliked all auditors. He called me to his office and said he had read all my audit reports for the past two years and they all had one thing in common - they all stunk. He said he wanted to make it clear that the first report I issued he did not like he would reduce Internal Review one personnel space. He said, "There are seven of you. The seventh report you issue that I do not like is your job. Regulations say I have to have an Internal Review FUNCTION, not an Internal Review OFFICE, and after you are gone I will assign the function to the Management Office." He was serious and if I stuck to my guns I would cost six other people their jobs.

We made our audit schedule and made our audits. We put everything we found in the working papers. We then issued a report stating that we had made an audit of such and such an organization and we had no findings we wished to report. Eventually he called me to his office and said he was concerned we were not finding anything wrong as he was convinced there were a lot of problems at the depot. I told him that we were finding plenty wrong and were documenting it but did not care to report it as we did not want our jobs eliminated. I told him the working papers were available and I was sure external audit agencies would review our working papers and provide him reports later on. He insisted that I must report all findings but in a manner that would not be objectionable to anyone. I refused and he wrote a new job description for my job. The personnel officer reviewed the job description and told him it was not a job description but a performance standard. We were still in the middle of this one when he was selected for Brigadier General and reassigned.

I will refer to the next commander as Colonel Bob Baler. Bob got all the key people together and made a little speech. He said basically that the last two commanders had broken our butts making general and that we should relax as he had been told fifteen years ago that he would never be anything but a third rate Ordnance Officer. He said we were not going to try to set any records while he was commander. He said we would try to stay as good as we were but if it got in the way of having fun and enjoying life and our jobs, then by damn we would have to just slip a little. He said there was more to life than being the best damn depot in the system.

Bob was as good as his word. He would chew you out when you messed up and then laugh and buy you coffee or ask you to stop by his house for supper. He would load up his station wagon with depot employees on the weekends and take them to his place in Florida. He told them anyone mentioning the depot or treating him like a commander would have to walk home, because they would conduct no business there. His bark was terrible but he would not harm a fly. I loved Bob Baler. And guess what? People just busted their butts for him and we had a better depot than we had ever had.

Our Comptroller took a job with NASA as Financial Manager for Cape Canaveral. Bob called me in his office and told me I would be the new Comptroller. The paper work was all set to process but on the day before the promotion a man named Fred Hollister called from Benecia arsenal and said Benecia was closing and he had been notified he had transfer rights to our Comptroller position and he was accepting it.

It did not really bother me. I made a very in-depth analysis of our Internal Review program and prepared a detailed report and gave it to Fred when he arrived. I could tell in a week that Fred Hollister was the best Comptroller in the system and was more effective than I would have ever been. He was a natural born Comptroller and no one could beat him at the job. Bob Baler was upset about Fred coming in and taking what he referred to as "Tom's job." I told him to cool it and support Fred. He told me he would but the next damn promotion that came open was mine.

Fred Hollister called me in and said he had a problem as he was setting up a deputy comptroller position and I had given him more support than anyone on the depot but I had no budget experience. I told him I would be angry if he selected anyone but John Edmondson, Chief of the Budget Office, for the job. He selected Johnny and the two of them made an outstanding team.

The only two problems Fred Hollister ever had were stuttering and spending his personal money. He stuttered so bad it was almost pitiful and he spent money like it was going out of style. Fred would make a trip to Washington and if he ran out of underwear would go out and pay $75.00 for a set. His evening meal often was more than three hundred dollars for two or three people. Fred's philosophy was "Nothing but the best." Everyone was reluctant to travel with Fred.

The chief of equipment management was a man named Frank Gilliam and Frank stuttered worse than Fred. He asked me one day if I would tell Fred that he stuttered. I asked him why and he said he wanted to meet him but was afraid if he went in Fred's office and started talking Fred would hit him before he knew he was not mocking him. By the way, Frank went to Florida once and said he was almost out of gas and finally found a lone station in the country. He said he pulled in and the owner said, "Wha wha wha what ca ca can I do do do for for for for you you you you?" He said he told him, "Fi fi fi fill it it it it up up up up up." He said the guy got red as a beet and said, "Ge ge ge get ou ou out, you you you sma sms smar smart assed S S S O O O B B B." He said he tried to tell the guy he stuttered too and the guy got a shotgun and he had to get out. He ran out of gas before he found a station.

The Chief of Management was a large pink skinned character who had a bad twitch in one eye. I used to go in Fred's office for a branch chief's meeting and I would start stuttering like Fred and twitching like Pinky (the pink skinned one). Fred knew I loved and respected him and took it good naturedly but Pinky would get furious.

The depots finally reached the computer age and all depots were to get IBM 305 computers, with all card input. Charlie Heard, the Depot Civilian Executive Assistant, went to Washington with a proposal to put a more advanced tape system at Anniston. He took a slide projector loaded with his proposal but no one would let him in their office. Charlie took a sheet from the hotel and had two guys to help him. He started nabbing people in the hall and two guys would hold up the sheet and Charlie would make his pitch in the hall. He nabbed the right man and Anniston was approved for the best computer system in the world at that time.

Most depots put the computer organization under the director for services and a couple put it under the comptroller. Anniston and Sacramento put it under the Director for Supply. The Chief of Stock Control at Anniston was given the job of getting it going and after it was installed elected to move from Stock Control to Chief of Data Processing. The big problem was that he was an alcoholic and a lush and a thief and much more. Charlie Heard pulled some strings to get him offered a higher paying job in Huntsville. The next day Bob Baler called me in and said, "Congratulations on your promotion." I asked him what he meant and he said I was going to be his Chief of Data Processing. I told him I knew nothing about computers and did not qualify and Bob replied, "You qualify for anything I tell those crooked SOB's in personnel you qualify for." He called the personnel officer in and told him what he wanted and he thought awhile and said that since the future of data processing would be mainly financial applications that I qualified. At that time, Charlie Heard was over both supply and maintenance operations at the depot and the rightful selecting official. I went to Charlie and told him what Bob had told me and that I did not want to take the job as he was the one who should be making the selection. Charlie just smiled and said, "I did make the selection, I just let Bob think it was his idea."

With much trepidation and a tremendous feeling of insecurity and inadequacy, I decided to accept. Before I did, I went to Data Processing and talked to all those who qualified for the job. All but one told me they did not want the job and would like to see me take it and would support me fully. The other one said he wanted it badly but knew he would never get it and the one that would get it if I did not take it was not capable of handling it. He said he would support me fully if I took it.

Charlie Heard, the best boss I ever worked for, told me that he would send his Deputy, J.L. Smith to take over Data Processing until I got my feet on the ground and as soon as I felt I could handle it I could send J.L. home. J.L. was responsible for the maintenance end of the Directorate for Supply and Maintenance. J.L. went to Data Processing early the first morning while I was processing in the Civilian Personnel Division. I finished about ten A.M. and went to Data Processing. J.L. was sitting at my desk and I just told him, "You can go home now, J.L. and thanks for helping out." I think J.L. had thought he would be there about three months but as far as I was concerned, it was now or never.

I introduced myself to the people and everyone seemed to accept me initially. I started checking out the operation. My office walls were lined with charts, including one they referred to as the blood chart as it took blood, sweat and tears to make it. I asked what external or internal reports were made from the charts and found that none were. I reviewed all the charts and called Charlie Heard and asked him if he used any of them. Charlie did not need them and I did not need them. I found one person was spending full time making and updating the charts. I called Doc Brown in and talked to him. Doc made the charts. I told Doc to take them all down and dump them in the trash can and to quit making them. He asked about the blood chart and I told him he could have it if he wanted it. I found during my discussion that Doc was a bright person capable of doing much more than making charts. I told him to not worry about a job.

I checked the clerical staff and found that one division chief had two secretaries. One worked half her time on data processing paperwork and the other half on the division chief's outside business interests. The other spent full time on his outside business interests. I abolished both secretarial positions and told him my secretary would handle his paperwork in her spare time.

I found that we had two individuals in that division chief's organization who were on temporary promotions to GS-12 and that the Chief, Position and Pay management Branch, Civilian

Personnel Division was extremely unhappy about the promotions and ready to cut them back to GS-11's. Both had GS-12 jobs lined up in Huntsville. I got with the Chief, Position and Pay Management and Chief, Manpower Office and worked out an agreement to divide the Programming Division into three programming divisions with a GS-12 over each one.

The Chief, Programming Division came to my office and said he worked for prestige, not money, and if I changed his division into three divisions and he only had a third of the people he would go to a job he already had lined up in Huntsville. I handed him my phone and told him to call and arrange a transfer date and I would approve it. He called and they asked how much notice I wanted and I told them none. He told them he needed thirty days.

I went to New Orleans to a programming school. Helen Saxon, a computer operator, and Stan Magness, a budget analyst for the comptroller, went with me. We learned almost nothing about programming except it was a difficult job to do right. Tic Vinson, one of the new programming division chiefs, called me while I was there and said the division chief that was going to Huntsville had gone to the military director for supply and maintenance, Major Johnson, and told him I was ruining Data Processing and that the Major told him he would fire me. I called Major Johnson and asked him about it and he said it was all settled and that Colonel Baler agreed with him and I was going to have to find another job.

We rode back to Anniston in Stan's car and I got home at two A.M. I called Colonel Baler at two o'clock in the morning and when he answered the phone I told him, "Bob, you are a no good SOB." He asked who I was and then asked if I was drunk. I told him what Major Johnson had told me and he said he had not even talked to Johnson and if the depot was not big enough for me and Johnson both then Major Johnson would have to get the hell out. He told me to go to sleep and come see him Monday.

I went to Johnson's office Monday morning after I talked

to Bob Baler and Johnson called the personnel officer in and they started talking about jobs I could transfer to. I told them I was staying where I was and they said I could not do that. I told Johnson that if he and I could not get along then he would have to get his butt off the depot. I said it loud enough for twenty or thirty people to hear. Johnson continued to tell me I was through and I told him to go see Bob Baler immediately or I would have the provost marshal come take him to his office. Johnson left and was gone an hour. He came back in and did not bat an eye when he said, "You and I have no problems, Tom. You run Data Processing and I will run the rest of the directorate." He then asked if Colonel Baler and I were friends and I told him we were bosom buddies and he needed to remember it. The Major never gave me another problem while he was there. I went back to Data Processing and told the departing division chief to get on the phone and get an immediate transfer worked out or he would not have a job to transfer from. He left for Huntsville that week.

I found that three of the programmers had transferred in from the Management Division when the Data Processing organization was set up and none of the three knew how to program and had made no efforts to learn. I called them in and gave them thirty days to find another job. Two went to Huntsville and one went to Virginia. I found we were very low on people who actually knew how to program. I set up a trainee program with six spaces I had eliminated in the directorate. The six selected started out as GS-5 trainee programmers, with periodic promotions guaranteed until they reached the GS-9 level, subject to satisfactory performance. I selected Doc Brown for one of the jobs and let the programming supervisors select the remainder. All six turned out to be excellent programmers.

When I first went to Data Processing we had an IBM 650 Tape/RAMAC system. The big problem was that the tape portion was called a tape data selector and was a real monster to work with. The other depots could handle cards only and we could handle tape. This made us several times faster than the depots with the IBM 305 Card/RAMAC system. It also meant we were not compatible with system wide procedures and had to write all our own procedures and send them to the procedures agency. This kept at least one analyst occupied almost full time. Another problem was that we had to do a selling job to get the more advanced computer and our people had promised to do the total data processing job with 61 people and we really needed over a hundred.

Equipment was controlled very closely by utilization and it did not matter that a system would not run without a particular piece of equipment, if it was not used a certain number of hours you had to write a total justification monthly, and fight to keep it. We had an IBM 407 that was used about 24 hours a month and every month we were spending 40 hours in our fight to keep it. I called the Chief of Operations in and told him to start showing 720 hours per month usage. Headquarters never did ask the first question after that and the division chief thought I was some smart cookie to think of that.

Every month we got call after call from headquarters asking for our equipment usage breakout in a manner we could not possibly break it out. I called other depots and found Headquarters needed it for a Congressional report and no one had it that way but they kept calling many times every month. I sat down and made a spread sheet and put down a sheet full of figures that I just made up. The next time Headquarters called I told them I had them informally and read them off on the phone and they copied them down. They called back the next day and had three figures they thought were way out of line. They called off one of them and I asked if they thought it was too high or too low. They said it was at least ten times higher than they expected. The figure was something like 146 and I told them they copied it down wrong as it should be 14.6. We did the same thing on the other two figures and they were happy. Next month they called back on just one figure. When I was fairly sure they were happy with the figures I had a programmer make up a simple program to just adjust the figures up or down a little each month and print them out. I started mailing the report then. Headquarters called and said no other depot was able to provide the information we did so they were just multiplying our figures by the number of depots and sending it to Congress and Congress was very happy with it. I was so glad I could help out. I was telling lies to Congress before Ollie North ever thought about it.

The greatest problem was probably that we had a lot of supply applications on computer and not too much else. There were hundreds of processes that needed automating but the computer was in the Directorate for Supply and most of the computer workload was naturally supply. Another problem was that computer processing was programmed to handle transactions the way people manually handled transactions. Finally, there had been a trend toward selecting programmers and analysts from the people who knew the applications on computer. This created two large problems. One problem was that the people were not programmers or computer analysts and never would be. The other problem was that the people were frequently the most knowledgeable in their area of supply and there were no qualified people to replace them in the functional areas. They therefore tended to continue to spend most of their time in the functional area. I recognized that we had to start selecting on the basis of programming skills or potential.

Finally, the equipment took so long to justify that it was outdated before it was delivered. This is a common problem in government. The approval cycle needed to be shortened but the people in headquarters wanted to lengthen it to justify the number of people they had on board working in the approval cycle.

A good example of equipment problems is that we had a thirty six megabyte hard drive that was hydraulically operated and weighed two full tons. The raised flooring had to be braced again every two weeks to keep the hard drive from falling through the floor. The movement of the hydraulic actuators literally pounded the huge piece of equipment into the floor. Those same vibrations also created disk errors. The equipment was the finest of its day but its day had passed before we ever got it.

I suppose it was inevitable with so many depots using

similar computers that a project like SPEED would be born. SPEED was the acronym for System-wide Project for Electronic Equipment at Depots. Someone decided the Army would save a fortune if the computers were standardized and one central agency was designated to write the programs for all depots. This would supposedly reduce the number of programmers required overall.

The Commander, Bob Baler, was notified that a meeting was being held at Rossford Ordnance Depot in Ohio and he should attend, along with his Director for Data Systems. I decided to go by train and Bob was going to fly, so I left a day before Bob. The next day there was a two inch snow and all flights in the South were cancelled and Bob was unable to go. I was notified that I represented both the Commander and Director for Data Systems.

There were 175 people present and a presentation was made on SPEED and the charts showed savings in the hundreds of millions of dollars, mostly in programmer salary savings. The meeting was opened for questions and I raised my hand and was acknowledged. I merely said that I knew that figures did not lie but it was obvious that liars had been figuring. A two star general ran from the back of the room and bounded onto the stage and said, "Sir, I will have you know that these are my figures." I said something to the effect that 'now we know', followed by a comment that I did not retract my statement. The general commented that I was calling him a liar in front of 175 people and I said I had not made a head count. He said he wanted to talk to my commander and I told him Bob got snowed in. He said he had commanders from areas that had ten feet of snow and my commander could not make it because of a two inch snow. I said at least he was honest and I think our conversation degenerated after that. The Data Processing people from Headquarters were telling me to shut up and I told them I would speak my piece. There were more than twenty depots at the time and the average programming staff was about twenty. We had sixteen at Anniston. There was no central programming group at the time. The plan was that the central agency would be staffed with a maximum of sixty people and each depot would lose sixteen programmers. There would be a savings of about 20 times 16 (320) minus 60 for the central staff, or a net savings of 260 people. It is getting ahead of myself but eventually, under Project SPEED, the average depot programming staff increased to thirty five and the central group had a staff of about 300.

There was a cocktail party that night and the general came over to me and said, "You are the one who claims I am lying!" and I said, "I am the one who knows your figures are a lie." He said he was going to have Bob Baler straighten me out. All of the other depot data processing people came over one by one and shook hands and said they agreed with me but I would not be around very long.

I left on the train during some of the worst winter weather I ever saw. We got to Nashville, Tennessee and could go no further. We stayed in the train overnight and the next morning there was four inches of ice all over the floor and it was bitterly cold. I had less than a dollar with me. I went to the dining car and found I had enough money for one cup of coffee. There was another man at my table and he asked if I was going to eat breakfast. I told him I had not cashed a check before I left Ohio and was broke except for enough to get a cup of coffee. He took out his billfold and handed me a twenty dollar bill and his business card and told me to mail it to him when I got home. He just about saved my life.

I had a message waiting when I got back to work to come see Colonel Baler. I went to his office and Bob glared at me, bit his cigar real hard and said, "Tom, why in the hell did I send you to that meeting?" I said, "Bob, you sent me because of my great tact." Bob mulled that one over and came back with, "Tom, you got about as much tact as a meat axe." We then talked the whole thing over. Bob said he had been requested to fire me on the spot when I got home but he felt I had told the truth as I saw it and there would never be a day when he fired someone for telling it like they saw it. He said to get to work and he would call the general and tell him to go to hell. The old man took a beating for defending me and I am sure no commander I ever had after that would have done it.

Project SPEED involved visiting every computer manufacturer submitting a bid on the standard equipment. It also involved depot support. The central group was based on a small organization that had been writing depot procedures and none of their people knew anything about computers. Each depot was given a number of programmers they would have to provide on temporary duty at Rossford Ordnance Depot to help write programs. Anniston had to furnish eight programmers full time. This was half of our staff. The depot had to pay the travel and per diem cost. We asked for volunteers and got four. The other four had to be selected, and periodically bring one or two home and rotate others to Rossford. The effort took more than two years. Programming began without even knowing the final equipment. It turned out that an IBM 1410 and IBM 1401 were selected.

All programmers had agreed to travel as part of the acceptance of the position. I had to keep bringing people home and rotating new ones. We got to the point that all had been except one female programmer with a four month old baby. I had travel orders prepared for her and she refused to go. Her husband was six foot six inches tall and weighed more than two hundred and fifty pounds. He came to my office and threatened me and I ordered him out. Finally the female programmer went to Huntsville and found jobs for both herself and her husband. She gave me two weeks notice. Then a week before time to leave she came in and said she had thought it over and decided I was right. She wanted to go on travel and take her turn and then when she had done her job she would go to Huntsville. That is what happened and I admired her very much for her decision.

We built a temporary computer room next to the old computer room and moved our IBM 650 system into it and remodeled the old room for the new IBM 1410/1401 systems. When it was our turn to convert, the central group was prepared to send a large team in to help with the conversion. I made a decision that we would do our own conversion without help and we did it despite dire predictions about what would happen to us. We made the smoothest conversion and in the shortest period they had seen. We were on Project SPEED and having relatively few problems. We had the best people in the system.

It eventually became obvious that the IBM 1410/1401 systems would not handle the applications the depots wanted to put on the computer systems and it would be necessary to move to larger and more modern systems. A new acronym was coined - Project SPEEDEX, which was nothing more than System-wide Project for Electronic Equipment at Depots - EXtended. The federal government had an anti-trust suit against IBM and it was a safe bet we would not get IBM equipment this time. The equipment we ended up with was a Control Data Systems 3300, which was really a communications system with a Business Data Processor front end. It was obvious to even the most uninitiated that the CDC 3300 was a poor choice for depot data processing.

I made an attempt to get SPEEDEX deferred five years. I made a speech to members of The Armed Force Management Association and my speech was reproduced in The Defense Manager, a national publication distributed at all levels of government and to every Congressman and Senator. Within an hour of distribution of the Defense Manager, John Gilbert, AMC Director of Management Information Systems (GS-17) was on the phone with the Anniston Army Depot Commander, demanding I be fired that day. At the same time, Ralph Tappen, Chief of the Logistics System Support Center, (GS-15) was on the phone with Charles Heard, Anniston Army Depot Civilian Executive Assistant, demanding I be fired that day. Charles Heard had guts and backed me one hundred percent, to his own personal detriment, and I not only survived but Charles Heard insisted the Commander approve an Outstanding Performance Award and a Sustained Superior Performance Award for me.

Army Materiel Command sponsored a committee consisting of representatives of AMC, the Logistics System Support Center and the Director for Management Information Systems of each SPEEDEX depot. The group elected a Chairman and I was elected Chairman two times. The directors knew I would fight for what I thought was right. I had their support and loyalty, and even better, their respect. When my second term ended I was presented with a poem that the group felt expressed what I stood for. This poem, "Never Give an Inch", is my proudest possession.

One very bad problem with the CDC 3300 was the environment it had to have to even have a chance to run. Temperature control had to be maintained within plus or minus two degrees and humidity control had to be maintained within plus or minus five percent. Power had to be almost perfect. The equipment ran on DC current, requiring DC motor generators. Steam had to be available to help control humidity. It cost each depot a fortune to build a new computer room and utility room and it had to be built by every depot as no depot had a computer room that would support the Control Data Corporation requirements.

Construction money was not available and every depot had to classify large portions of the computer room as equipment. Even walls had to be classified as equipment and screws were driven in instead of nails to make it look like panels were demountable. It made liars of every engineering department in the depot system.

While all this construction was going on, the depots were once again sending their programming staffs on temporary duty to do the programming. Eventually the botched up systems were released to the depots and the depots began to operate the new Control Data 3300 systems. We learned the difference between IBM and CDC immediately. When there was a problem with IBM equipment an IBM systems technician used the appropriate test equipment and within minutes or hours had the problem identified and the equipment operational. The CDC technicians were equipped with test gear that was strange to us, consisting primarily of a comb, a plastic hammer, a hair dryer and a can of freon. They would run a test program and one technician would sit at the console while others took turns rubbing a comb across rows of cards to see if there was a vibration problem. Then they would use the hair dryer to blow hot air on the cards to see if there was a heat related problem. If this failed, they would spray freon on cards to see if there was a cold related problem. If none of this disclosed the problem they would take plastic hammers and beat on the cards to see if there was a shock related problem. Frequently, during the hammer phase the console technician would yell and we would ask if that meant they had found a bad card. The response was always that they had either found a bad card or had made a card bad from the beating. If all else failed they would do what they called 'turn up the margins.' This meant they would increase voltage a certain percent to see if they could burn something out completely, making it easy to spot by the smoke.

The local engineers were reluctant to call for outside help and we had to push them unmercifully to get them to admit defeat and call in outsiders. For awhile it seemed like the outside crew was very good as they usually found the problem rather quickly and fixed it. We noticed that we always had a series of nagging problems for a week or two after the National crew left. We finally learned why the locals really hated to call in the outside help. The outsiders were no better than the locals but had a higher margin approval level. This meant they were allowed to increase the power more than the locals and burn the system out faster. The locals hated this because they knew they would be busy for weeks replacing burned out components.

When we were using IBM equipment we had never known what even a 24 hour downtime was because the equipment had never been down for 24 hours at a time. It was not unusual at all for Control Data Corporation equipment to be down three solid weeks and on two occasions it was down for much longer periods. This was complicated by the fact that even when the equipment was running perfect there was no way it could process one day's input within twenty four hours. That meant we were on a constant schedule of batching input and running a cycle every two or three days. We were never current when we ran CDC equipment. When we were down for three weeks it took weeks and weeks to catch up. We found that we could run six cycles with two days input in each much faster than one cycle with seven days input - or even four days input - because when the volume reached a certain level the equipment sat there for days and did practically nothing.

From a personal standpoint, I had opposed selection of the CDC equipment, even getting into print with a publication distributed to every member of congress. There were demands at the time from all levels that I be fired. I had no input into the selection process, I had no input into the central programming, I had no authority to fire contractor engineers, I had no input into any of the areas affecting the entire process - yet I was the guy they blamed when the equipment would not run and the functional people could not get their output. To compact it further they were planning on selecting certain depots to have computers and other depots being served by them via communication lines. This meant that other depots were saying everything was great in an effort to be selected as a central processing site. Headquarters Data Processing people played one depot against another. When our commander raised hell with headquarters about our computer problems they would select a team from headquarters and other depot people and come in and make us look like monkeys. Other depots were not getting their work done on computer but were processing manually and playing politics.

Eventually we installed an Uninterruptible Power System costing in excess of a million dollars. We replaced the buggy CDC memory with memory from another company and replaced the disk drives with third party equipment. We got to the point that we could sometimes run almost a week without major problems. We were still not able to process a full day's input in twenty four hours. Life was hard and miserable for a long, long time.

I think most of my problems in Data Processing were caused by my efforts to give my supervisors full control of their operations. I did not like to hold a supervisor responsible for running his organization and then impose my style of management on him. If the results of their supervision were acceptable I did not want them to feel they had to achieve those results the same way I would have.

I also did not want to make their personnel selections as I felt they were responsible for the operation and entitled to select the people they would have to perform the job. I felt that many selections for promotions were not the best, certainly not the people I would select, but I felt strongly that if they were observing Equal Opportunity laws then they should make the selections. The only people I selected were my secretary and my division chiefs. As a result, we got programmers who could never program and analysts who could never analyze. A lot of them were good old boys and fine fishing and hunting buddies and nice drinking buddies but did not have much to offer in terms of data processing.

One division chief appeared to take great delight in conforming with regulations down to the minute letter of the law to prevent accomplishment of many of my objectives. The man who took my place when I left simply moved him off the job. I could never bring myself to do that as I knew in his own way he was doing his job. I knew he was doing it to make my job more difficult but he was still doing his job and I could not bring myself to cause him heartache over that.

Another big problem was that I never had enough people to do the job right. I had to take on many, many jobs myself because there was no one else to do it and those jobs had to be done. The more of them I did, the less time I had to properly manage the organization. The average strength of my Directorate for Management Information Systems was between 85 and 90 people. We had every job to do that other depot DMIS organizations had to do, yet the average strength among all the depots was 125 to 135 people. It is hard to compete when you have 40 to 50 fewer people. I spent an average of 14 to 16 hours per day at the depot, for 25 years. I never drew a penny in overtime. I also took a brief case full of work home with me and managed to work another two or three hours per day on depot work at home.

I could never get much cooperation from other directors. I had the only director's office on the depot that was not carpeted. The Director for Services and Chief, Depot Facilities Division refused to approve it. The entire office and conference room were carpeted two weeks after I retired and the new director took over.

There were too many programs and projects that did not relate to accomplishment of the mission. There were annual fund drives, savings bond participation programs, suggestion programs, zero defects programs, command performance parties, officer's club participation, Armed Forces Management Association, direct deposit of paychecks, performance standards, and on and on - and you were expected to approach one hundred percent participation in all of them.

There were visiting dignitaries and you were required to sit in at the briefings for them and attend the parties for them. There were weekly staff meetings and at times daily staff meetings and you had to be at all of them. I frequently found myself in a three day meeting when I had what seemed like a million pressing problems. When it was over I would find my in-basket overflowing and my division chiefs living in a relaxed atmosphere with little concern over any problem outside their own little world. Division chiefs would feud with one another and each would expect me to take his side in the feud. It was lonely at the top.

SPECIAL

I just wanted to mention some people I met while working for the Anniston Army Depot. They are not listed alphabetically or in order of importance or significance, or in any specific manner - intentionally.

◇◇◇◇◇◇◇◇◇◇◇◇◇◇◇◇◇◇◇◇◇◇◇◇◇◇

John C. Stanton   Chief of Internal Review

John gave me an opportunity when I badly needed it and I will never forget him for it. John had a dry sense of humor and was often heard to say, "It is an amusing thing to me." John was outstanding both as an auditor and a supervisor. He insisted on compliance with high standards of personal and professional conduct and on compliance with generally accepted accounting standards. Thank you, John, for all you taught me.

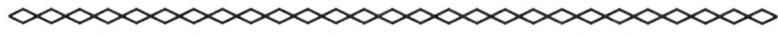

◇◇◇◇◇◇◇◇◇◇◇◇◇◇◇◇◇◇◇◇◇◇◇◇◇◇◇◇
Elsie Kilgore   Supervisor in General Supply Division

Elsie recognized me for the rookie I was on my first audit at Anniston Ordnance Depot. There I was trying to make sense out of a very complicated system that I did not understand so I could write criticisms against her. What does Elsie do? She gives me a crash course in the whole supply system and tells me to check with her before I make a fool of myself. I would check with Elsie and she would say, "We did this one right, you just overlooked this, but you are right on these twelve - we dropped the ball on all of them. If I had problems putting the finding in the proper supply terminology, Elsie would suggest some better wording. Elsie Kilgore was a true professional and more interested in getting things done than in covering her rear.

I saw Elsie walking through Building 362 one day and her bloomers fell down around her ankles. Elsie never missed a step, just kicked the bloomers up with one foot and threw them across her shoulders. I love you Kilgore. Thanks for all the kindnesses. Elsie passed away recently.

◇◇◇◇◇◇◇◇◇◇◇◇◇◇◇◇◇◇◇◇◇◇◇◇◇◇◇◇
Mary Alice Hollingsworth   Finance and Accounting Supervisor

Mary Alice had her office at the top of the steps leading down to the rest rooms in Building 53. Alice told me, "I smell them all." She was a grand lady trying to hide it. I was pushed for something to report one day and Alice opened her desk drawer and gave me a folder of documents and told me to check them. They all looked fine to me until Alice gave me a course in governmental accounting in one short hour. Every document represented a contract that had been released without committing or obligating funds for it. The reason was that there was no money to commit or obligate.

Alice was married to Buck Hollingsworth for many, many years and they had no children and then suddenly she was pregnant. I asked her a simple question, "Well how on earth did you do it?" Alice looked at me with that wicked grin of hers and replied, "Dog style, the best we can remember."

Thank you, Alice, for just being Alice.

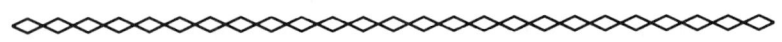

◇◇◇◇◇◇◇◇◇◇◇◇◇◇◇◇◇◇◇◇◇◇◇◇◇◇◇

Ed Melton   Controller of Anniston Army Depot

Ed Melton was my boss when I became Chief of Internal Review. We were very friendly enemies. I loved Ed but loved to needle him even more. Ed had one large fault in that he could only talk dirty and could only tell dirty jokes.

Ed and I would get in a peeing contest every now and then. One started out with me underlining a word in a memo to him. His response stated that you underlined words the recipient was too dumb to understand. His response had four or five words underlined. I replied with about twenty words underlined. His next reply had two full paragraphs underlined. I replied one more time and had every word in a two page response underlined. Ed then replied with just one sentence, no underlines. It said, "I am still your boss and I think you are smart enough to understand that."

I told Ed one time that I had a friend in Tuscaloosa who was a dead ringer for him, that I could not tell them apart. He got real excited and asked me what his name was. I told him, "I never did know his real name, Ed. Everyone called him Hog Jaw."

Part of my job was to coordinate with Army Audit Agency when they were on depot and Ed started doing this by having them come to his office and not inviting me. I complained and he apologized but asked if I minded having the meeting in his office. I told him that would be fine and we set up a meeting for the next day with the team chief of the Army Audit Agency team. I went to Ed's office at the appointed time and we started discussing the audit. The problem was that Ed and the team chief both spoke in Spanish and I did not know what in the hell they were talking about.

Ed accepted a job with NASA and went to Huntsville, then on to Cape Canaveral as financial manager of the Cape. Ed took many, many people with him, all getting promotions they richly deserved.

>>>

Fred Hollister Comptroller (Friendly Fred, Finagler of Federal Funds)

Fred Hollister, last of the big time spenders. Fred paid $75 for a suit of underwear. Fred sometimes spent more than $300 for a dinner for two. Fred knew how to live. Fred is dead and cremated and his ashes spread over Benecia Arsenal in California.

Colonel Baler had decided to promote me to Comptroller at Anniston Army Depot but had to wait to see if Fred wanted the job as Benecia Arsenal in California was closing and Fred had transfer rights. Fred called on the afternoon of the last day he had rights and accepted the job.

Fred arrived and it turned out he stuttered very badly, but it was soon apparent he was the best Comptroller in the Army and I was really proud our depot got him. As Chief of Internal Review, Fred was my boss and he was a good one. He let me run my operation my way and he supported me fully. I loved Fred. I was sad when he died of cancer.

Fred was playing golf with Woody Strange when Woody

had a heart attack and died instantly. He was asked how it was at the next staff meeting and Fred said, "It was terrible. Hit the ball and drag Woody. Hit the ball and drag Woody. I thought I would never make it to the eighteenth hole."

Fred was really crazy about his wife's Mother, who lived with them. There were six of us as pall bearers at her funeral, including me and Fred. Fred said, "They should have eight pall bearers instead of six and after the funeral we would have two foursomes for golf."

Fred was one of my few friends but was always a true friend. I trusted Fred completely to do anything he said he would do. I miss you, Fred, old buddy.

◇◇◇◇◇◇◇◇◇◇◇◇◇◇◇◇◇◇◇◇◇◇◇◇◇◇◇

Paul Crockett   Chief, Production Control, Directorate for Maintenance

No one was impartial toward Paul Crockett. You either hated him or you loved him. I loved Paul Crockett.

Paul was not just Chief of Production Control at Anniston Army Depot; Paul was Mr Production Control in the Depot System. He was the very best and he knew the job and how to produce the highest quality products at the absolute lowest cost better than anyone in the Army. Paul was a real talker but he also got results.

There were plans to model production control on computer under Project SPEEDEX after the system at Sacramento Army Depot as Sacramento had the project. Paul and I made several trips to Sacramento to fight for the Anniston system. Paul made it clear that they were modeling after an operation that rebuilt radio equipment and when projects changed in midstream the radios could be thrown in a corner or swept under a rug. He made the point that you do not sweep 250 tanks under a rug or pile them in a corner. He won a lot of points for Ordnance depots, with little support from the other depots.

Paul and I had some time to kill in the San Francisco

airport while waiting on our flight and he took me in tow and we visited every ticket counter. Paul would ask if CORE or NAACP had left tickets for Crockett or Bowerman. He would explain that we were professional pickets and ready to go to the next demonstration. He would then say that maybe the demonstration is here in town and we would visit every automobile rental booth and he would ask the same thing.

We were eating dinner in a restaurant and Paul started telling the waitress how pretty she was and then how far he was from home and how lonely his room was. He finally told the girl that he just needed it bad but no one cared about his needs. The waitress left and in about ten minutes she came back with her coat on and told him she was ready to go. Paul asked her where she wanted to go and she told him they were going to his room. He asked her why they would do that and she said for sex and hurry up. Paul gave her his innocent look and told her he was married and could not do that. She asked him why he had asked her if he did not want to do it and Paul told her his wife let him talk about it but she wouldn't let him do it. She was really angry and told him she had to beg hard to get off work and she was ready to do it and she would find someone else to do it with. She left in a huff and Paul grinned at me and said he bet he did somebody a real favor.

We were going through the airport in Atlanta and there were a lot of Black people carrying strike signs. Paul had to stop and ask this one Black guy what he was doing. The guy said he was striking and Paul asked him what he was striking for. The guy said he was striking for more money. Paul told him that if he had a guy working for him and he started just walking around carrying a sign he would not pay him anything, much less more. The guy told him he did not understand, that he would quit carrying the sign when he got more money. Paul told him that it sounded more like blackmail than striking and they got in a heated argument. I had to drag Paul away before he got mobbed.

Paul had a heart attack and passed away. The depot was never the same without him and I always missed him. Paul will have Heaven on schedule long before the rest of you get there.

◇◇◇◇◇◇◇◇◇◇◇◇◇◇◇◇◇◇◇◇◇◇◇◇◇◇

Bill Purdy Finance and Accounting Officer

I take full responsibility for my actions in hiring Bill Purdy when I was Chief of Internal Review. No, seriously, Bill was tops. He made a good Finance and Accounting Officer. I told Fred to make him Chief of Internal Review when I left for Data Processing and Fred did it. Bill did a good job.

I can only remember one thing that disappointed me with Bill. We had been boss and employee and friends a long time and then when Bill went to Finance and Accounting we were associates and friends. I got in a real financial bind and someone I owed threatened to report me to the depot and that is the worst news you can get after AIDS. I had been paying on a thousand dollar bond by the payroll deduction method and the bond had passed maturity date. I knew that $750 would put me in good shape and it was scheduled to be mailed the next week. I asked Disbursing to let me have it over the counter and they said it took too much time to find it. I knew it would take under a minute but they refused. I went to Bill and told him I had never asked for a favor but I was really in a bind and asked him to get my bond for me. Bill refused and I could never bring myself to forgive him. I had to go to a finance company and make a short term loan to pay my debt. I still love you though, Billy.

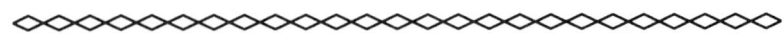

◇◇◇◇◇◇◇◇◇◇◇◇◇◇◇◇◇◇◇◇◇◇◇◇◇◇

Eleanor Rhodes   My Secretary for twenty five years

Eleanor is originally from Maine and I owe a lot to the circumstances that got her to Alabama as she was the finest Secretary in the world and I was most fortunate to have her.

Eleanor was the fastest and most accurate typist ever, and did the neatest job. She did this with hands that hurt her constantly. She was also a good friend and avid supporter and if every employee I had was just half as good at their jobs as Eleanor was, then I would still be there.

Eleanor typed my Master's thesis and several more that I wrote for other people. I could write a Master's thesis over a week-end and Eleanor could type it faster than that. We could have easily turned out two per week.

What can I say? Eleanor was my best employee and was more professional at her job than anyone else I had. Our relationship was purely professional and as friends. Long live Eleanor Rhodes.

Eleanor and I dated about once a week for awhile but I think she found me boring and the last time I asked her out she said, "Oh I don't know." I took the hint.

◇◇◇◇◇◇◇◇◇◇◇◇◇◇◇◇◇◇◇◇◇◇◇◇◇◇◇◇

Herman Tidmore Coker   Computer Systems Analyst

Herman T. Coker was a long time friend of my wife and her family and became one of my employees when I was selected as Director for Data Systems. Herman was on temporary duty in Italy when I first went to Data Processing. Herman was in demand everywhere and traveled frequently.

Herman knew every form used in the supply system by name and number and knew what they were used for, how many copies there were, who got each copy, and what they did with it. When procedures were changed he could sit down and write a new manual without referring to the old manual. He could write a new manual in a very short time frame. The people responsible for system wide manuals often asked him to rewrite a manual for them. He knew the supply system better than anyone in the country. Herman had a heart of gold. He was often suspected of being gay but no one ever proved it. But gay or straight, he was worth his weight in gold in any data processing organization. It was a blow when he retired and we were always glad when he visited after retirement so we could get answers to the questions we had saved up - as well as just being glad to see him.

Herman died, apparently from cancer of the stomach, and many, many of us attended his funeral in Collinsville, Alabama.

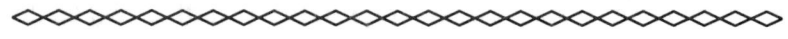

◇◇◇◇◇◇◇◇◇◇◇◇◇◇◇◇◇◇◇◇◇◇◇◇◇◇◇◇◇◇◇◇◇◇◇◇◇◇

J.D. Brittain   Director for Services

J.D. Brittain was promoted to GS-14 the same day I was. I think J.D. knew his job better than anyone else on the depot knew theirs. He was responsible for a wide range of highly technical activities but always seemed to know the fine details of each one, whether it was procurement, depot property, depot facilities, vehicle maintenance, or whatever.

J.D. did his job in a professional manner and was not afraid to tell a commander, "You can't do that." He was not negative in his attitude and was equally good at pointing out how something could be done legally.

I was truly sorry when J.D. retired as it took some of the fun out of working when he left. I missed him shuffling paper in a notebook at staff meetings to annoy the commander and I missed him butting in with his, "I'd like to say this about that." I miss you pal.

◇◇◇◇◇◇◇◇◇◇◇◇◇◇◇◇◇◇◇◇◇◇◇◇◇◇◇◇◇◇◇◇◇◇◇◇◇◇

I cannot call some commanders by name without fear of being sued. I will use code names for those individuals. I served under fifteen different commanders while I was at the Depot and at least five of them were promoted to Brigadier General and I had some part in effecting those promotions, as part of Depot management. I supported each and every one of them and never did anything against any of them, although one was convinced I did by his guilty conscience. I will not speak of them in any particular order, just as they come to mind.

<()><()><()><()><()><()><()><()><()><()><()><()><()>

Colonel Horace Mane

Colonel Mane was short. Too short. His lack of physical stature clouded his judgement. He was a very intelligent man but his ego was much too large. I was acting Chief of Internal Review when he came.

Colonel Mane operated basically by creating fear in his subordinates, feeling they would be afraid not to do a good job. He never felt that anything could be done well unless it was done his way and he had no confidence in anyone. He had a plan to be promoted to General and that plan was to show how poor the depot was when he arrived and how good it was when he left.

He told me that a part of my job was to check up on all external audit findings and see if corrective action had been taken and to report to him when it had not been. I told him it was the job of his directors to keep him informed on the status of audit finding corrective actions and I would not be a spy for him. We had some bitter arguments on that one point but I refused to budge.

It seemed that every audit I made I ran into something Col Mane had done wrong. During a travel audit I found he was being paid mileage for driving his personal car when he had actually used a government sedan. The Finance and Accounting Officer refused to take him a collection voucher and collect for the overpayment so every time I found such a voucher I would have a clerk make a collection voucher and I would go get him to write a check to The Treasurer of the US for it. He finally demanded to know what percentage of his vouchers were being checked and I told him all of them were. He glowered at me and finally asked me to bring one collection voucher when I finished the audit.

I audited the Officer's Club and found where the Club Secretary had given him an estimate for a party. He had marked all the prices down fifty percent or more and told the Club Secretary to bill him for that amount. I wrote the Secretary a note asking if all members could reduce their prices. The Secretary took him the note and he called me in and asked me if I thought he was dishonest. I told him I thought he was very dishonest and if he had been six inches taller he would have come across the desk at me. I laughed at him and he became furious. I gave him a bill for the remainder of the charges for the party and he paid it.

Before he left the depot he had a book prepared that was close to a foot thick. Every supervisor on the depot was forced to write a section stating how poorly they were operating when the Colonel arrived and how good they had become under his guidance. I stated that Internal Review was not operating as well and refused to write a section on Internal Review. Ed Melton begged me to do it for him and I finally wrote a brief section stating that before the Colonel arrived we needed good professional auditors to audit the depot and we had received so much practice from auditing him personally that now we could do the jobs with monkeys from the zoo. I took it direct to the Colonel and he made Ed write one for his book. His book had a fifteen page cover letter stating basically that the depot had a good reputation when he arrived but they gained it mainly because they had always had unlimited funds and resources. He said those funds and resources were drying up at the time of his arrival and his planning and forward thinking saved the depot from disaster.

Just before the Colonel left he called all depot employees into a warehouse and made a speech telling them all he had done for the depot. Everyone on the depot was laughing at him. We later learned his book was very popular in headquarters. It was the only thing heavy enough to serve as door stops.

<()><()><()><()><()><()><()><()><()><()><()><()><()>
Colonel Tim Parson

Colonel Parson replaced Colonel Mane. This meant we had two in a row bucking for Brigadier General.

Colonel Parson called me to his office shortly after arriving. He pointed to a huge pile of my Internal Review audit reports and said he had read every audit report I had issued since taking over Internal Review and they all had one thing in common - they all stunk. He said he had been a procurement officer in his last assignment and he hated all auditors with a passion as they all criticized everyone except themselves and they loved to step in right before you were ready to move out on something and say they had heard you planned so and so and they objected.

He said he was not going to argue with me as regulations required he have an Internal Review function and there was no requirement for an Internal Review Office. He said that for every audit report I issued that he did not like I would lose one auditor space. He said there were seven spaces and the seventh report he did not like would cost me my job and he would then assign the function to the Management Engineering Office.

I told him that was fine with me and all the time he was there we just documented our findings in work papers and issued a report that just said we had made a certain audit and no findings were being reported. He finally called me in and said he did not understand why my reports did not have more substance. I told him he had called the shots and to just refer to his Internal Review by our new name, which was Silent Service. He became very angry and tried to rewrite my job description. His proposed job description mainly talked about how I had to be courteous to everyone I audited and had to issue my reports without upsetting anyone, etc. The personnel officer told him he had a performance requirement instead of a job description and refused to issue it. This argument ended when he was promoted to Brigadier General and reassigned.

<()><()><()><()><()><()><()><()><()><()><()><()><()><()>
Colonel Bob Baler

Colonel Baler was what the depot needed badly when he arrived. He had visited the depot as project officer of a test track that was being built for the depot and Charlie Heard had given him a tour of the depot. Bob asked Charlie who the next depot commander would be and Charlie, as was his way, said he did not know but he was sure he would be a SOB. Not too long after that, when Colonel Baler had left, we learned the next commander would be Bob Baler. When Bob got there he looked for Charlie and told him, "Here the SOB is." Charlie thought he was in for a lot of trouble but his fears were ungrounded.

Bob Baler got everyone together the next day and made a little speech. He said, basically, the following: "Relax fellows. The last two commanders damn near broke your back making general. I ain't bucking for nothing. I was told fifteen years ago that I would never be anything but a third rate ordnance officer. We ain't going to try to set no records and we ain't going to try to make any improvements. We are going to have some fun and try our best to hold what we got. If holding what we got gets in the way of having some fun, then damn it we will just have to slip a little. All you gotta do to get along with me is to just act like you are trying to do your job. If somebody screws up once in awhile I will take the blame."

Colonel Baler stuck to his promises and he was there five delightful years. He might roar at you now and then but he would not harm a fly and I loved the old man. Anyone on that depot would fight you if you said anything bad about Bob Baler. Bob Baler was a true gentleman.

When Ed Melton left the depot Woody Strange went in to see Bob and asked him about getting the job of depot controller. Colonel Baler jumped up laughing and left his office. He went down the hall, stopping everyone he met and telling them old Woody wanted to be controller and could not even keep a golf score. You had to know Woody to appreciate the humor. Woody was a charming and gentle type and would have been brutalized as controller.

Woody was in Bob's office on another occasion and Bob told him, "I love you, Woody." Woody asked him why and Bob pointed at his twenty year old dog snoozing in the corner and said, "You have eyes just like my dog." Woody said he could never figure Bob.

Colonel Baler frequently loaded his old beat-up station wagon with people from the depot and took off to his place in Florida. He had just one rule and that was, no mention of the depot from the time they left till the time they got back. On one trip, Roland McKendree, who ran most of Maintenance at the time, had a problem on his mind and cornered Bob and started talking depot talk. Bob interrupted him and told him if he said one more word he would walk back to Anniston. Those trips did a lot for the depot as Bob Baler was truly just another guy with no more privileges than anyone else except the one reserved privilege to stop any talk about the depot. On one trip he and Ken Baerwald, the Director for Supply, got in a shouting contest on the way back and Ken completely lost his cool. He challenged Bob to stop the car and get out and fight, and that was totally out of character for Ken. Bob just wheeled over on the shoulder of the road and stopped. Ken jumped out of the car and Bob just sat there. Ken yelled for him to get out of the car. Bob gave Ken his sweetest smile and said, "I'll hold your coat." Ken got back in the car and they changed the subject.

Bob Baler selected me for Director for Data Systems, knowing I had never even seen a computer. He said they had plenty of people that knew about computers and what they needed was someone who knew about people. He said he would guarantee I would know all there was to know about computers in nothing flat. About three weeks after I went on the job I called Bob and said, "Hey, Bob, I now know all there is to know about this damn thing." He cheered and said he had told me I would know all there was to know about computers in nothing flat. I said, "Hey, hold on man, I ain't talking about computers. I mean I know all there is to know about this damn push button phone. I ain't had time to look at the computer yet." He got a real charge out of that.

Colonel Baler was not allowed to accept a gift when he left the depot and no one would have embarrassed him by offering him one. The huge color television set and two lounge chairs that showed up in his van when he got to Minnesota must have been a real surprise to him. If we had our way we would have bought him a home anywhere he wanted it to match the home he had in all our hearts.

Bob Baler visited the depot a few years after he had retired and we had a secret party for him. I knew when I saw him that he had had a stroke since he retired. I spoke to him and knew that he knew who I was but he pretended not to even know me. Charlie Heard started trying to explain who I was and Bob grinned at him and said, "I know the SOB. He called my general a liar." I decided I would needle him back. He obviously had lost control of one side when he had his stroke because he had one hand tucked under his belt. I said, "What's wrong with your damn hand?" Bob just looked at me and said, "You are the only one that noticed so keep your big mouth shut." Bob died a few months later and there went the country's last big hope for a great president in my time.

<()><()><()><()><()><()><()><()><()><()><()><()><()>
Colonel Stan Bell   Depot Commander

One commander arrived at the depot and remained five long and miserable years. I shall refer to him as Colonel Stan Bell. His arrival was a sad day for the depot and for me in particular. He disliked me more than any other person on the depot and I was his favorite target while he was there.

We had an annual fund drive due shortly after his arrival and he appointed me as fund drive coordinator. It was the first year we could use pledges and payroll deductions and we had the largest amount pledged and contributed in the history of the depot. I always knew it was due to the new payroll deduction plan more than anything I did and I did not ever attempt to get a lot of credit for it. Colonel Bell had not contributed and I made him aware of it and finally he made a monthly pledge and then attempted to say he contributed the same amount as Charlie Heard. I reminded him that his contribution was monthly and Mr. Heards contribution was bi-weekly and for every dollar he gave, Mr Heard was giving a little more than twice as much.

This infuriated him and he ordered me to state in the fund drive report that the Commander and CEO gave the same amount. I refused to make that comment as it was not true. He then invited the community civic leaders to the depot and introduced Mr Holman, Director for Administration, as the fund drive coordinator. The civic leaders presented him with a letter of commendation. They had his middle initial wrong and he went into a rage about it. They apologized and offered to correct it and he told them he would have his secretary make the correction and send it to them for signatures as most of them might be able to spell their own names correctly. I had been working with them and they asked that I be called in to the meeting. I was called in and when I saw what Colonel Bell was doing I told them I would just let Mr Holman and Colonel Bell explain how they had handled the drive, and I left. Colonel Bell told me to stay and I told him I obviously had no business at a meeting where they were discussing their great success and I left.

Colonel Bell called me in after the group left and told me I was to never walk out of his office like that again. I told him he made me sick and leaving was preferable to vomiting on his carpet.

That was the beginning of five years of harrassment by Colonel Bell. He took every opportunity after that to do anything to me he thought he could get away with. I let him know he was my boss and I would support him anytime it was legal and ethical to do so but if he ever made an attempt to fire me, he would get more than he bargained for.

Not too much later, I made a speech at the depot that was reported in a national publication that went to everyone in congress and in the pentagon. I was critical of the computer selection process that resulted in selection of an inferior computer system for every depot in the country. A GS-17 in our Washington headquarters and a GS-15 at the Logistics System Support Agency were on the phone almost immediately demanding that the Colonel fire me. The Colonel directed that a panel be set up to review my actions and recommend appropriate action. The panel called me to testify and I refused on the basis they were not established in accordance with Army regulations. Regulations required that I be given a written document and that the panel be established by a command general order. The Colonel kept trying to comply with regulations without giving me my rights, so I just kept refusing to talk to the panel. Mr Heard asked me to meet with the panel and at least explain my position. I did that and the panel voted to make a finding that I had done nothing wrong and dissolve the panel. Charlie Heard then wrote a performance rating and rated me as outstanding and recommended a cash award. He went to Colonel Bell's office with it and did not come back until Colonel Bell agreed to sign it. I owe Charlie Heard a lot as you do not win battles like this without a friend and Charlie was a true friend.

I will not dwell on my personal problems with Colonel Bell at this point. I will list a few things Colonel Bell did and let you draw your own conclusions:

Colonel Bell stocked his government quarters with batteries, tires, sheets, pillow cases, pecans, oil and many other items and coerced government employees and members of the military into buying from him.

Colonel Bell went into the produce business and used the receiving area in a major warehouse for storing the produce to the extent that it hampered depot supply operations. Orders were taken by phone and delivered by the depot taxi system, making it impossible many times for depot employees to use the taxi system.

Colonel Bell would have as many as three depot directors waiting to see him for hours and his produce business partner, a depot employee, could walk in immediately and discuss the produce business while depot business was put on hold.

Colonel Bell turned a supply meeting into a search for a part for his car, to see who could get the lowest price.

Colonel Bell would have travel orders issued for a Fort near his home town and go home for week ends on travel orders and never visit the Fort.

Colonel Bell would negotiate for a cheap room when on travel by telling the motel management that he was thinking of sending a large group of depot employees there and might ask them to stay at that motel.

Colonel Bell loaned his own Father money and then foreclosed on the property serving as collateral. He stated his father was a spend thrift and deserved to lose the property.

Colonel Bell had money in many, many banks and had a system for withdrawing and transferring money that would result in double interest on the money for 10 days a month.

Colonel Bell would buy something on sale that he never intended to keep and then return it after the sale was over and get refunded at the regular price.

Colonel Bell would require someone to ride with him on temporary duty because he got two cents per mile more if he had a rider. Then he would not stop for his passenger to use a rest room as it took extra gas to stop and start. When he arrived at the destination he would not take them to the motel they wanted to stay at. He would usually stay with a friend and dump them at the closest motel.

Colonel Bell, when he did stay at a motel would go to the room of a traveling companion and make local calls to avoid having them charged to his room.

Colonel Bell once found a "hamburger war." His traveling companion said he was asked what size coke and had the waitress bring all three glasses and to put water in one of them. He poured the water back and forth to determine the best value. He then said he had a stomach condition and ordered coke without ice to get more coke. He then spooned ice into the coke from the water glass of his traveling companion. He had several cokes and hamburgers and asked the waitress how much he owed. She told him 91 cents and he handed her his glass and told her to bring 9 cents worth of coke to round it to a dollar. As they left, he looked at his bill and it was 98 cents and he returned to the table and held up his coke glass and attempted to get the attention of the waitress. She appeared to be looking elsewhere to avoid him. Colonel Bell sighed and went to the register and gave them the dollar and instructed them to give the change to the waitress. They went back to Colonel Bell's car and he sat there a long, long time without starting the engine. He finally sighed and said, "I have been told all my life that leaving a tip made you feel better. That was the first tip I ever gave in my life and I feel like hell. I am just out two cents."

The above are just samples. There are hundreds more and some are about the same and some are even worse.

Colonel Bell and I had many clashes. I refused to go along with his nonsense. He finally decided to make a move and was afraid to fire me so he attempted to put me in a situation in which he felt I would quit. He called me in, with witnesses, and said we had to get ready for Project SPEEDEX and he was assigning me as project officer full time and was assigning my deputy as the Director for Data Systems. He wanted me in headquarters building and was assigning the comptroller as my point of clearance and I was not to leave the building without clearing with the Comptroller. I was assigned an office, with a typewriter but no desk. I was given an assignment of typing a thousand page report on the status of Project SPEEDEX. I had to get a trash barrel and lay a board across it for a desk.

Periodically, I was told to prepare a briefing for the depot command staff and directors. I would prepare flip charts and start the briefings at the appointed time. Almost immediately the commander would start calling people out of the briefings until I was the only one in the conference room. I would just continue to give the briefing as though the room was filled.

Everyone was warned to stay away from me and Fred Adams was the only one who would visit my office. All the others were afraid to be seen with me. I had my little office with a filing cabinet, chair, typewriter, and a garbage can with a board across it for eight long months. I went to the Colonel's office three times every week and told him how much I loved the job and appreciated the opportunity to study SPEEDEX without worrying about routine assignments. I would tell him I had been about ready to resign and the project officer assignment gave me new hope and I had decided to remain with the depot because of it.

The Colonel would send for me now and then and tell me who was doing what to me. He told me of people I thought were my friends and how they were cooperating with him by telling me what I had told them. He told me one day, "People call me when you say something about me and they call so fast that sometimes I can still hear your voice echoing." He told me this once and then said I had called him an SOB 172 times, an old bum 146 times and beetle butt 97 times. I told him he had better get after those people as obviously he was only getting about ten percent reported. I told him that I usually used an adjective also, such as a crooked SOB or a Cheap bum.

I went to the data processing building without permission one day and decided I may as well tell the Colonel myself. I went to his office when I got back to headquarters and he held his fingers to his lips and motioned for me to sit down. I was able to listen to two people telling him I had been there. Both people were telling me privately how they were supporting me and were on my side. They were very vicious in their comments. I never trusted anyone after that, other than Fred Adams. Fred was an accountant and his support meant nothing, other than there was one person I could count on. Charlie Heard was not at the depot at this time. Charlie had got disgusted and retired.

Finally Colonel Bell retired and a new commander came in. I will refer to him as Colonel Mark Wheat. Colonel Wheat called me to his office and asked me to sit down. He had several sealed envelopes on his desk. He called his secretary in and handed them to her and told her he wanted those envelopes opened at the shredder and shredded without reading. She left with them and Colonel Wheat told me that Colonel Bell had given him files on several people and most of them were on me. He said he had them sealed without reading them and had ordered them shredded. He said he would form his own opinion of people at the depot, without being influenced by someone with an axe to grind. He said he intended to talk to a few people that day and would see me again the next day. The next day he called me in and said he had several discussions about me and needed to know one more thing. I asked him to just name it and he said he wanted to know what my attitude was going to be towards people who had not supported me or had worked against me if I went back to my job. I told him I felt all of that was brought about by the fear tactics of Colonel Bell and as far as I was concerned it would be over. I told him I would always have a hurt but I refused to hurt others just because I had been hurt. He shook hands and told me to get back to work.

Colonel Wheat was an alcoholic and had many problems in his personal life, but he had integrity and his integrity saved me. I was forever in his debt.

<()><()><()><()><()><()><()><()><()><()><()><()><()>
Colonel Mark Berg   Depot Commander

Colonel Berg came in so new as a Colonel that he drew his first pay as a Colonel while at Anniston. He had an exalted opinion of himself, not proven by ability. He never made a single command decision while at the depot. If you do not make decisions you cannot do anything wrong. He forced the directors to do their jobs and his job too. He spent most of his time at the drawing board explaining math to us, and designing charts guaranteed to show only the good things about the depot and bury the problems.

Colonel Berg liked to jog and at least as long as he was out jogging he was not in his office screwing something up. I always wished he would jog twenty-four hours a day.
Colonel Berg came up with the wild idea of Tanks for Anniston, putting all our eggs in one basket. We lost wheeled vehicle and Army Personnel Carrier and many other rebuild jobs, thanks to this Colonel.

His claim to fame was a method to give credit back to the depot when they performed better than they bid. He was known throughout the system as "Base Line." He managed to stay at the depot a full year after be was promoted to Brigadier General while he feathered his nest by setting up a Depot Systems Command at Letterkenny Army Depot.

Colonel Berg finally left, as all pests eventually do and good riddance to a millstone around the neck of the depot. He guaranteed certain promotions before he left.

<*><*><*><*><*><*><*><*><*><*><*><*><*>

Colonel George Master   Depot Commander

Colonel Master was a great big guy and full of love for all of us. He beat his breast and screamed but he loved us and we knew it. When morale was low in a certain unit it seemed that George was the first to know and you would see him sitting with his arm around someone telling them it was going to be all better.

George would pound the table at a staff meeting and scream, "Balls - I apologize for my language but nothing else will cover this situation." He did not do this all at once. He would tap the table and say something in a low voice and then slap the table and talk a little louder. He would pound a little harder each time and talk just a little louder. He would work himself up to the pounding and yelling.

George would chew you out and then apologize and say regulations required him to do it and then he would put his arm around you and take you for a cup of coffee.

During one staff meeting he talked to two or three directors about how sorry data processing was and I got so mad I went back and wrote a letter of resignation and sent it to him. George personally came to my office and put his arm around me and told me he loved me. I said something like, "Go to hell you big SOB." He looked at me and said something like, "You know I do some dumb things at times. Tell me what I did and I will straighten it out." I told him what he did and he said, "Hell, I was talking about them data processing guys, not you, Tom." I asked him if he had ever considered I was those data processing guys and he said hell no.

George called the people who he had made to the statement to, and me, to his office and told them he had made a dumb damn statement and wanted to apologize to Tom and make sure they all knew he knew Tom was the best in the business. He did it all over again at the next staff meeting. When George told you something, you could bank it.

I hated to see George Master go. He was our first Texas Aggie commander as far as I knew. I love you George, wherever you are.

<*><*><*><*><*><*><*><*><*><*><*><*><*><*><*>

This book would not be complete without mention of some people from off the depot who influenced my life.

<*><*><*><*><*><*><*><*><*><*><*><*><*><*><*>

Howard Allen   Director for MIS Atlanta Army Depot

Howard Allen was my best friend among the other depot Directors for Management Information Systems. Howard was a great guy. He and I hit it off from the day we met. Howard was a tall man in excellent physical condition and even took some equipment for work-outs on trips. I was really shocked when his deputy called me and said Howard died. Howard cut the grass in his yard and got something cool to drink and just died.

Howard was a displaced Yankee. He was always kidding the South. He told me when he first drove to Georgia he got lost and saw a farmer plowing a field. He said he stopped and asked the farmer how to get to Atlanta. The farmer scratched his head and started pointing and talking and then stopped and said that was not right. He scratched his head and started pointing three more times and always stopped. Finally he told Howard he just could not get there from where they were. Howard was ready to give up when the farmer started again and said, "Now, if you go back the way you came from three miles and turn right and go two miles, and then turn right on the highway, you can get there. And it is a good gravel road all the way into Atlanta."

We made a lot of trips to meetings and I usually called Howard and got his flight plan so I could go to Atlanta and take the same flights. We got to have some good long discussions that way. One time I went to Orlando, Florida for a training course and did not even know Howard was going. We had picked the same hotel and met in the lobby. Howard had driven and I flew but I rode back to the Atlanta Airport with Howard.

I missed you Howard, after you ratted out on me and died. Life was never quite as pleasant after you left and I have missed you.

<*><*><*><*><*><*><*><*><*><*><*><*><*>
Al Lis (The Fox) Director for MIS Tooele Army Depot

Al became my best friend after Howard died. His friendship was something to hold on to in a crazy mixed up world. Al and I usually coordinated our flight plans so we could travel at least part of the way together on our trips. At the least, we tried to arrive about the same time so we could share a rental car. Al was also a great guy and he and I were very close. We frequently found ourselves on the opposite side of the fence from LSSA and AMC and sometimes several of the other directors. We were well aware of the politics played by many of the directors.

Al had a terrible telephone at Tooele and he also talked very low. We found that if he squeezed the phone the volume increased. I used to yell at him to squeeze the phone.

Al and I are both retired now. Al has Parkinson's Disease and is slowly drawing over. He says he looks like a walking cane. He is not able to write but I write him and he calls now and then.

Hang in there, Al, I cannot lose you.

<*><*><*><*><*><*><*><*><*><*><*><*>

James T. Wheeler Director for MIS Red River Army Depot

Tom Wheeler perceived himself as the leader among the depot directors. Tom had a lot of ability and had been around a long time and may have been the real leader, it is hard to say. Tom was a good talker and he talked professionalism a lot. He always compared his operation with a commercial enterprise. His supervisors were managers, not division or branch chiefs and the depot directors were department heads. It all added up to the same thing; we were at the mercy of higher headquarters and the politicians.

I liked Tom Wheeler then and I like him now. He is also retired. I see him or get a phone call from him when he is traveling and in the area. I think what bothers me is that when I was a depot director and the depot directors were working so closely together to save ourselves from destruction, I had a feeling of closeness like family and I felt the other directors had the same feelings. When we started retiring, suddenly we were not family anymore, not even distant cousins. I was depending on those relationships to carry me through the future and now they are not there for me and do not really seem to care if I even survive or not. I wrote letters that were not even answered, and appeared to receive very cool responses eventually.

I don't know. I still think very highly of Tom Wheeler and always will. Hang in there, Tex.

<*><*><*><*><*><*><*><*><*><*><*><*>
Julius Cohen (Jookie) Civilian Executive Assistant Pueblo Army Depot

Jookie was a CEA but took on the job of DMIS as an added duty while he was looking for a new director. Jookie offered me the DMIS job at Pueblo and I turned it down because I did not think my financial status permitted me to make a move. It was a good decision as Pueblo eventually closed as a depot and I would have been in trouble.

There was never a doubt in my mind that Jookie was the most influential CEA in the depot system. He was a good thinker and long range planner and knew his job well. I once thought he ranked above Charlie Heard but toward the end I knew Charlie was the greatest.

The people at Pueblo eventually seemed to turn against Jookie and Jookie retired. It was not long after he retired that the command began to whittle away on Pueblo and it kept losing status and finally dropped out as a depot. I firmly believe it would have remained open if Jookie had stayed on.

I always liked you, Jookie, and I still do.

<*><*><*><*><*><*><*><*><*><*><*><*><*>

Jim Gossett   Adjutant, Red River Army Depot

Jim Gossett was Adjutant at Anniston Ordnance Depot at one time. I did not know him then but my wife knew him. Jim went to Red River Army Depot and was made Adjutant there, a Civil Service position.

Jim was always the one I saw first when I visited Red River Army Depot, and I visited there dozens of times. Jim and I would chat for quite awhile and he would fill me in on all the changes at Red River since I had been there. Jim was a great guy and I liked him. Jim had a serious drinking problem and he is dead now,

I miss you, Jim old Buddy. You were one of the best.

<*><*><*><*><*><*><*><*><*><*><*><*><*>

```
Al Woronowycz     Director for MIS      Tobyhanna Army Depot
Lee Browder       Director for MIS      Letterkenny Army Depot
Al Smart          Director for MIS      Atlanta Army Depot
Elmer Bossom      Deputy Dir for MIS    Letterkenny Army Depot
Floyd Landgraf    Chief Programmer      Red River Army Depot
George Kyer       Friend                Red River Army Depot
Sherman Rose      Friend                Red River Army Depot
Herman Morrison   Friend                Red River Army Depot
Jo                Wheeler's Sec         Red River Army Depot
Herb Freeman      Dir for Supply        Red River Army Depot
Mr. Mountz        Dir for Maint         Red River Army Depot
Buford Seales     Dir for MIS           Sacramento Army Depot
```

Black Bart	Dir for MIS	Sacramento Army Depot
Steve McDonald	Deputy Chief	Logistics Systems Support
Harold Krueger	DMIS	Supply & Maint Cmd
Bobby Sealock	Deputy DMIS	Atlanta Army Depot
Gordy Foster	Friend	LSSA
Jim Nielsen	Director for MIS	CC Army Depot
Frank Dubiel	Deputy Dir MIS	Tobyhanna Army Depot
Jim Hannon	Director for MIS	Tobyhanna Army Depot
Ralph Tappen	Chief, LSSA	LSSA
John Cianflone	Deputy DMIS	AMC Headquarters
Lou Wiggins	Deputy DMIS	Supply & Main Cmd
John Gilbert	DMIS	Army Materiel Cmd

<*><*><*><*><*><*><*><*><*><*><*><*><*>

Extract from "The Defense Manager" Vol. 3 No. 6   January 1970 ANNISTON CHAPTER MEETINGS FEATURE "KNOW YOUR DEPOT"

Anniston Army Depot Chapter's excellent newsletter for December contains a "KNOW YOUR DEPOT" write-up of their big mission: "To Get the Material to the Field for Use at the Earliest Practicable Date, in Class A Condition."

This interesting series illustrates the great value of an AFMA Chapter to its sponsor Command. It is a prime example of unofficial interdepartmental communications which do much to meld the operations of a complex military establishment into an efficient whole.

At the November meeting the incoming chapter president, Mr. Thomas R. Bowerman, Director for Data Systems of the Depot, was principal speaker and made an excellent presentation on SPEEDEX and its import upon the Depot's operations. A digest of his speech is reprinted herein.

Anniston Chapter is to be congratulated on this management-oriented "KNOW YOUR DEPOT" series. This chapter has no problem in finding principal speakers of great value—right at home.

"SPEEDEX"

By Mr. Thomas R. Bowerman

The presentation began with a short movie called "Computer Glossary." This movie explains the operations of a computer and defines technical terms in layman language. At the conclusion of the movie, the speaker commented as follows:

As most of you know, SPEED is the acronym for System wide Project for Electronic Equipment for Depots. It started as a project under the Chief of Ordnance and was carried over to the Supply and Maintenance Command. It began with six Ordnance Depots—Anniston, Erie, Pueblo, Red River, Tooele, and Letterkenny. Under the Supply and Maintenance Command, Erie was closed and Sacramento, Lexington, Tobyhanna, Atlanta and Sharpe were added. The basic concept was that all depots would get identical computers and a central agency would do the programming for all, rather than each depot doing its own programming!

The IBM 1410 and IBM 1401 were selected and installed at each of the depots. The Logistics System Support Center was established at Letterkenny Army Depot to do the programming. It was done by depot personnel on TDY for the supply portion. All other applications were assigned to individual depots. Anniston did payroll and ammunition. The systems have never been highly responsive to required changes.

This leads us up to SPEEDEX. SPEEDEX refers to SPEED EXtended to ARADMAC, New Cumberland and Granite City, making 13 depots; and extended to include Data Processing Management, Appropriation Accounting and Management Information as new systems.

The SPEEDEX specifications were sent out to many manufacturers. Bids were received only from IBM, General Electric and Control Data Corporation. The equipment proposed by CDC—the CDC 3300 system—was selected as the SPEEDEX equipment, subject to a benchmark test and successful operation of a prototype at Letterkenny. The benchmark has been passed and the prototype test is scheduled for April 1970.

Approval was granted to construct computer rooms at Letterkenny for the Systems Support Center test equipment and the depot prototype. These rooms have been built and the test equipment is now being installed. The depots have been given approval to develop computer site projects, but cannot begin construction until the prototype has proved successful.

Our first job at Anniston will be to provide space for a computer room. We have decided to build it in the room where the EAM and key punch equipment are located now. It will take a succession of moves to get that space available. This is the order of the moves:

First, PIO, Security Control, Manpower and the portion of Civilian Personnel in the Northern-most part of Building 53 will move upstairs in Building 64.

Second, Purchasing and Contracting will move to the North end of Building 53.

Third, Ammunition and Surveillance will move to Building 22.

Fourth, Systems and Programming, my office and BILI will move to the East end of Building 362.

Fifth, Key Punch will move to the Snack Bar area in Building 362.

Sixth, EAM will move to the area vacated by Systems and Programming and BILI. Hopefully, we can also provide a slight increase in space for Transportation Division.

Seventh, the IBM Customer Engineer will move in the new EAM area. This will vacate the area for the Computer Room. My present office will be the new magnetic tape vault. The area just North of my office will be used as a Control Data Corporation Customer Engineer room and a storage area for paper and cards.

The new Computer Room, Tape Vault, Customer Engineer Room and Storage area will have a raised floor, which will serve not only to provide space for electrical and signal cables, but will also serve as a plenum for the latest type under-floor air conditioning.

Our immediate access storage units will be housed in a separate glassed-off area to reduce dust and muffle noise. This will be within the main computer room. There will be either three or four of these boxes and each one will have its own separate hydraulic unit. The hydraulic units require a chilled water cooler. There are two large generators. They will be located in the warehouse.

The Computer Room will have four tape drives, several boxes for memory units, a card reader, card punch and two high speed printers. There will also be micromation equipment for recording data directly from tape to microfilm. (This is not Control Data Equipment.)

It is hoped that we will be able to release the IBM 1401 and 1410 six months after the CDC equipment is installed. We plan to relocate the EAM equipment to this room when it is released. This will place our card punch, EAM and computer equipment in the proper arrangement.

In addition to the equipment in the Computer Room, there will be many remote units installed around the depot. The exact number of remotes has not been determined, but the number originally specified is 62. These are visual display units, typewriters, keyboards, printers, card readers and card punches. The largest configuration will be in Shipment Planning, which will have a visual display unit, a high speed printer, card punch, card reader and typewriter with keyboard. The keyboard is necessary to inquire. Some stations will have typewriters that will print out but cannot inquire.

The remotes are connected to the computer through controllers and communication modems. One type controller will handle twelve remotes and another type will handle six. The remotes in Building 362 will be cable connected. All others will be connected through telephone lines. As an example, telephone lines will be installed from the computer to the North end of

Building 53. This will require what we call a communications modem at each end of the line. In Building 53, the controller will be connected to the modem. They can be 25 feet apart. We can then connect up to twelve remotes to this controller, provided they are within 1,000 feet. This should take care of Purchasing and Contracting, Civilian Personnel, IAF, Cost Accounting and Stock Fund. A separate modem and controller at the other end of the building will serve the Commanding Officer, Executive Assistant, Comptroller, Manpower Office, Management Engineering Division and Director for Administration.

Each Director will have a visual display unit, which resembles a TV set. He will be able to select a large number of reports and have any one displayed. The unit will also print a hard copy of the report if desired. Each depot will program its own reports.

So far, the system sounds good. There are a few problems. One major problem so far is that the Control Data Corporation does not have software as yet that will operate this equipment with all these remotes. They are working on it. Another big problem is that the training they have been providing so far has been poor. Programmers have felt ill- prepared after their training, to say the least.

I contend that our beginning programs will reflect the training we receive. Later, the better programmers will learn for themselves, but in the beginning all programmers will be handicapped by inadequate training. Some will always be handicapped, but most will eventually overcome it.

This may be rambling, but I think at this point I should mention·a few problems we are encountering in the plans to construct a Computer Room for Control Data Corporation equipment. Control Data insists on reviewing our plans in minute detail. They have given us quite a few requirements.

The air conditioning must be so effective that the room temperature will not vary more than plus or minus two degrees. Seventy-two degrees is optimum and the equipment will turn itself off if it exceeds 74 degrees. Humidity must remain within plus or minus five percent. Some components take in cool air at floor level and discharge it at ceiling level. Other components take in cool air at ceiling level and discharge it at floor level. There is a danger that the hot air from one component will knock out another component. We hope this is overcome by installation time.

This air conditioning must operate seven days a week twenty-four hours a day. If we turn it off, we are responsible if the equipment fails when we restart.

Cards to be processed must be in the same air conditioned and humidity controlled environment for at least 24 hours prior to processing.

Control Data states that even our remote sites must be air conditioned and humidity controlled—seven days a week and 24 hours a day. These sites will cost a large amount to construct. We are considering the use of modular labs—a sort of pre-fab deal. If we fail to build them to Control Data Corporation specifications, they will not be responsible for malfunctions.

It seems to me that the installation and operation of third generation computer equipment is going to be a very expensive operation. Just getting the 13 depots up to the installation point is going to require a one-time expenditure of a large amount of money. The difference in our present costs and the rental cost of the new equipment will cost another considerable sum each year. In view of the present fund shortages and the necessity to fire thousands of permanent civil service employees, I suggested a five-year deferment of SPEEDEX. My suggestion was sent to Washington, but hasn't been returned as approved. This was in the form of an employee suggestion rather than an official action.

Since we installed the SPEED equipment and SPEED systems, we have been able to make program changes to take care of requirements our depot managers felt were essential. This was possible because of three things:

    1. We have a local programming staff that can do the job.

2. The Logistics System Support Center allowed us to do so provided we coordinated with them.

3. We have the basic source deck programs.

Under SPEEDEX we have been told that we will not be permitted to make changes. To assure that we don't make them, we are being crippled three ways:

1. Our programming staff is being reduced 10% in Calendar Year 1969 and an additional 20% in Calendar Year 1970.

2. The Logistics System Support Center will not permit changes under SPEEDEX and they have full backing of AMC.

3. We will have only object programs under SPEEDEX, which means we can't make changes even if we had the programmers and permission.

The effect on this depot will be that every manager will operate with SPEEDEX output whether he likes it or not. Changes must be requested from LSSC and will be made only if LSSC decides it is best for all depots.

This is one reason I stress full support of SPEEDEX at Letterkenny Army Depot on TDY by our functional people. One of these days you will awaken to what has happened to you, but it will be too late.

To sum up, we have many problems and they will continue to grow in size and complexity as installation and implementation time gets closer. We are going from a central system to a remote system, from IBM to Control Data, from second generation to third generation and from AUTOCODER to COBOL programs. We have a lot of people to shuffle and a big construction job. We are losing people in the depot RIF and a special RIF of programmers. We have to operate two systems during a conversion period, with fewer people—not more. Don't throw away your pencils yet— you may need them.

************ END ************

Comment: The Defense Manager is distributed throughout all levels of government, including every Congressman and

Comment: The Defense Manager is distributed throughout all levels of government, including every Congressman and Senator. Within an hour of distribution in Army Materiel Command, John Gilbert, AMC Director for Data Systems (GS-17) was on the phone with the Anniston Army Depot Commander demanding that I be fired. At the same exact time, Mr Ralph Tappen, Chief of the Logistics System Support Center (GS-15) was on the phone with Mr Charles Heard, Anniston Army Depot Civilian Executive Assistant, demanding that I be fired.

A board of inquiry was established to investigate me. The board informally suggested I just resign. I refused. I was variously accused of leaking classified information and many other improprieties. I found every statement in my speech in unclassified documents.

What finally resulted in failure to fire me was that no one had the nerve to put the charges against me in writing and providing me a copy and I proved this to be a requirement. The inquiry finally evaporated.

Throughout the entire process, Charles Heard had the guts to stick with me one hundred percent and even insisted that the commander approve an outstanding performance appraisal and sustained superior performance award for me.

Charles Heard is the only Civilian Executive Assistant Anniston Army Depot has ever had. Another now bears the title but bears no resemblance to a Civilian Executive Assistant.

Test of a Manager

The test of a Manager is the fight that he makes
   The grit that he daily shows.
The way he stands on his feet and takes
   Fate's numerous bumps and blows.
A coward can smile when the risk is small,
   When theres nothing his progress to quench.
But it takes a man to stand straight and tall,
   And never give an inch.

It isn't the victory after all,
   But the fight that a brother makes.
The manager who, driven against a wall,
     Still stands erect and takes
The blows of fate with never a flinch,
   Is the man who'll win in the by and by,
For he'll stand his ground what ere the fight
   And never give an inch.

It's the bumps you get and the jolts you get
   And the shocks that your courage stands.
The hours of sorrow and vain regret,
   The prize that escapes your hands
That test your mettle and prove your worth.
   For it isn't the hours of toil at the bench,
But the blows you take on the good old earth,
     That show your stuff, so—
NEVER GIVE AN INCH!!

We had one EAM operator with a lot of potential, but who did not feel he was being recognized rapidly enough who transferred to Fort McClellan. He knew he made a mistake and wanted to come back and was permitted to do so. His name is of no consequence. I will just call him Charlie..

I set up six trainee programmer positions beginning at GS-5 and leading automatically to GS-9, subject to satisfactory performance. Charlie was selected for one of those positions and received class room and on the job training. Charlie convinced Civilian Personnel that he had some other qualifying experience. One GS-11 position came open and was to be filled before the trainees had qualifying time. Charlie convinced me and the people in Personnel that we should remove him from the trainee program and consider him for the GS-11 job. I did it and he was selected for the GS-11 position. When the trainee's finished and qualified for GS-11 there were no openings at that time and Charlie was the only trainee to be promoted. I looked back at it and knew he had been given unfair advantage.

Charlie volunteered as a system programmer and there was no doubt his job was the hardest programmer job we had. Charlie then came in and demanded to be promoted to GS-12 or he would ask for reassignment to a regular GS-11 programmer job and I could see if I had anyone else who could do the job. I told him convincing Personnel his job had more responsibility would be difficult as they separated responsibility from hard jobs and were not about to promote because a job was harder to do. He could not see that and began to write me long letters asking what I had against him and what he had done to cause me to dislike him, etc. I really had no say in the matter and had requested Personnel to survey his job several times and they always said it was GS-11.

Charlie then concentrated on the Chief of Position and Pay Management in Civilian Personnel and eventually she asked me if I could do something so Charlie could be promoted. I reorganized again and Charlie was promoted to GS-12. Charlie immediately started in for a GS-13 and eventually I selected him as a GS-13 Division Chief by making some ridiculous organizational changes to pyramid a division.

Charlie was ready for a GS-14 before he even got his GS-13. I knew Charlie was already stabbing me in the back in an attempt to make my bosses unhappy with me. Things were not going fast enough and the Director for Management Information Systems job came open at New Cumberland Army Depot and Charlie applied for it. I was called by John Gilbert in AMC and John told me the commander at New Cumberland wanted him to make the selection and he seemed to remember Charlie had a drinking problem. Well, Charlie did have a drinking problem to the extent of having the shakes all the time but I lied to John and Charlie got the job and left the depot.

I thought everything was resolved and did not think about Charlie again until I heard he had applied for Charlie Heard's old job - Civilian Executive Assistant, GS-15. There was no way Charlie could get this job as General Line, former depot commander at Anniston, had required that the job be given to Nathan Hill, who had helped him set up the Depot Systems Command.

Colonel Walker, Depot Commander, had Nathan Hill ask if I would accept a job on his staff. I told Nathan I was already on his staff but he said it was a special project. He did not want to talk grade so I talked to Personnel and they said the job proposed for me would probably be a GS-11, a reduction from my GS-14. I refused the job and Nathan started on a reorganization that would remove most of my grade supporting functions and place them in a new office under the Comptroller. No one would tell me what was happening.

I went to the Equal Opportunity Office and signed a form stating I perceived myself to be a Black Male. I then filed a discrimination complaint based on age and race. A team was sent in from Washington to investigate my complaint and I won. Colonel Walker was required to apologize and to discontinue his reorganization plans.

Suddenly Charlie showed up at the depot and I thought he was on a visit but learned the depot had hired him, using the application he had submitted for CEA (GS-15) and just scratching through lines and writing in different data. He was under the impression I would be demoted by the time he got there and would be a GS-14. I did not cooperate and they assigned him as GS-13 and to his old GS-13 job, which was vacant at the time. They were just leaving him in headquarters and I insisted that if he was on one of my division chief jobs he would jolly well do the job. They finally forced him to come take the job but he was very uncooperative and had his old pals in his office all the time whispering to them.

A new effort began. The Commander felt a need for a Data Processing Officer, reporting direct to him. They started writing a new job description and all the words in it were taken from my job description. I talked to Personnel and they said if they approved the new job it would be a GS-14 and my job would be reduced to GS-12, which meant all my programmers would be reduced to GS-9 and my division chiefs would be reduced to GS-11.

I filed another complaint and it was taken up with the new Commanding General of Depot Systems Command. He returned the depot commander's request for organizational changes disapproved. The disapproval had no more than arrived when a new approach was begun.

The problem for me was that Nathan and Charlie were friends and drinking buddies and Nathan wanted my job for Charlie and Charlie would never let him stop pushing until he got that job. I called Charlie in and had a real heart to heart talk with him, pointing out that I had four sons and had never done as much for any of them as I had for Charlie and that I knew Charlie was just out to get my job regardless of what he had to do. Charlie openly admitted it and claimed he felt bad about it but that was the way it was.

I went home that night and thought about all of it and I did something I had never done in my life before. I cried like a baby. I had never cried in my life, not even when my Brother and Father died. I went to the doctor the next day and had a long talk with him. He signed a statement that I was too ill to perform my duties and recommended I be put on sick leave until my sick leave ran out and then be retired.

I went to the depot and took the doctor's statement to the Depot doctor and processed out that day. It was 1983 and I was sixty-one years old and I was on sick leave pending regular retirement. I had enough sick leave to last well into 1984.

Several months later Colonel Walker left the depot and Colonel Pigas came in as the new commander. I decided I would see if the new kid on the block could be more reasonable. I went back to my doctor and told him I felt I had recovered and he agreed and signed a statement saying I was ready to return to work. I went back to the depot and took my statement to the depot doctor. He needed time to consider if I was really able to come back to work (meaning he had to talk to Colonel Pigas). I went back a couple days later and there was no decision so I went and talked to Colonel Pigas. He was of the opinion I was not ready to come back to work. I called my doctor and it developed he was a general in the reserve and not without considerable influence. He convinced Colonel Pigas that he should accept his diagnosis.

Colonel Pigas told me that he and I had no problems and he was happy to get someone with my experience in the job and we should all put the past behind us and move forward. I took him at his word, little realizing he was not speaking the truth and the truth was not in him. The truth was that his Director for Management Information Systems at his former assignment was a close friend of Charlie and had already given Colonel Pigas the story about me that Charlie wanted him to have even before he came to Anniston.

Colonel Pigas was very sly in dealing with me, always saying he was satisfied with my work but always saying otherwise behind my back. He started yet another reorganization project. Dave Stanley, the Director for Maintenance, came to me one day and said the most diabolic plan ever conceived against a human was in process against me. He said they knew I would appeal anything they did to me so every time the command group contacted headquarters they led the conversation around to data processing and then made a casual comment like, "Our DMIS is senile, you know." He said when they made their move no one in headquarters would take anything I said seriously as the idea I was senile would be firmly embedded.

The final straw came when a friend called me from Fort Monroe, Virginia. He said Colonel Pigas was there for a briefing and after he briefed him he mentioned that he knew Tom Bowerman at Anniston Army Depot. He said Colonel Pigas looked at him and said, "Don't mention that guy's name to me. He has never done a damn thing for Anniston Army Depot." It was unbelievable almost as Colonel Pigas and I had a discussion the day before he went to Fort Monroe and he had told me he was very pleased with the way I was running my operation.

I went to Colonel Pigas' office and confronted him with what my friend had told me. He said the man was a liar and he had said no such thing and if I wanted him to, he would call the man and tell him he was a liar. I told him I wanted him to and he said he did not have his phone number and I gave him the number. He tried to bluff my friend and my friend would not back down so he told my friend to keep his mouth shut and stay out of our depot business. He then admitted he may have said it but was just kidding. I told him we now knew who the liar was.

I went back to my doctor and told him it did not work out and he said he thought I ought to get away from the dummies at the depot and gave me another statement. The next day I processed out again. When I was finished I went to headquarters and Colonel Pigas was in the hall talking to several people. I snapped my fingers and told him I wanted to see him in his office immediately. He was ticked off as he had no idea I no longer worked for him. We went to his office and I told him that I was the type person who could not work for someone they did not respect and I had searched my soul trying to find one tiny thing in him I could respect and could find nothing, therefore I quit. I turned and left him sputtering.

I then went to Nathan Hill's office and told Nathan that all I had to say to him was that the depot had never had but one Civilian Executive Assistant and it was not him and he would never be one, no matter how long he might serve on the position.

I acted with great restraint as my original plan had been to stand on top of Colonel Pigas' desk and take a full circle urination, then go to Nathan's office and do the same. I guess the only thing that made me change my mind was the realization that some poor janitor would have to clean up the mess.

Chapter Twenty

Retirement

Retirement was, is and always will be an unenjoyable situation. I have always worked and worked hard. My idea of work hours has always been from "Can to Can't." When I first retired I had a lot of things I thought I wanted to do, such as paint the house, clean the windows, work on the yard, clean the grill, go fishing, plant hedges, clean out the ditch, and on and on. Once you have done all that, what do you do for an encore? Trying to teach my dog, Margo, how to use a computer was a complete flop. She would not even use paper.

I bored everyone I knew with a flurry of letter writing but after awhile they quit replying and one way correspondence is not much fun. I found myself sitting in a chair in the yard and looking at the clouds and talking to Margo about life. She understood but never said anything.

I went to work at Radio Shack in Oxford, trying to sell computers. Rudy Irwin had been there forever and no one wanted to talk to me about a computer. They preferred to wait until Rudy was available. I quit that job and later went to work at the Radio Shack in North Anniston. I had good luck there and was top salesman in the district for a long time. I enjoyed working for Frank Villalpando, no matter how sloppy and disorganized he was. Then Rudy left Radio Shack and I was sure I would be selected to replace him but they selected another employee with about one percent of my experience and I quit again.

Things were so boring that I went back to Radio Shack, working for Frank again. Employees that knew nothing about computers were selling computers and I was having to support the ones they sold and I finally quit again. A little later Rudy opened a store front computer store and I went to work for him.

I worked for him well over a year but he had an awful temper and it got to the point I could not work with him and quit.

I was running a computer Bulletin Board Service all this time and spending more and more time on it. It was difficult as I was dependent on contributions and expenses were several times higher than contributions. Then BBS systems started springing up all over Anniston, Oxford and Jacksonville and contributions fell off more, with expenses going up. I was getting a few small repair jobs here and there and had one consulting client, but expenses were so much greater than the miscellaneous income that I had to close the BBS totally. That left nothing much to do.

I gave my BBS equipment to Mike Stultz, my adopted grandson. Mike had Cerebral Palsy and a spirit larger than all outdoors. I helped Mike keep the system going until he learned his way around.

I opened another BBS and ran it awhole longer but it was too expensive and I had to quit again.

And that brings us to the present. The present is a life of some bitterness and much boredom. Retirement is not what it is cracked up to be. I spent most of my time taking care of Frances. Not that I resented it. I am sure Frances knew I never minded taking care of her and if she had lived I would have taken care of her forever. We stopped being lovers in 1984 and about 1991 or 1992 we began to be very close friends.

Chapter Twenty-One

Bulletin Board Systems

I started a BBS in 1978, using a small computer and a 300 Baud Modem. The Modem was really an acoustic coupler and when someone called I had to manually insert the phone in the acoustic coupler and hope I could get it seated before the carrier signal was lost. Most of the people calling were using terminals instead of computers and there was no way they could download files. The BBS catered to message traffic at local level.

I got a CP/M computer with a ten megabyte hard drive, something I was sure would never fill up. I got a 1200 baud external Hayes Smartmodem. We were beginning to get calls from all over the world and most callers wanted to download files. I managed to get a 32 megabyte hard drive to work and we were really big-time.

I finally went to an external 2400 baud modem to work on the old Kaypro and suddenly we were famous. We had boards calling from all over the world. The expenses went on and on and very few people were able or willing to contribute. The cost of running a BBS were getting too high to continue. I knew I had to do something.

I had things all to myself in the early days as a BBS was very difficult to set up and learn. I had switched to a Tandy 1000 SX to run the BBS and everything looked okay.

BBS software became easy to obtain and run. It did most of the old things we once had to do manually. With the advent of smart BBS software it suddenly became feasible to set up and run a BBS and it seemed that everyone wanted in on the act and BBS' started springing up everywhere. Many of the BBS' were free and the new Sysops would call my BBS and leave mail asking users to switch to their board. Some of the new BBS' used larger and more powerful computers and in some cases convinced users that their BBS software was more user friendly.

Eventually there were so many BBS' that it was not possible to get continued support and I had to close my BBS. The BBS had been my life for fifteen years and it was a real shock to discontinue.

Scott Gray, a real friend, went into the computer business and sold me a 386DX 40 MHZ with 340 megabytes hard disk space. I installed three CD ROM drives and obtained 40 CD ROM shareware disks. I also changed to ROBOBoard/FX, a graphic BBS system and users could view files in VGA mode. It was a very sophisticated system, really superior to anything the dozen or so BBS' in the area had to offer. I was still unable to get callers to share expenses through cash donations and had to quit after seventeen years.

It has always seemed odd to me that users would spend from $1500 to $2000 for a computer but were unwilling to make even a $5 or $10 donation to a BBS. New and free boards keep cropping up but most last a short while and die.

The ultimate insult was an article in the Anniston Star about BBS' that covered three relatively new boards and did not even mention mine when mine was the first BBS in Alabama and the 9th or 10th in the USA.

Chapter Twenty-Two

The Declining Years, Waiting for the Fat Lady

I do not have a job and am on a very limited income. I was forced to discontinue my Bulletin Board System as I could no longer afford it and did not have a computer capable of running a decent BBS. Scott Gray, a friend in the military at Fort McClellan, went in the computer business and sold me a 386 DX 40 MHZ computer on monthly payments, at cost, and with no interest. I have spent a lot of my time running bulletin boards but have reached the point where I can no longer afford to run one. (But I am running it anyway.)

So where do I go from here? I am too old to get a job. People seventy four years old are not employable. No one wants to be around them. Actually, I am going nowhere. Frances broke her hip in February of 1993, and I spent most of my time at home taking care of her. She could do almost nothing for herself. She sat in a chair in the kitchen all day watching television and I did the cleaning, cooking, laundry and all the other assorted chores. I did not mind the work. I was bothered by the confinement as I had to be there for her all the time. I did not resent it. I was supposed to be there for her. Then January 9, 1995 my beloved Frances fell and broke her arm and her other hip and eleven days later, January 20, 1995, she passed away.

I met a really nice lady in Laurel, Mississippi by mail. Her husband was an Armed Guard in WWII and I sent him a shipmate listing. She returned it and told me he had passed away. I wrote her and she wrote me again and we have continued our correspondence. She is a grand lady and I just wish I was younger.

I also met a super lady in New Hampshire. A friend of a

friend asked me to write to her and I did. We have been corresponding a few weeks and enjoy writing to one another very much. She is a blonde, which is what Frances always threatened to find for me.

Recently, in May of 1996, my friend, Mike Stultz passed away. I loved Mike very much. Mike was born with Cerebral Palsy and had very little use of his hands, but his mind and his heart more than made up for it. He was a little man with a huge heart and a love for everyone.

The simple answer to the question of who cares is that no one cares anymore. What is one old man to anyone? The right answer is no one. I am not in a feeling sorry for myself mood. I have nothing to feel sorry about. The truth is that the fat lady is about ready to sing on me. I will soon be gone and long be forgotten. I regret only that there will not be time to do some of the things I have always wanted to do.

May I remind you that these few words below are how I would like to be remembered:

Test of a Manager

The test of a Manager is the fight that he makes
   The grit that he daily shows.
The way he stands on his feet and takes
   Fate's numerous bumps and blows.
A coward can smile when the risk is small,
   When there's nothing his progress to quench.
But it takes a man to stand straight and tall,
   And never give an inch.
It isn't the victory after all,
   But the fight that a brother makes.
The manager who, driven against a wall,
      Still stands erect and takes
The blows of fate with never a flinch,
   Is the man who'll win in the by and by,
For he'll stand his ground what ere the fight
   And never give an inch.
It's the bumps you get and the jolts you get
   And the shocks that your courage stands.
The hours of sorrow and vain regret,
   The prize that escapes your hands
That test your mettle and prove your worth.
   For it isn't the hours of toil at the bench,
But the blows you take on the good old earth,
   That show your stuff, so—
NEVER GIVE AN INCH!!

Mike Stultz and Deb Clay

Reference Data

This is an effort to leave some memories behind. My life has been far from perfect. I ve had my share of incidents I was not proud of. I could say that if I had it all to do over ain I would do it in a different way, but I doubt I would.

I am proud of all my children. They have made me proud and given me nothing to be hamed of. I regret I did not have the foresight to start a college fund for each of them. In y personal opinion, a college degree does not provide happiness or security and in many ses may well work the opposite. It is no shame to not have a college education. My ucation may have provided a few breaks for me but I never did consider it all that valu- le.

I hope I will be remembered awhile. I always tried to help others and never intention- y hurt anyone. To those I leave behind, I say something I always had a problem saying; "I ve you."

Thomas Roy Bowerman, Sr.

Dates

A. Mother's Birthday	7 Feb	1898
B. Father's Birthday	2 Nov	1882
C. Herman's Birthday	26 Nov	1916
D. Juanita's Birthday	22 Oct	1919
E. My Birthday	6 Apr	1922
F. Charles Henry	26 Oct	1947
G. Thomas Roy, Jr	9 Jan	1957
H. Terry Adrian	13 Feb	1958
I. Barry Lynn	26 Sep	1959
J. Tom & Frances Anniv	14 Apr	1956
K. Frances' Birthday	2 Sep	1918
L. Frances Died	20 Jan	1995

Important People

Important People in my life

A. Mrs Eunice Bales Bowerman - My Mother - I owe it all to her
B. William Henry Bowerman - My Father - I love him
C. Frances Erline Johnson Bowerman - My wife, Mother of my Children
D. Charles Henry Bowerman - My son by my first wife
D1. Charles Ray Bowerman - Son of Charles Henry
D2. Sandi Bowerman - Daughter of Charles Henry
D3. Terri Bowerman - Daughter of Charles Henry
D4. Charles Nicholas - Son of Charles Ray - My Great Grandson
D5. April Nicole Bowerman - Daughter of Sandi - My Great Granddaughter
E. Thomas Roy Bowerman, Jr - Mine & Frances' first son
F. Terry Adrian Bowerman - Mine & Frances' second son
G. Barry Lynn Bowerman - Mine and Frances' third and last son
H. Susan Butler Bowerman - Tom Jr's wife
I. Shelby Burgess Bowerman - Chris' Mother
J. Christopher Bowerman - Barry & Shelby's son - my grandson
K. Chase Bowerman - Barry & Shannon's son - my grandson
K1. Cylie Bowerman - Barry & Shannon's daughter - my grand daughter
L. Thomas Roy Bowerman, III - Tom & Susan's son - my grandson
M. Tiffany Bowerman - Tom & Susan's daughter (sigh) my grand daughter
N. Suzy Bowerman - Terry's first wife
O. Joy Bowerman - Terry's second wife
P. Eleanor Rhodes - My Secretary for twenty-five years
Q. Chip Bowerman - Dog who flew Henry Kissinger to China - & much more
R. Mike Stultz - My adopted Grandson
S. P.L. Montgomery - Always busy but never too busy to help
T. Deborah Clay - Always a laugh
U. Joe Magee - True Support
V. Tom Walker - True Support
W. Louise Yorath Hillman - I fell in love with her in Cardiff, South Wales
X. Bettye Simmons - Puppy Love in Monroe, Louisiana
Y. Mabel Day - A passing fancy in Cincinnati, Ohio
Z. Bennie Andrus - A real Buddy in Galveston, Texas
1. Sally Grenner - War-time drinking pal in Brooklyn, New York
2. Tim and Nickie Engle - BBS Pals
3. George and Cindy Falcone - BBS Pals

Important Numbers

A. Social Security Number - myself   - 420-36-0530
B. Social Security Number - Frances   - 419-05-2524
C. Telephone Number   - (205)237-8754
D. Navy Service Number   - USNR 604 79 36
E. Army Serial Number   - RA 14 209 231
F. Air Force Serial Number   - AF 14 209 231

Genealogy One

```
* Jacob Otto Bales m. Catherine Minka
.              m. Sadoni Schmidt
. * Henry J Bales m. Nancy Caroline Manuel
. .            m. Lula Martha Dorn (22-Jan-1870) -
. . * Ross Bales
. . * Eunice Bales (7-Feb-1898) - (13-Jul-1989)
          m. William Henry Bowerman (2-Nov-1882) -
. . . * Herman Henry Bowerman (26-Nov-1916) - (1955)
          m. Jimmie Mae Cook
. . . . * Jo Evelyn Bowerman
. . . * Juanita Bowerman (22-Oct-1919) - (25-Sep-1987)
          m. Harry Simon Berman, Jr (11-May-1916) - (26-Jul-1988)
. . . . * Carol Ann Berman (16-Jun-1948) -
            m. (14-Jul-1968) John Keegan
. . . . . m. (23-Nov-1979) Miles Shipman Brooks
. . . . * Susan Lee Berman (05-Apr-1953) -
. . . * Thomas Roy Bowerman (6-Apr-1922) -
     m. (14-Apr-1956) Frances Erline Johnson (02-Sep-1918) - (20-Jan-1995)
. . . . * Thomas Roy Bowerman, Jr (09-Jan-1957) -
            m. Susan Butler
. . . . . * Thomas Roy Bowerman III (29-Dec-1980) -
. . . . . * Tiffany Bowerman
. . . . * Terry Adrian Bowerman (13-Feb-1958) -
. . . . * Barry Lynn Bowerman (26-Sep-1959) -
            m. Shelby Burgess (06-Apr-1958) -
. . . . . * Christopher Bowerman
            m. (1993) Shannon
. . . . . * Dustin Chase Bowerman
. . . . . * Cylie Bowerman
. . * Loys Bales (07-Nov-1903) - (22-Feb-1978)
          m. (07-Sep-1923) Robbie Lura Bales (25-Mar-1909) -
. . . * Robert William Bales (11-Jan-1925) - (09-Dec-1929)
. . . * Charles Edward Bales (30-Oct-1935) -
     m. (28-Feb-1964) Helen Marie Harrison
. . . . * Betty M Harrison (16-Feb-1950) -
. . . . * Randall Harrison (28-Oct-1957) -
. . . . * Kelly L Harrison (21-Nov-1962) - (07-Mar-1987)
. . . * James Henry Bales (22-Jan-1937) - (21-Jan-1991)
          m. (11-Jun-1963) Angel Courtney
. . . . * Andrea M Bales (04-Aug-1968) -
. . . . * J Anthony Bales (20-Feb-1979) -
. . . * Martha Carolyn Bales (11-Nov-1945) -
          m. (09-Aug-1963) Roger Beavers (09-Nov-1945) -
. . * William Otto Bales
. . * Joseph James Bales m. Frances Ellen Burdette
. . . * Joseph James Bales, Jr. (08-08-1932) -
. . . * Betty Bales
. . . * Jo Evelyn Bales
```

Genealogy Two

```
* Hardy Johnson (About 1777) -          m. Bettie Libran (About 1780) -
. * Henry Johnson (Unknown) -
. * Oliver Johnson
```

```
.   * Howell Johnson
.   * Stephen Johnson (19-Feb-1814) - (15-Mar-1883)
        m. (25-Jul-1839) Martha Carol Brown (15-Feb-1815) -
.   .  * A. Marshall Johnson (15-Sep-1840) -        m. Penelope Cruise
.   .  * John W Johnson (09-Dec-1841) -        m. Mollie Berry
.   .  * William M Johnson (04-Dec-1843) - (At early age)
.   .  * Leecie Ann Johnson (07-Dec-1845) -
            m. (30-Sep-1860) Samuel Sellers
.   .   .  * Samuel Sellers
.   .   .  * Ella Sellers
.   .   .  * Viola Pearl Sellers
.   .   .  * Edwin Sellers m. Edwina Sellers
.   .   .   .  * Palmer Bell
.   .   .  * Calvin Sellers
.   .   .  * William Sellers m. Unknown
.   .   .   .  * William Sellers Jr
.   .   .   .  * Edwin Sellers
.   .  * Margaret C Johnson (08-Mar-1848) -
.   .  * Mary Frances Johnson (29-Jun-1850) -        m. John Lee
.   .   .  * Mary Lee
.   .   .  * Mattie Lee
.   .   .  * Stephen Lee
.   .   .  * Calvin Lee
.   .   .  * Minnie Lee
.   .  * Almon E Johnson (18-Dec-1852) -        m. Eliza Cochran
.   .  * Stephen Libran Johnson (20-Dec-1857) - (30-Dec-1927)
                    m. Mary Bradley (       ) - (1882)
.   .   .           m. Frances Carter
.   .   .           m. Lucy McKinney
.   .  * Willie Johnson
.   .  * Martha Leggett Johnson (20-Dec-1857) - (About 1929)
                    m. Robert Schooler (       ) - (1884)
.   .   .           m. (1897) Jackson Henderson
.   .   .  * Ella Schooler
.   .   .  * Pearl Schooler
.   .   .  * Hugh Henderson
.   .   .  * David Henderson
.   * Hardy Johnson, Jr
.   * Martin Johnson

.   * Jane Johnson
.   * Emilene Johnson
.   .  * David A Johnson (14-Jun-1855) - (21-Jun-1921)
        m. (13-Dec-1879) Bedford Forrest Cochran (About 1862) -
.   .   .  * Stephen Lynch Johnson (30-Aug-1882) - (30-Jun-1952)
            m. (09-Jun-1918) Beuna Othella Bagley (04-Dec-1886) -
.   .   .   .  * Frances Forrest Johnson (13-Jan-1919) -
                m. (19-Jun-1945) Jackson Ashurst Carr (01-Jan-1917) -
.   .   .   .   .  * Jane Carr (30-Apr-1946) -
                    m. (12-Feb-1966) Roger Bell Ingram
.   .   .   .   .  * Ann Carr (04-May-1948) -
.   .   .   .   .  * Beth Carr (06-Apr-1951) -
.   .   .   .  * Martha Isabel Johnson (06-Nov-1922) -
            m. (15-Sep-1950) Charles Barnett Robinson (11-Aug-1923) -
.   .   .   .   .  * Cynthia Meer Robinson (10-Jun-1951) -
.   .   .   .   .  * Stephen Charles Robinson (23-Jun-1953) -
.   .   .   .   .  * Kathy Elaine Robinson (03-Jul-1956) -
.   .   .  * Alvie Hendrix Johnson (16-Sep-1884) - (23-Oct-1958)
                m. (07-Oct-1906) Nelle Bryce Lucas (04-Oct-1884) - (25-Dec-1971)
```

```
.   .   .   .   * Maudie Mae Johnson (29-Jul-1907) -
                    m. Sydney Grady Browning (21-Mar-1906) - (21-Jan-1961)
.   .   .   .   .   * Donald Grady Browning (10-Nov-1933) -
                        m. (07-Jan-1955) Sue Reedy
.   .   .   .   .   .   * James Edward Browning (27-Nov-1955) -
.   .   .   .   .   .   * David Brian Browning (26-Nov-1959) -
.   .   .   .   .   * Charlotte Aileene Browning (17-Nov-1937) -
                        m. (15-Jun-1957) Frank W Guy
.   .   .   .   .   .   m. (04-Apr-1963) Belton B Usrey
.   .   .   .   .   .   m. Ralph Blackmon
.   .   .   .   .   .   * Bradford Leigh Guy (19-Apr-1958) -
.   .   .   .   .   .   * Kimberly Sue Usrey (27-Feb-1964) -
.   .   .   .   .   * Bobby Browning (    ) -(At early age)
.   .   .   .   * William David Johnson (31-Oct-1909) - (21-Jan-1973)
                    m. (24-Jun-1933) Vera Nunnally (23-Nov-1909) -
.   .   .   .   .   * Barry Kern Johnson (16-Oct-1934) -
.   .   .   .   .   * Marshall Hendrix Johnson (20-Mar-1912) - (29-Aug-1967)
.   .   .   .   .   * Frieda Mildred Johnson (07-Oct-1915) - (03-May-1917)
.   .   .   .   .   * Franklin Stephen Johnson (02-Sep-1918) -
                    m. (03-Aug-1942) Charles Elizabeth White (04-Dec-1921) -
.   .   .   .   .   * Frieda Lynn Johnson (29-May-1943) -
                m. (26-Mar-1969) Charles Farned Norris
.   .   .   .   .   .   * Charles Stephen Norris (17-Jan-1970) -
.   .   .   .   .   .   * Daniel Joseph Norris (22-Dec-1971) -
.   .   .   .   .   * Anita Charles Johnson (25-Aug-1950) -
.   .   .   .   .   * Franklin Stephen Johnson, Jr (11-Aug-1951) -
.   .   .   .   .   * Rita Ann Johnson (07-Aug-1954) -
.   .   .   .   .   * Elizabeth Lee Johnson (29-Dec-1957) -
.   .   .   .   .   * Frances Erline Johnson (02-Sep-1918) -
                m. (01-Jan-1938) Melvin Welch Caton (12-Jun-1916) - (05-Jun-1955)
.   .   .   .   .   m. (14-Apr-1956) Thomas Roy Bowerman (6-Apr-1922) -
.   .   .   .   .   * Thomas Roy Bowerman, Jr (09-Jan-1957) -
                        m. Susan Butler
.   .   .   .   .   .   * Thomas Roy Bowerman III (29-Dec-1980) -
.   .   .   .   .   .   * Tiffany Bowerman
.   .   .   .   .   * Terry Adrian Bowerman (13-Feb-1958) -
.   .   .   .   .   * Barry Lynn Bowerman (26-Sep-1959) -
                        m. Shelby Burgess (06-Apr-1958) -
.   .   .   .   .   .   * Christopher Bowerman
                            m. (1993) Shannon
.   .   .   .   .   .   * Dustin Chase Bowerman
.   .   .   .   .   .   * Cylie Bowerman
.   .   .   .   * Eleanor Louise Johnson (25-Feb-1925) -
                    m. (26-May-1956) James Stewart Hinds
.   .   .   .   .   * Marsha Nell Hinds (25-Aug-1951) -
                        m. Michael K Norred (08-Oct-1950) -
.   .   .   .   .   .   * Chrysta Mae Norred (03-May-1978) -
.   .   .   .   .   .   * Melissa Anne Norred (03-May-1978) -
.   .   .   .   .   * Michael Stewart Hinds (20-Jan-1953) -
                        m. Lynne Mundy (29-May-1959) -
.   .   .   .   .   .   * Lindsey Michelle Hinds (02-Nov-1982) -
.   .   .   .   .   .   * Allison Marie Hinds (03-Dec-1986) -
.   .   .   .   .   * David Mark Hinds (26-May-1955) -      m. Rita Unknown
.   .   .   .   * Margaret Ann Johnson (22-Apr-1928) -
                    m. Stephen Gracie, Jr (05-Sep-1927) -
.   .   .   .   .   * Stephen Gracie, III (30-Aug-1952) -
.   .   .   .   .   * Jo Ann Gracie (27-Nov-1956) -
.   .   .   .   .   * David Graham Gracie (23-Jan-1963) -
```

Tuscaloosa High School

Superintendent of Education   Dr H.G. Dowling

Through high school they fly! Seven hundred and more a year, our young people - thin ones, fat specimens, dull, brilliant, plain, exquisite, courteous and gentle, rude with the ignorant haste of youth, patient and industrious, lazy beyond description, bane of the teacher's existence, and also ample reward for every effort! Hullabaloo in the wide hallways, regular beat of cheering from the pep sessions, roars from the football field, sweet harmony in band and chorus rooms, secret whisperings of clubs and cabals, rumors of heavy thinking in Math and Science and English halls! And then all too suddenly the last day of school is here;we hand them a little parchment roll, give them a friendly pat upon the shoulder,and send them out to ways that neither we nor they have properly foreseen.......... H.G. Dowling   1940

Secretary to Superintendent of Education   Miss Susie Mae Smith

Miss Smith was formerly Principal of Tuscaloosa Junior High School

Board of Education:

    Mr J. Gordon Madison
    Mr Hayse Tucker
    Mr J.A. Duckworth
    Mr Rueben Wright
    Mrs Sam Wiesel
    Dr H.G. Dowling

Principal of Tuscaloosa Senior High School   Miss Clara Verner

You come to us as freshmen, wide-eyed, expectant, uncertain in your new surroundings. You leave us three years later, poised, perhaps even a bit sophisticated. In the interval we hope you have experienced the exhilaration of play, the inspiration of dreams, the satisfaction and pride that comes to those who can truly say, We have fought the good fight; we have finished our course." Clara Verner (Miss Clara)   1940

The Faculty

MISS EVELYN ASHLEY	Latin & French. Sponsors the Latin & French Clubs. Began classes with "Now, people."
MISS ANNA BROWN	Literature & English. Guides the Jennie Brown Club. Began classes with "All right, students."
MR KARL BRUDER	Art. Art staff of the Black Warrior under his wing. Remarks, "Just relax and let yourself go."

MR CARLETON BUTLER	Band & Instrumental Music. Master mind of the red coats and majorettes. "Jeez, let's get going."
MISS MARGARET CAMPBELL	Vocational Home Economics. Adviser for the Future Homemakers of America. When lifting gum, "You look very nice today, dear, except for one thing."
MISS VERNON CLARKE	Distributive Education. Directs the Salesmanship Club. "Get out your notebooks and get to work."
MRS M.W. CLINTON	Health and Girls' Physical Education. Sponsors the Pep Squad and works with Girl Scouts. Warns, "I can't pass you if you won't dress."
MR MATTHEW W. CLINTON	English and Social Studies. Royal Director of R.O.F.B...."I WILL NOT talk above you. When you get through, I'll begin."
MISS WILLIE DAFFRON	Librarian. Asks, "Now just what do you think I ought to do to you."
MISS EM DONOHO	Chemistry and Photography. Faculty adviser for the Camera Club and the Science Club. Heard to say, "You must get understandings."
Mr CHARLES EBERSOLE	Industrial Arts. Even above the machines you can hear, "Now fellas."
MISS JEWEL ECHOLS	English and Social Studies. Hi-Life consultant. Rationalizes, "You can go if you give a good reason for it."
MISS HELEN McGIFFERT	Plane Geometry and Economic Geography. Adviser for the Motion Picture Committee. Most familiar theorem; "Get to work now."
MISS SUE McCLEOD	Home Economics and Boys' Social Problems. Guiding light of the C.G. and C.O.B.... Takes pride in saying, "Let me tell you about my boys."
MISS VENA MORROW	Stenography and Typing. Student Placement Bureau organized under her supervision. Business-wisely asks, "Is that business-like?"
MISS PEARL PATTON	English and Social Studies. also French II. Collects with the Stamp Club. Encourages with, "I think that would be very interesting."
MISS RUBY PATTON	Biology. Adviser for the Biology Club. Says often, "Now, students."
MISS MYRTLE PAYNE	Bookkeeping and Business Training. Puns, "I'm

	a Payne, but I can't help it."
MR TORREY FULLER	English and Journalism. Responsible for the Hi-Life. Parting shot, "Goodbye now."
MRS W.A. GRAY	Senior Math and Freshman Algebra. Philosophizes: "If you don't get it this year, you'll get it next."
MISS RUBYE GULLEY	Algebra and Geometry. Busy with the business staff of the Black Warrior. Constant Query: "Where's my pencil."
MR FRANK KENDALL	Coach and Boys' Physical Education. Advises Red Letter Club. Also regularly advises: " Let's get 'em on, boys."
MRS VIVIAN LAWSON	Librarian... Sotto voces:"Move to another table."
MISS IRMA McDAVITT	Stenography and Typing. Urges "Limber up."
MISS LOUISE PHIFER	American History and Vocational Guidance. Pilot of the Boys' Hi-Y. Practices what she preaches: "Act Natural."
MR VINCENT RAINES	Speech. Taskmaster of the Greasepainters and Debaters. Also well known to the Motion Picture Committee. Urges, "Up and at 'em."
MISS ELIZABETH ROSE	English and Social Studies. Sponsors Honor Society. Mento for the editorial staff of the Black Warrior. Always wants to know, "Where's my purse."
MISS FANNIE SCHMITT	Head Librarian. Quiets with, "Quiet please."
MRS FESTUS SHAMBLIN	Chorus Music. Shelters the A Cappella Choir "I won't go another inch until you all get quiet."
MRS MAURICE STUCKEY	Utley's Assistant in D.O.... Diversified comment, "Be seated, students."
MRS E.D. THAMES	Senior English. Ring leader in Remedial Reading Familiar quotation:"Now, my little dears."
MR T.D. UTLEY	diversified Occupations. Faculty sponsor of the D.O. Club. Comments with, "I wonder."
MR EDGAR E. WEAVER	American History and Occupations. His word to the wise, "Let us study."
MR GEORGE ZIVICH	Physics. Paralyzes with, "I see a zero from here."

Tuscaloosa High School Senior Class - 1940

Abbott, Fontaine
Attwood, Marion
Barksdale, Amy Jean
Bates, Billy
Bowerman, Thomas
Burnum, John
Channell, James
Clarke, Florinne
Cleere, Mason
Cole, Jimmy
Copeland, James
Cummings, Louise
Drew, Polly Ann
Durham, Wilson
Elliott, Gus
Fehler, George
Gaines, Byron
Goode, Betty
Gray, Kathleen
Haley, Mollie
Hanna, Barbara
Hardin, Jack
Herndon, Nan
Hinton, Jimmy
Holliman, Marie
Hubbard, Mary Snow
Hunter, Jessica
Jacobs, Gene
Johnson, Melvin
Jones, Lucia
Koster, Frances
Larsen, Keith
Manderson, Margaret
Mayfield, Margie
Mize, Norman
Morton, Max
O'Gwynn, Jean
Parker, Ava Nelle
Partrich, Mary Lee
Pearson, Robert
Ray, Elizabeth
Savage, James
Shirley, Margaret
Smalley, Noah
Stallworth, Nancy
Sullivan, Elaine
Thrower, W.G.
Tucker, Elsie
Waldrop, Rosemary
Williams, Billy
Wright, Gene

Adams, Lottie
Avery, Marion
Barlowe, Eugene
Bates, Winsley
Browne, Elizabeth
Burroughs, Dorothy
Chancey, Robert
Clary, Rick
Cobb, Lucy Lee
Conner, Ellis
Cox, June
Dailey, Mildred
Driskill, B.C.
Easterling, Mary
Ellis, Grace
Fields, Lorene
Gibbons, Howard
Goode, Grace
Gresham, Edward
Hamby, Margaret
Hannah, Helen
Harris, Ruth
Hicks, Eloise
Hobson, Henry
Hopper, J.T.
Hughes, Pat
Hutchins, Margaret
Jamison, Billy
Johnson, Nellie
Kartzinel, Shirley
Krebs, Joe
Larsen, Laurene
Marlowe, Forrest
McLane, Dorothy
Moore, Jean
New, Bobby
Oliver, Charles
Parker, John
Patterson, Anne Lou
Phillips, Gena Grace
Ray, Frances
Schuyler, Imajean
Sikes, Virginia
Snow, Dorothy
Stein, Lenora
Swindle, Sam
Tillman, Elaine
Tucker, Opal
Watson, George
Wilson, Lois
Wright, James

Apperson, Roger
Bailey, G.E.
Barr, Lorraine
Bidgood, Willis
Burkhalter, Kathleen
Causey, Minnie Evelyn
Chappell, Mary Helen
Clayton, Margie
Colburn, Leo
Copeland, Billy
Crisler, James
Darden, Margaret Bell
Duncan, Virginia
Echols, John
Englebert, Betty
Fowler, Edris
Glass, Louise
Grace, Julia
Gulledge, Jane
Hanley, Mary Martha
Hanson, Gloria
Herndon, Joyce
Higginbotham, Nell
Holley, Jeanne
Hubbard, Bonham
Hughes, Sarah
Jackson, E.S.
Johnson, Janice
Jones, Hal
Kirkley, Eathon
Lancaster, A.D.
Little, Frank
Mashburn, Ruby
McPherson, Lucille
Moorer, Ruth
O'Connor, Billy
Panabaker, Jack
Partain, Betty Jo
Patton, Dorothy
Pruett, Ruth
Reuben, Marvin
Sewell, Joe
Skelton, Ruby Dean
Snyder, Beth
Strickland, Nell
Thornton, Lois
Tubbs, Robert
Turner, Betty
Weaver, Inez
Wooley, George

CCC - Stevens Pass

Stevens Pass Side Camp

G.R. Hodges	E.S. Griffin	W.H. Vickery
T.A. Williamson	K.B. Taylor	C.G. Lilly
M.L. West	H. McCurry	L.O. McBryde
E. Lee	C.R. Moon	T.L. Lay
O.J. Davidson	L.D. Peck	D.A. Parker
F.G. Ozbolt	D.A. Curl	E. Thomas
J.W. Rogers	G.E. Sledge	C. McClung
C.A. Cates	T.R. Bowerman	B. Cowan
C.C. Connell	B.G. Montgomery	J.P. Crosswhite
O.W. Hicks	G.L. Jackson	M.T. Enis
H.F. Creasy	B. Browning	B. Brown

CCC - Chatter Creek

Chatter Creek Side Camp

E. Edwards	C.L. Fletcher	H.E. Hogan
R.D. Phillips	H.E. Cobb	C.L. Parker
R.S. Norwood	C.L. Chapman	W.G. Osborn
C.B. Redd	C.C. Robbins	R.T. Chandler
E. Lisby	E.A. Minton	J.R. Sellers
T.E. Cost	A. Peek	H.L. Stephenson
O. Hocutt	S.E. Hindman	R.L. Pennington
G.W. McElyea	H.A. Muncher	J.L. McCowan
P.J. Lindsey	E.H. Mayes	R. Allred
J.T. Hollingsworth	B. White	E. Harris
P.Z. Walker	J.E. Allen	

CCC - Main Camp - Camp Icicle

G. Kirk	A.A. Powers	H.F. Wilburn
T.L. Burden	W.P. Morrow	J.A. Hyatt
M. Elliot	A.A. Fuller	C. Franks
C.E. Wylie	L.I. Haynie	H.W. Poteete
W.T. White	E.W. Thomas	J.E. Watson
H. Eubanks	L.J. McGahuey	W.L. Wright
A. Franklin	E. Hamilton	C.R. Burnell
H.G. Campbell	J.E. Kelly	C.J. McCreless
C.J. Perry	P. Jones	B. Gillis
W.F. Glasgow	W.J. Eason	J.H. Pike
J.H. Hall	F. Beard	C.C. Whitehead
H.L. Adams	J.D. Dailey	V.I. Gold
C.L. Smith	B.E. Henson	L.C. Carpenter
J. Sproul	J.J. Howard	V.L. Parish
L.Z. Bragg	O.F. Williams	W.W. Turney
Z.A. Trotter	M.B. Walker	J.T. Crane
T.J. Minton	J.E. Wilson	W.E. Singleton
J.C. Sanders	E.L. Vinson	L.H. Page
C.H. Garrett	M.I. Wright	H.A. Gilchrist
G.R. McMullan	J.W. Tucker	P. Bell

W.C. Hanks	H.P. Cobble	O.V. Riggs
F.J. Moss	J.E. Swindle	P.P. Vest
H.I. J. Moore	A.W. Butler	E.W. Tidwell
E.D. Letson	C.H. Brucke	W.E. Johnson
D.L. Davis	B.L. Knight	C.R. Heaton
E.L. Williams	C.W. Holland	W. Gilchrist
V.H. Nelms	J.D. Williams	A.R. Hamilton

World War II Navy Documents

Diary of the Armed Guard Gunnery Officer on the S.S. Charles Sumner

Charles L. Sawyer - Commanding
July 29, 1943

Charles Sumner - Liberty - 7176 Tons
July 29, 1943

Type of Vessel.......Liberty Ship
Type of Cargo.U.S.Army & Explosives
Owner of Vessel:
  U.S.War Shipping Administration
Chartered to:
  Coastwise Transportation Company
  Boston, Mass.
Port of Departure...New York, N.Y.
Average Speed.......9.5 Knots

Sawyer, Charles L.	LT(j.g.)
Archung, Phillip J.	Coxswain
Bowerman, Thomas R.	GM3c
Hazuka, George E. Jr.	GM3c
Arthur, William L.	S1c
Byrne, Edward R.	S1c
Campbell, Frank J.	S1c
Clark, Victor D.	S1c
Fenton, Robert H.	S1c
Foster, Horace C.	S1c
Miller, Raphael M.	S1c
Morgan, Alvin E.	S1c
Newton, Harold P.	S1c
Oliver, Donald	S1c
Pribble, Clarence N.	S1c
Rinehart, Charles L.	S1c
Rouster, Irvin M.	S1c
Seth, Ralph	S1c
Shuey, John W. Jr.	S1c
Smith, John R.	S1c
Stockwell, Kenneth	S1c
Stroud, Thomas G.	S1c
Taflinger, Francis L.	S1c
Chittum, Casper Aley	S1c
Meyers, Jacob Edward	S1c
Dodrill, Arthur E. Jr.	SM3c
Mulqueen, Thomas H.	SM3c
Stumpf, Louis L.	RM3c

Diary of the Armed Guard Gunnery Officer on the S.S. Charles Sumner

Charles L. Sawyer - Commanding
July 30, 1943

Charles Sumner - Liberty - 7176 Tons
July 31, 1943

0700 - Condition three watches set.
Section four on duty.
0715 - Reveille
0720 - Breakfast

0515 - General Quarters.
0600 - General Quarters secured.
Number 5 and 6 guns cocked and
loaded.

0730 - Underway
0900 - Muster. All present or accounted for. Various orders for trip published. Articles 14 through 36 of "The Articles for the Government of the United States Navy" read at muster.
1000 - Inspected entire ship and magazines.
1130 - Dinner
1700 - Supper
2000 - General Quarters drill with gunners buzzer. Crews of 3 and 4 inch gun drill. Number 7 and 8 guns cocked and loaded.
2015 - General Quarters, inspected all stations.
2100 - All stations secured.

0700 - Reveille.
0720 - Breakfast.
1120 - Dinner.
1300 - Muster. All present or accounted for. Articles 37 through 70 of "The Articles for the Government of the United States Navy" read at muster.
1545 - Convoy exercised in turns.
1700 - Daily inspections of magazines. Temperatures, small arms 80-85; 4 inch 82-86; 3 inch 76-80. Powder samples in good order. Supper
1940 - Drill in manning gun stations
1945 - General Quarters. Firing circuits and lights reported in good order. Guns trained and elevated through full arc. Working properly. Sight set at 800 yards scale at midpoint.
2045 - Secured from General Quarters Condition three maintained throughout 24 hours.

Diary of the Armed Guard Gunnery Officer on the S.S. Charles Sumner

Charles L. Sawyer - Commanding
August 1, 1943

Charles Sumner - Liberty - 7176 Tons
August 1, 1943 (Continued)

0415 - General Quarters. Firing circuits checked and working properly.
0520 - Secured from General Quarters.
0700 - Reveille.
0720 - Breakfast.
0830 - Muster. All present or accounted for.
0830-0930 - Section one class in blinker. T. Mulqueen, SM3/C in charge.
0900 - Recoil fluid checked in 4 inch gun.
0900-1000 - Section four class in knots. P. Archung, Cox, in charge.
1000-1100 - Section one class in knots. G. Stroud, S1/c in charge.
1120 - Dinner.
1320 - Received permission to test fire guns.
1330 - Recoil liquid checked in 3 inch gun.
1340 - Test fired 4 inch gun. One round at zero degrees elevation. Three rounds at seventy degrees elevation.
1400 - Guns, mounts, bolts and ship supporting structure examined and

exercised in turns. Several ships test fired. Misfire on #7 20MM during test firing. No casualties.

found in good condition.
1430-1530 - Section three class in
blinker. A. Dodrill,SM3/c in charge
1700 - Supper.
1700 -Daily inspection of magazines
Temperatures: Small arms - 78-80.
4 inch gun 80-82. 3 inch 76-78.
1940 - Drilled in manning gun
stations.
1945 - General Quarters. 3 and 4
inch guns firing circuits & lights
checked. Guns elevated and trained
through their full arcs. Night
range of 800 yards and midpoint
deflection set. Position of spare
life jackets checked - satisfaction
2050 - Secured General Quarters.
Condition three watch maintained
throughout the 24 hours. Convoy

Diary of the Armed Guard Gunnery Officer on the S.S. Charles Sumner

Charles L. Sawyer - Commanding
August 2, 1943

0345 - General Quarters. Firing
circuits tested on 3 and 4 inch
guns. Guns and sights trained and
elevated through their full arcs.
Found in working order.
0700 - Reveille.
0720 - Breakfast.
0830 - Muster. All present or
accounted for.
0835-0930 - Section two class in
blinker. A. Dodrill, SM3/c
instructor.
0900 - Daily inspection of magazines. Temperatures, Small Arms
76-80, 4 inch 76-82, 3 inch 74-78.
0930-1030 - Section four knots and
splices. P. Archung, Cox instructor
1000-1100 - Section one knots and
splices. G. Stroud, S1/c instructor
1100-1130 - Gun drill on 4 inch gun
Entire crew.
1120 - Dinner.
1300 - Fire and emergency sounded
on General Alarm. All stations
manned. Abandon ship drill by
Merchant Marine crew. Battle
stations all hands. Merchant crew
drilled and instructed in their
battle station duties.
1400 - Battle drill secured. Gas
mask issued to all Merchant Marine
not on watch.
1430-1530 - Class in blinker

Charles Sumner - Liberty - 7176 Tons
August 3, 1943

0415 - General Quarters. 3 and 4
inch guns firing circuits and lighting circuits checked, guns and
sights moved through their full arcs
Working properly. Sights set at 2000
yards.
0515 - Secured from General Quarters
0700 - Reveille.
0720 - Breakfast.
0830 - Muster. All hands instructed
in launching of rafts. Sea routine
for the day.
1100 - Drill on the 4 inch gun. The
complete crew drilled at all
stations.
1120 - Dinner.
1135 - Secured from 4 inch gun drill
1230 - Daily inspection of magazines
Temperatures, small arms 76-78, 4
inch 76-80, 3 inch 74-76.
1300 - Drill with 3 inch gun crew
surforce. Instructed crew in anti-
aircraft fire control.
1400 - Secured from 3 inch gun drill
1630 - Supper.
1945 - General Quarters. 3 and 4
inch guns firing and lighting
circuits checked, guns and sights
moved through full arc. All working
properly. Fathometer operated during
General Quarters. Oscillation very
distinct in sound powered head sets.
Capt. Anderson advised. Sights set

section three. T. Mulqueen, SM3/c conductor.
1640 - Supper.
1925 - General Quarters. 3 and 4 inch guns lighting and firing circuits checked, guns trained and elevated through their full arcs. Sights moved through full arcs. All working properly. Sights set at range of 800 yards deflection at midpoint.
2030 - Secured from General Qtrs.
2400 - Clocks set ahead one hour.
Condition Three watch maintained throughout the 24 hours.

at night range of 800 yards.
2045 - General Quarters secured. Blackout reported complete.
2400 - Clocks advanced 1 hour. Condition three watch maintained throughout the 24 hours. Several ships exercised their guns during the day.

Diary of the Armed Guard Gunnery Officer on the S.S. Charles Sumner

Charles L. Sawyer - Commanding
August 4, 1943

0515 - General Quarters. 3 and 4 inch guns firing circuits tested, guns and sights moved through their full arc. Working properly. Day range of 2000 yards set.
0700 - reveille.
0720 - Breakfast.
0800 - Fog.
0830 - Muster. Instruction and practice in securing rafts.
1120 - Dinner.
1630 - Supper.
Very low visability. Whistles sounded frequently for aid in station keeping. Running lights and cargo cluster lights burning at night. Masthead on and off when sighting light ahead.
1730 - Daily inspection of magazines. Temperatures, small arms 68-78, 4 inch 70-78, 3 inch 64-68. Condition three watch maintained throughout the 24 hours.

Charles Sumner - Liberty - 7176 Tons
August 5, 1943

0700 - Reveille.
0720 - Breakfast.
1120 - Dinner.
1200 - Daily inspection of magazines. Small arms 66-72, 4 inch 68-72, 3 inch 64-68.
1700 - Supper
1915 - General Quarters. 3 & 4 inch guns and sights moved through their full arc. Working properly. Blackout reported complete.
2115 - Secured from General Quarters Condition Three maintained throughout the 24 hours. Visibility till noon bad. Whistles used.

Diary of the Armed Guard Gunnery Officer on the S.S. Charles Sumner

Charles L. Sawyer - Commanding
August 6, 1943

0500 - General Quarters. 3 & 4 inch guns firing circuits checked, guns and sights trained through their full arc. All working properly. Secured at range of 2000 yards.
0600 - Secured from General Qtrs.
0700 - Reveille.
0720 - Breakfast.

Charles Sumner - Liberty - 7176 Tons
August 7, 1943

0500 - General Quarters. 3 & 4 inch guns firing circuit checked. Guns & sights moved through their full arc. Working properly. Range set at 2000 yards.
0600 - Secured from General Quarters
0700 - Reveille.
0720 - Breakfast.

0830 - Muster. Daily inspection of magazines. Temperatures, small arms 63-67, 4 inch 65-68, 3 inch 60-64.
1120 - Dinner.
1300 - Fire and boat drill all hands.
1315 - Battle station drill. 20MM loaders and tension men drilled.
1345 - Drill with 3 inch gun crew and antiaircraft fire control.
1415 - Secured from drill.
1700 - Supper.
2015 - General Quarters. 3 & 4 inch guns lighting and firing circuits checked, guns & sights moved through their full arc. All working properly. Secured at a range of 800 yards. Blackout checked and reported complete.
2115 - Secured from General Qtrs.
2400 - Clocks advanced one hour. Condition three watch maintained throughout 24 hours.

0900 - Muster. Daily inspection of magazines. Temperatures, Small Arms 63-65, 4 inch 65-68, 3 inch 60-63.
0910 - Section two drilled at four inch gun.
1000 - Section one drilled at four inch gun.
1120 - Dinner.
1700 - Supper.
2130 - General Quarters. 3 & 4 inch guns lighting and firing circuits checked. Lights working properly. Ground wire disconnected on 3 inch gun. 4 inch working properly. Guns & sights moved through entire arc. Range of 800 yards set for night.
2210 - Secured from General Qtrs. Condition three watch maintained throughout the 24 hours. Number 8 20 MM taken down and cleaned. Number 6 20 MM taken down and cleaned.

Diary of the Armed Guard Gunnery Officer on the S.S. Charles Sumner

Charles L. Sawyer - Commanding
August 8, 1943

Charles Sumner - Liberty - 7176 Tons
August 9, 1943

0515 - General Quarters. Guns were trained and elevated through full arc. Sights moved through full arc. Firing circuits checked. Working properly. Range of 2000 yards set on 3 and 4 inch guns.
0615 - Secured General Quarters.
0700 - Reveille.
0720 Breakfast.
0900 - Muster. Daily inspection of magazines. Temperatures, Small Arms 65-70, 4 inch 62-67, 3 inch 55-60.
1000 - Two illuminating rockets fired. Numbers 7 & 8 20MM's fired with barrels from 20 MM guns numbers 2,3,4, and 5.
1045 - Guns secured, taken down and cleaned.
1120 - Dinner.
1700 - Supper.
1730 - Fuzes set on anti-aircraft projectiles, labels placed on each. Merchant Marines fuze setter drill.
2130 - General Quarters. 3 & 4 inch guns firing circuits & lights checked. Guns and sights trained & elevated through their full arcs. Reported working properly. Range of 800 yards set for night.

0530 - General Quarters. 3 & 4 inch guns firing circuits checked, guns & sights trained & elevated through their full arcs. Reported working properly. Range of 2000 yards set for day.
0700 - Reveille.
0720 - Breakfast.
0900 - Muster. Section two drill on 4 inch gun.
0930 - Section three drill on 4 inch gun.
1100 - Daily inspection of magazines Temperatures, Small Arms 67-67, 4 inch 64-68, 3 inch 56-60.
1120 - Dinner.
1700 - Supper.
2100 - Enemy submarines reported in vicinity. General Quarters. Guns firing and lighting circuits checked, guns & sights trained and elevated through full arcs. Reported working properly.
2300 - General Quarters secured. Condition two watch set.
2400 - Clocks advanced one hour.

2400 - Clocks advanced one hour.
Condition three watch maintained
throughout the 24 hours.

Diary of the Armed Guard Gunnery Officer on the S.S. Charles Sumner

Charles L. Sawyer - Commanding
August 10, 1943

0530 - General Quarters. Guns firing circuits checked, guns and sights trained & elevated through their full arcs. Range of 2000 yards set for the day.
0630 - General Quarters secured, condition three watch set.
0700 - Reveille.
0720 - Breakfast.
1120 - Dinner.
1300 - Fire and boat alarm. All hands to their respective stations. Battle station alarm. All hands to battle station. Merchant Marine crew drilled in their duties. Two cases of 20 MM ammunition brought from magazine. Merchant Marine party greased and loaded empty magazines. All hands secured as drill completed.
1400 - All hands secured.
1430 - Daily inspection of magazines. Temperatures, Small Arms 65-68, 4 inch 66-70, 3 inch 56-62.
1700 - Supper.
2200 - General Quarters. Guns firing & lighting circuits checked, guns & sights trained & elevated through their full arcs. Reported working properly. Range of 800 yards set.
2300 - General Quarters secured. Condition three watch maintained from 0630 to 2400.

Charles Sumner - Liberty - 7176 Tons
August 11, 1943

0500 - General Quarters. Guns firing circuits checked, guns and sights trained and elevated through their full arcs. Reported working properly. Range of 2000 yards set for day.
0600 - General Quarters secured.
0700 - Reveille.
0720 - Breakfast.
1120 - Dinner.
1300 - Muster.
1330 - Daily inspection of magazines Temperatures, Small arms 63-65, 4 inch 68-72, 3 inch 63-65. 4 inch and Small Arms magazines opened for airing.
1430 - Magazines closed and locked. 3 inch magazine opened for airing.
1500 - 3 inch magazine secured.
1700 - Supper.
2200 - General Quarters. Guns firing circuits and lights checked, guns & sights trained and elevated through their full arcs. Range of 800 yards set. Reported working properly.
2245 - General Quarters secured.
2400 - Clocks advanced 1 hour. Land at 1400. Running lights during hours of darkness. Condition three watch maintained throughout the day.

Diary of the Armed Guard Gunnery Officer on the S.S. Charles Sumner

Charles L. Sawyer - Commanding
August 12, 1943

0700 - Reveille.
0720 - Breakfast.
0900 - Muster.
0915 - Section 2 & Section 4 class in Morse code.
0930 - Section 3 class in Morse code.
1000 - Daily inspection of magazines. Small arms 64-70, 4 inch

Charles Sumner - Liberty - 7176 Tons
August 13, 1943

0700 - Reveille.
0730 - Breakfast.
0900 - Muster. Port instructions stressed. Liberty to be granted from 0930 until 2400 alternate days for each watch section.
0915 - Daily inspection of magazines Temperatures, Small arms 65-68, 4 inch 66-68, 3 inch 60-68.

68-73, 3 inch 58-70. Litmus test satisfactory.
1120 - Dinner.
1300 - 20 MM guns cleaned and secured for port.
1700 - Supper.
1800 - Pilot aboard. Condition 3 secured, gun watch posted.
1900 - U.S. Naval Liaison Officer representative aboard. Port orders received. Instruction for Armed Guard Crew published. Gangway and roving watch constructed.
2230 - Docked. Gangway and roving watch posted. Gear secured and locked. Ready boxes and flood valves locked.

0930 - Inspection of quarters and security of gear, found to be satisfactory. Morse code exam all seaman 1/C.
1130 - Dinner.
1300 - Crew paid.
1630 - Dinner.
Gangway and roving watch maintained throughout the day.

Diary of the Armed Guard Gunnery Officer on the S.S. Charles Sumner

Charles L. Sawyer - Commanding
August 14, 1943

Charles Sumner - Liberty - 7176 Tons
August 15, 1943

0700 - Reveille.
0730 - Breakfast.
0900 - Muster. Bowerman, GM 3/C not present.
1200 - Thomas R. Bowerman 604 79 36 GM 3/C USNR. Restricted one (1) day of shore liberty as penalty for absence from muster.
2400 - Clocks retarded one hour.
Daily inspection of magazines. Temperatures, small arms 67-70, 4 inch 60-70, 3 inch 58-68. G. Hazuka GM 3/C assigned to shore patrol duty.

0700 - Reveille.
0900 - Muster.
0915 - Inspection of quarters and daily inspection of magazines. Temperatures, small arms 67-70, 4 inch 68-72, 3 inch 68-68. T.Bowerman assigned to shore patrol duty.
K. Stockwell S1/C bruised right foot while on deck.

Diary of the Armed Guard Gunnery Officer on the S.S. Charles Sumner

Charles L. Sawyer - Commanding
August 16, 1943

Charles Sumner - Liberty - 7176 Tons
August 17, 1943

0700 - Reveille.
0900 - Muster.
0915 - Daily inspection of quarters and magazines. Temperatures, small arms 66-70, 4 inch 67-70, 3 inch 66-68. Guns inspected and barrels wiped out. Gangway and roving watch maintained. P. Archung Coxswain assigned to shore patrol duty.

0715 - Reveille.
0900 - Muster.
0930 - Daily inspection of quarters and magazines. Temperatures, small arms 67-72, 4 inch 69-72, 3 inch 64-66. Gangway and roving watch maintained throughout the day.

Diary of the Armed Guard Gunnery Officer on the S.S. Charles Sumner

Charles L. Sawyer - Commanding
August 18, 1943

0715 - Reveille.
0900 - Muster.
0915 - Daily inspection of quarters and magazines. Temperatures, small arms 65-70, 4 inch 67-70, 3 inch 68-72. G. Hazuka assigned to shore patrol. Gangway and roving watch maintained throughout the day.

Charles Sumner - Liberty - 7176 Tons
August 19, 1943

0715 - Reveille.
0900 - Muster.
0915 - Daily inspection of quarters and magazines. Temperatures, small arms 65-70, 4 inch 67-70, 3 inch 62-66. T. Bowerman GM 3/C assigned to shore patrol duty. Gangway and roving watch maintained throughout the day.

Diary of the Armed Guard Gunnery Officer on the S.S. Charles Sumner

Charles L. Sawyer - Commanding
August 20, 1943

0715 - Reveille.
0900 - Muster.
0915 - Daily inspection of quarters and magazines. Temperatures, small arms 62-70, 4 inch 62-69, 3 inch 60-68.
1030 - Flight Lieutenant Twining aboard with party of RAF officers and ratings for inspection of ship and armament. P. Archung, Coxswain assigned to shore patrol duty. Gangway and roving watch maintained throughout the day. Crew paid.

Charles Sumner - Liberty - 7176 Tons
August 21, 1943

0715 - Reveille.
0900 - Muster.
0915 - Daily inspection of quarters and magazines. Temperatures, small arms 64-72, 4 inch 64-70, 3 inch 62-70. Gangway and roving watch maintained throughout the day.

Diary of the Armed Guard Gunnery Officer on the S.S. Charles Sumner

Charles L. Sawyer - Commanding
August 22, 1943

0715 - Reveille.
0900 - Muster.
0930 - Daily inspection of quarters and magazines. Temperatures, Small Arms 65-75, 4 inch 68-75, 3 inch 64-74.
1500 - Investigator for U.S. Army aboard to check loss of a can of fruit on the dock. R. Miller, Sea1c USNR stated M.P. had brought an unlabeled can to the gangway during his watch, and had asked him to set it on the deck for him and that he would get it at 2400 when he was off duty. G. Hazuka, GM 3/c assigned to shore patrol duty. Gangway and roving watch maintained throughout the day.

Charles Sumner - Liberty - 7176 Tons
August 23, 1943

0700 - Reveille.
0830 - Muster.
0845 - Lt.(jg) C. Sawyer, P. Archung Coxswain, A. Morgan, S1/c, K. Stockwell, S1/c, V. Clark, S1/c, C. Chittum, S1/c, J. Meyers, S1/c, and Merchant personnel, A. Esposito, G. Goldberg, H. Smith, H. Suggs, A. Westflagg, Mohamed Badowy, ashore for two day course at D.E.M.S. AA School. Liberty cancelled until return of class.
1700 - Liberty granted.
1730 - Daily inspection of quarters and magazines. Temperatures, Small Arms 60-70, 4 inch 64-68, 3 inch 58-66. T. Bowerman, GM 3/c assigned to shore patrol duty.

Diary of the Armed Guard Gunnery Officer on the S.S. Charles Sumner

Charles L. Sawyer - Commanding
August 24, 1943

0700 - Reveille.
0830 - Muster.
0845 - Party for AA school ashore. Liberty cancelled.
1000 - Reported breaking of elevating stop of No. 7 20MM to US Naval Liaison Officer.
1700 - Liberty granted.
1730 - Daily inspection of magazines. Temperatures, Small Arms 60-68, 4 inch 62-66, 3 inch 60-68. P. Archung Coxswain, assigned shore patrol duty. Gangway and roving watch maintained throughout the day.

Charles Sumner - Liberty - 7176 Tons
August 25, 1943

0700 - Reveille.
0900 - Muster. Liberty to expire at 2400. Starboard 20MM stripped and cleaned.
0930 - Daily inspection of quarters and magazines, Temperatures, Small Arms 62-70, 4 inch 64-68, 3 inch 60-70.
1000 - K. Stockwell 622-88-99 S1/c USNR sent to USN Liaison Officer for medical attention, and right foot not properly healed. G. Hazuka GM3/c 642-14-12 sent to USN Liaison Officer for medical attention for itching rash spotted on arms & legs. Gangway and roving watches maintained throughout the day.

Diary of the Armed Guard Gunnery Officer on the S.S. Charles Sumner

Charles L. Sawyer - Commanding
August 26, 1943

0400 - Away from dock and anchored in the Mersey. Gun watch set.
0700 - Reveille.
0730 - Breakfast.
0900 - Muster. Gear broken out and distributed. Phones checked. Port 20MM's cleaned and checked.
1130 - Dinner.
1200 - Daily inspection of quarters and magazines. Temperatures, Small Arms 58-70, 4 inch 59-70, 3 inch 56-69.
1630 - Supper.
2200 - Taps.

Charles Sumner - Liberty - 7176 Tons
August 27, 1943

0700 - Reveille.
0715 - Departure.
0730 - Breakfast.
0900 - Muster. Life jackets inspected.
1100 - Physical Drill.
1130 - Dinner.
1200 - Daily inspection of magazines Temperatures, Small Arms 65-73, 4 inch 68-73, 3 inch 62-69.
1300 - Fire drill, boat drill and battle stations drill. 20MM crew's drill.
1325 - Drill secured.
1630 - Supper.
1800 - Condition 3 watch set. Gun watch secured.

Diary of the Armed Guard Gunnery Officer on the S.S. Charles Sumner

Charles L. Sawyer - Commanding
August 28, 1943

0715 - Reveille.
0730 - Breakfast.
0900 - Muster.
1100 - Physical drill.
1130 - Dinner.
1600 - Daily inspection of

Charles Sumner - Liberty - 7176 Tons
August 29, 1943

0545 - General quarters. Guns and sights trained and elevated through their full arcs. Firing circuits checked. Range of 2000 yards set on sights.
0645 - General quarters secured.

magazines. Temperatures, Small arms 66-72, 4 inch 70-75, 3 inch 64-70.
1700 - Supper.
2100 - General quarters. 3 and 4 inch guns trained and elevated through their full arcs, lights and firing circuits checked. Sights set at a range of 1000 yards. Black out reported complete.
2200 - General quarters secured. Condition 3 watch maintained throughout the 24 hours.

0715 - Reveille.
0730 - Breakfast.
1130 - Dinner.
1330 - Muster. Articles one through eighteen of the Articles for the Government of the United States Navy read to crew.
1400 - Drill with 4 inch gun crew.
1430 - Drill with 3 inch gun crew.
1500 - Daily inspection of magazines Temperatures, Small Arms 62-64, 4 inch 64-66, 3 inch 62-62.
1630 - Physical drill.
1700 - Supper.
2115 - General quarters. Guns trained and elevated through full arcs. Lights and firing circuits checked. All reported in good working order. Lights checked. Range of 800 yards set for the night. Blackout reported complete.
2230 - General quarters secured.
2400 - Clocks retarded one hour. Condition 3 watch maintained throughout the 24 hours.

Diary of the Armed Guard Gunnery Officer on the S.S. Charles Sumner

Charles L. Sawyer - Commanding
August 30, 1943

Charles Sumner - Liberty - 7176 Tons
August 31, 1943

0515 - General quarters. Guns and sights trained and elevated through full arcs, firing circuits checked. Reported working properly. Range of 2000 yards set on both guns.
0715 - Reveille.
0730 - Breakfast.
0900 - Muster. Articles 19 through 41 of the Articles for the Government of the United States Navy read to the crew.
0930 - Pointer, trainer and sightsetter drill on 4 inch gun.
1000 - Pointer, trainer and sightsetter drill on the 3 inch gun.
1130 - Dinner.
1300 - Daily inspection of magazines. Temperatures, Small Arms 62-64, 4 inch 65-67, 3 inch 60-62.
1700 - Supper.
2045 - General Quarters. Guns and sights trained and elevated through full arcs. Lighting and firing circuits checked. Reported in proper order. Blackout reported complete.
2130 - General quarters secured.

0530 - General quarters. Guns trained and elevated through their full arcs. Firing circuits checked, reported in good working order. Range of 2000 yards set on sights.
0615 - General quarters secured.
0715 - Reveille.
0730 - Breakfast.
1130 - Dinner.
1300 - Daily inspection of magazines Temperatures, Small Arms 62-64, 4 inch 63-65, 3 inch 58-62.
1700 - Supper.
2115 - General quarters. Guns and sights trained and elevated through their full arcs. Reported working properly. Lighting and firing circuits checked. Range of 800 yards set for the night. Blackout reported complete. Extremely rough day. Some water on deck of small arms magazine
2400 - Clocks retarded one hour. Condition three watch maintained throughout 24 hours.

Condition three watch maintained throughout the 24 hours.

Diary of the Armed Guard Gunnery Officer on the S.S. Charles Sumner

Charles L. Sawyer - Commanding
September 1, 1943

Charles Sumner - Liberty - 7176 Tons
September 2, 1943

0445 - General Quarters. Guns and sights trained and elevated throughout their full arc. Firing circuits checked and reported in good working order. Range of 2000 yards set on sights.
0545 - General quarters secured.
0715 - Reveille.
0730 - Breakfast.
1130 - Dinner.
1300 - Muster. Article 42 through 70 of "The Articles for the Government of the United States Navy" read to the crew.
1400 - Daily inspection of magazines. Temperatures, Small Arms 58-60, 4 inch 62-64, 3 inch 60-60.
1700 - Supper.
2030 - General quarters. Guns and sights trained and elevated through their full arcs. Lighting & firing circuits checked. Reported working properly. Blackout reported complete.
2130 - General quarters secured. Condition three watch maintained throughout 24 hours.

0515 - General Quarters. Guns trained and elevated throughout their full arcs. Firing circuits checked. Reported working properly.
0600 - General quarters secured.
0715 - Reveille.
0730 - Breakfast.
0900 - Muster.
1000 - Three (3) inch AA projectiles found in ready box started from their case. Due to roll of ship. Wood strips placed in ready box as a preventive.
1100 - Physical drill.
1130 - Dinner.
1300 - Daily inspection of magazines Temperatures, Small Arms 60-62, 4 inch 62-64, 3 inch 58-60.
1700 - Supper.
2045 - General quarters. Guns and sights trained and elevated through their full arcs. Lights and firing circuits checked. Reported working properly. Blackout reported complete Range of 800 yards set for night.
2145 - Secured from general quarters
2400 - Clocks retarded one hour. Condition three watch maintained throughout the 24 hours.

Diary of the Armed Guard Gunnery Officer on the S.S. Charles Sumner

Charles L. Sawyer - Commanding
September 3, 1943

Charles Sumner - Liberty - 7176 Tons
September 4, 1943

0500 - General Quarters. Guns and sights trained and elevated through their full arcs. Firing circuits checked. Reported in good working order.
0615 - General quarters secured.
0715 - Reveille.
0730 - Breakfast.
0900 - Muster.
0930 - Daily inspection of magazines. Temperatures, Small Arms 60-62, 4 inch 60-64, 3 inch 58-62.
1100 - Physical drill.
1130 - Dinner.

0530 - General quarters. Guns and sights trained and elevated through their full arcs. Firing circuits checked. Reported working properly.
0630 - Secured from general quarters
0715 - Reveille.
0730 - Breakfast.
1130 - Dinner.
1230 - Muster. T. Bowerman reported H. Foster, S1/c completed his 48 hours of extra duty.
1630 - Physical drill.
1805 - Left convoy and set course for St. Johns, Newfoundland. Boiler

289

1300 - General alarm. Battle stations drill. Loading drill on 3 and 4 inch guns. Loading drill on 20 MM guns.
1310 - Secured from battle stations and fire stations manned.
1320 - Secured from fire stations and Abandon ship stations manned.
1330 - Drill secured.
1700 - Supper.
2000 - General quarters. Guns and sights trained and elevated through their full arcs. Lights & firing circuits checked. Reported in good working order. Blackout reported complete.
2100 - Secured from general quarters. Condition three watch maintained throughout 24 hours.
trouble cause of change in destination.
2030 - General quarters. Guns and sights trained and elevated through their full arcs. Lights and firing circuits tested. Reported in good working order. Blackout reported complete.
2130 - General quarters secured. Condition three watch maintained throughout the 24 hours. Magazine temperatures, Small Arms 60-60, 4 inch 60-62, 3 inch 58-60.

Diary of the Armed Guard Gunnery Officer on the S.S. Charles Sumner

Charles L. Sawyer - Commanding
September 5, 1943

0445 - General Quarters. Guns and sights trained and elevated through their full arcs. Firing circuits checked. All working properly.
0715 - Reveille.
0730 - Breakfast.
0900 - Muster. Daily inspection of magazines. Temperatures, Small Arms 60-62, 4 inch 58-62, 3 inch 56-60.
1100 - Physical drill.
1130 - Dinner.
1700 - Supper.
At anchor in St. Johns. Radio silence broken at noon to call for tugs. We were disabled at harbor entrance. Clocks advanced 30 minutes. Condition three watch secured and gun watches set. Navy gear checked and locked up.

Charles Sumner - Liberty - 7176 Tons
September 6, 1943

0715 - Reveille.
0730 - Breakfast.
0900 - Muster. Inspection of quarters and magazines. Temperatures Small Arms 62-67, 4 inch 60-68, 3 inch 56-60.
1100 - Physical drill.
1130 - Dinner.
1200 - Liberty granted.
1630 - Dinner.
1730 - P. Archung ashore for shore patrol duty.
2330 - Word received from U.S. Naval Shore Patrol that Ralph Seth, S1/c 753-02-82 USNR and Horace Foster, S1/c 351-06-64 USN had been turned over to them by Civil authorities for safe keeping. To appear in city court St. Johns, Newfoundland September 7, 1943 on charges of being drunk and disorderly. Gun watches maintained throughout the 24 hours.

Diary of the Armed Guard Gunnery Officer on the S.S. Charles Sumner

Charles L. Sawyer - Commanding
September 7, 1943

0715 - Reveille.
0730 - Breakfast.
0900 - Muster. Daily inspection of magazines. Temperatures, Small Arms

Charles Sumner - Liberty - 7176 Tons
September 8, 1943

0715 - Reveille.
0730 - Breakfast.
0900 - Muster. Inspection of quarters.

64-73, 4 inch 62-70, 3 inch 60-72.
1130 - Dinner.
1200 - Liberty granted. Ralph Seth
S1/c 753-02-92 and Horace Foster
S1/c 351-06-64 returned. Both were
convicted in Magistrates court St.
Johns, Newfoundland on charges of
drunkenness and disorderly conduct.
Punishment awarded was $5.00 fine
each, Newfoundland currency.
1630 - Supper.
Gun watch maintained throughout the
24 hours. T. Bowerman, GM3/c
assigned to shore patrol.

0930 - Daily inspection of magazines
Temperatures, Small Arms 63-75, 4
inch 63-73, 3 inch 62-73.
1100 - Physical drill.
1130 - Dinner.
1200 - Liberty granted.
1630 - Supper.
G. Hazuka GM3/c assigned to shore
patrol. Gun watches maintained
throughout the 24 hours.

Diary of the Armed Guard Gunnery Officer on the S.S. Charles Sumner

---

Charles L. Sawyer - Commanding
September 9, 1943

Charles Sumner - Liberty - 7176 Tons
September 10, 1943

0715 - Reveille.
0730 - Breakfast.
0900 - Muster.
0930 - Daily inspection of
magazines. Temperatures, Small Arms
62-73, 4 inch 66-75, 3 inch 60-72.
1115 - Received air raid notice
from USNLO.
1130 - Dinner.
1630 - Supper.
2315 - Air raid alarm, civilian
drill. Men at General Quarters
stations.
2400 - Secured from General
Quarters.
Gun watches maintained throughout
the 24 hours.

0715 - Reveille.
0730 - Breakfast.
0900 - Muster.
0915 - Daily inspection of magazines
Temperatures, Small Arms 66-72, 4
inch 68-74, 3 inch 60-69.
1030 - Physical drill.
1130 - Dinner.
1630 - Supper.
Gun watches maintained throughout
the 24 hours.

Diary of the Armed Guard Gunnery Officer on the S.S. Charles Sumner

---

Charles L. Sawyer - Commanding
September 11, 1943

Charles Sumner - Liberty - 7176 Tons
September 12, 1943

0715 - Reveille.
0730 - Breakfast.
0915 - Muster. Inspection of
magazines. Temperatures, Small Arms
67-72, 4 inch 68-74, 3 inch 58-71.
Turn to on issuing of sea gear.
Stripping, cleaning and inspecting
20 MM guns.
1130 - Dinner.
1630 - Supper.
1800 - Men at quarters for sailing.
1910 - Secured from quarters.
Set condition three watch. Guns
maintained till 1800. Condition
three watch maintained from 1910.

0530 - General Quarters. Out of
convoy and proceeding independently.
Guns trained and elevated through
their full arcs. Firing circuits
tested. Reported working properly.
0630 - Secured from General Quarters
0715 - Reveille.
0730 - Breakfast.
0900 - Muster.
1100 - Physical drill.
1130 - Dinner.
1400 - Daily inspection of magazines
Temperatures, Small Arms 69-75, 4
inch 67-75, 3 inch 62-69.
1500 - Supper.

Condition three maintained throughout the 24 hours. International fog signal and range light burned during fog.
2400 - Clocks advanced one half hour

Diary of the Armed Guard Gunnery Officer on the S.S. Charles Sumner

Charles L. Sawyer - Commanding
September 13, 1943

Joined Convoy
0715 - Reveille.
0730 - Breakfast.
1130 - Dinner.
1300 - Muster.
1315 - Daily inspection of magazines. Temperatures, Small Arms 66-69, 4 inch 66-69, 3 inch 63-63.
1630 - Physical Drill.
1700 - Supper.
2015 - General quarters. Guns and sights trained and elevated through their full arcs. Firing circuits & lights checked. Reported working properly.
2115 - Secured from general quarters.
2400 - Condition three watch maintained throughout 24 hours. Clocks retarded one hour. W. Arthur S1/c completed his 48 hours extra duty.

Charles Sumner - Liberty - 7176 Tons
September 14, 1943

0515 - General Quarters. Guns, sights, and firing circuits checked. Reported working properly.
0615 - General Quarters secured.
0715 - Reveille.
0730 - Breakfast.
1130 - Dinner.
1300 - Battle station drill. All hands. 20 MM crews drilled. 3 & 4 inch pointer and sightsetter drill.
1315 - Battle stations secured and proceeded to fire stations and abandon ship stations.
1530 - 20 MM guns cleaned. 3 and 4 inch guns checked and aired. Magazines secured and inspected. Temperatures, Small Arms 67-75, 4 inch 68-76, 3 inch 62-73.
1700 - Supper.
1930 - General Quarters. Guns, sights and firing circuits checked. Reported working properly. Range set at 800 yards. Blackout reported complete.
2030 - General Quarters secured. Clocks retarded one hour.

Diary of the Armed Guard Gunnery Officer on the S.S. Charles Sumner

Charles L. Sawyer - Commanding
September 15, 1943

0430 - General Quarters. Guns trained and elevated through their full arcs. Firing circuits checked. Reported working properly. Range set at 2000 yards.
0545 - General Quarters secured.
0715 - Reveille.
0730 - Breakfast.
1130 - Dinner.
1300 - Muster. Daily inspection of magazines. Temperatures, Small Arms 73-76, 4 inch 74-76, 3 inch 68-75.
1700 - Supper.
1915 - General Quarters. Blackout reported complete.

Charles Sumner - Liberty - 7176 Tons
September 16, 1943

0445 - General Quarters. Guns and sights trained and elevated through their full arcs. Firing circuits checked. Reported working properly. Range set at 2000 yards.
0545 - General Quarters secured.
0715 - Reveille.
0730 - Breakfast.
1130 - Dinner.
1300 - Muster. Turn to on the cleaning of guns.
1600 - Daily inspection of magazines Temperatures, Small Arms 74-80, 4 inch 75-80, 3 inch 72-78.
1845 - General Quarters. Guns and

1945 - Secured from General Quarters. Condition three watch maintained throughout the 24 hours.

sights trained and elevated through their full arcs. Lights and firing circuits checked. Reported working properly. Blackout reported complete
1930 - General Quarters secured. Condition three maintained throughout 24 hours.

Diary of the Armed Guard Gunnery Officer on the S.S. Charles Sumner

Charles L. Sawyer - Commanding
September 17, 1943

Charles Sumner - Liberty - 7176 Tons
September 18, 1943

0445 - General Quarters. Guns and sights trained and elevated through their full arcs. Firing circuits checked. Reported working properly.
0550 - Secured from General Qtrs.
0715 - Reveille.
0730 - Breakfast.
1130 - Dinner.
1300 - General alarm. Battle stations drill. 3 and 4 inch gun crews drilled. 20 MM crews drilled in loading. Fire and Abandon Ship drill. All hands.
1330 - Drill secured.
1600 - Muster.
1630 - Daily inspection of magazines. Temperatures, Small Arms 75-80, 4 inch 76-80, 3 inch 72-76.
1700 - Supper.
1845 - General Quarters. Guns and sights trained and elevated through their full arcs. Lights and firing circuits checked. Reported working properly.
1945 - General Quarters secured. Condition three watch maintained throughout the 24 hours.

0515 - General Quarters. Guns and sights trained and elevated. Range set at 2000 yards. Firing circuits checked. Reported all working properly.
0615 - Secured from General Quarters
0700 Reveille.
0730 - Breakfast.
0830 - Crew mustered, turned to on stowing gear.
1000 - Quarters inspected.
1100 - Magazines opened for airing. Temperatures, Small Arms 75-80, 4 inch 76-80, 3 inch 70-77.
1130 - Dinner.
1300 - Condition three secured, gun watch posted.
1630 - Supper
2000 - Liberty granted, starboard watch to 0900.
Deguassing questionary turned in to inspecting officer by Captain.

Diary of the Armed Guard Gunnery Officer on the S.S. Charles Sumner

Charles L. Sawyer - Commanding
September 19, 1943

Charles Sumner - Liberty - 7176 Tons
September 20, 1943

0715 - Reveille.
0730 - Breakfast
0900 - Crew mustered. All present or accounted for. Church liberty granted.
1130 - Dinner.
1200 - Liberty to 0900 granted to port watch. Daily inspection of magazines. Temperatures, Small Arms 74-80, 4 inch 77-82, 3 inch 72-75.

0715 - Reveille.
0730 - Breakfast.
0900 - Crew mustered, all present or accounted for. Turned to or assigned work. Daily inspection of magazines, Temperatures, Small Arms 76-82, 4 inch 78-86, 3 inch 72-78.
1200 - Liberty granted to Starboard watch.
2000 - T. Bowerman GM3/c requested the shore patrol to pick up Frank Campbell S1/c and John Shuey S1/c on

charges of drunkenness, having liquor on board in violation of general orders and fighting. Taken to U.S. Naval Armed Guard Center in Brooklyn. Men on subsistance one (1) meal.

Diary of the Armed Guard Gunnery Officer on the S.S. Charles Sumner

Charles L. Sawyer - Commanding September 21, 1943	Charles Sumner - Liberty - 7176 Tons September 22, 1943
0715 - Reveille. 0730 - Breakfast one half crew ashore at a time - all meals logged 0900 - Crew mustered. All present and accounted for. 1200 - Liberty granted to Port section. 1500 - Supplies received aboard. 1600 - Daily inspection of magazines. Temperatures, Small Arms 78-81, 4 inch 75-84, 3 inch 75-77. Men on subsistance three (3) meals.	0715 - Reveille. 0730 - Breakfast. 0900 - Crew mustered, all present or accounted for, turned to on assigned work. Daily inspection of magazines, Temperatures, Small Arms, 74-78, 4 inch 76-84, 3 inch 72-76. 1200 - Liberty granted to Starboard Section. 1430 - Thomas R. Bowerman, GM3c 604 79 36 V-6 USNR detached. Mulqueen, Thomas Howard 618 67 30 SM3/c V-6 USNR detached. Foster, Horace Century 351 06 64 S1/c USN detached. Blackwell, Dewey Ransom, Jr. 2626826 SM3c USN reported for duty. Summerville, Sarford Thurl, 250 78 09 S1/c USN reported for duty Gear belonging to Campbell and Shuey sent to Armed Guard Center. Men on subsistance three (3) meals.

Diary of the Armed Guard Gunnery Officer on the S.S. Charles Sumner

Charles L. Sawyer - Commanding September 23, 1943	Charles Sumner - Liberty - 7176 Tons September 24, 1943
0715 - Reveille. 0915 - Crew mustered, all present or accounted for. Daily inspection of quarters and magazines. Temperatures, 4 inch 74-80, 3 inch 70-80. 1200 - P. Archung, Coxswain, A. Dodrill, SM3/c, E. Byrne, S1/c, D. Oliver, S1/c, G. Pribble, S1/c, K. Stockwell, S1/c, granted special liberty to 0900 September 27, 1943. Men on subsistance three (3) meals. Ammunition moved from Small Arms Magazine to four inch magazine.	0700 - Reveille. 0900 - Crew mustered, all present or accounted for. Daily inspection of quarters and magazines. Temperatures 4 inch 76-82, 3 inch 68-76. 1300 - Group No. 1; G. Antrim, C. Chittum, V. Clark, Acting P.O., S. Summerville, J. Meyers, R. Miller, A. Morgan, F. Tafflinger, ashore for Armed Guard Gunnery School. Men on subsistance three (3) meals.

Diary of the Armed Guard Gunnery Officer on the S.S. Charles Sumner

Charles L. Sawyer - Commanding
September 25, 1943

Charles Sumner - Liberty - 7176 Tons
September 26, 1943

0715 - Reveille.
0900 - Mustered crew, all present or accounted for. Daily inspection of magazines, Temperatures, 4 inch 77-84, 3 inch 72-79.
1130 - Dinner, end of subsistance. Three meals a day aboard.
1900 - Group No. 1 returned from gunnery school. Liberty granted.

0715 - Reveille.
0900 - Crew mustered, all present or accounted for. Daily inspection of magazines. Temperatures, 4 inch 74-84, 3 inch 68-75.
1200 - Liberty granted.

Diary of the Armed Guard Gunnery Officer on the S.S. Charles Sumner

Charles L. Sawyer - Commanding   Charles Sumner - Liberty - 7176 Tons
September 27, 1943

0700 - Reveille.
0715 - Group I returned to Gunnery School.
0900 - Crew mustered, all present or accounted for. Daily inspection of magazines, Temperatures, 4 inch 74-82, 3 inch 70-74.
1200 - G. Hazuka, W. Arthur, R. Fenton, G. Rinehart, R. Seth, G. Stroud, granted special liberty.
1700 - Group I aboard from Gunnery School.

Diary of the Armed Guard Gunnery Officer on the S.S. Lewis Luckenbach

Wednesday, December 8, 1943   Wednesday, December 8, 1943

S.S. Lewis Luckenbach
Type of vessel: Cargo
Type of cargo: General
Owner: Luckenbach Steamship Co. Inc
Chartered to: United States Army

Name	Rate	Service
McCarthy, Charles G.	Ens	I-V(S)
Roberts, Donald E.	Cox	USN
Bowerman, Thomas R.	GM2c	USNR
Newstad, Theodore M.	GM3c	USNR
Brzozowski, James A.	S1c	USNR
Harper, Louis C.	S1c	USNR
Lesesne, David M.	S1c	USNR
Strominger, Harry C.	S1c	USNR
Talaska, Edmund J.	S1c	USNR
Vaughn, Elwood E.	S1c	USNR
Volzer, Ted W.	S1c	USNR
Wilderman, Robert I.	S1c	USNR
Williams, Richard H.	S1c	USNR
Wilson, William H.	S1c	USNR
Wilson, Frank L.	S1c	USNR
Wright, John C.	S1c	USNR
Williams, Joseph R.	S1c	USNR
Wade, William D.	S1c	USNR

Ward, Keith A.	S1c	USNR
Watkins, David L.	S1c	USNR
West, Ralph M.	S1c	USNR
Westbrook, Estel W.	S1c	USNR
White, Robert L.	S1c	USNR
Young, Ralph J.	S1c	USNR
Zielinski, Robert M.	S1c	USNR
Kirksey, Oliver C.	SM3c	USNR
Lewis, Jack D.	SM3c	USNR
Smith, Richard P.	RM3c	USNR

Note: West, Ralph M. and Smith, R.P. and Zielinski, R.M. hospitalized in Cardiff, Wales.
Butler, Thomas George, RM3c, USN, assigned on duty in Cardiff, Wales, in substitution for Smith, R.P. Zielinski returned to ship just hours before departure. West had returned earlier.

Diary of the Armed Guard Gunnery Officer on the S.S. Lewis Luckenbach

Thursday, December 9, 1943
EWT 1900

Smith, R.P., R.M. 3/c complained of pain and running in his left ear. Ship had already been restricted prior to sailing. With the aid of Chief Gunner Vasburgh of the P.D.O. Army Base, took Smith to the Armed Guard Center where he was examined by Lt.Comdr. Nolan, who finally, though a little reluctantly said it would be all right for Smith to sail.

Mag Temp.: Fwd: 45 Aft: 47
Friday, December 10, 1943

EWT 0600
Undocked from Pier 4, Army Base, Brooklyn, N.Y. and got under way. Sea Watch (Cond. III) had previously been set.
EWT 0930
Muster for all hands except watch. Watches and how to stand them explained again. Lifebelt equipment distributed. Cigarettes (5 packs per man) distributed. Short talk on routine matters given, e.g. seriousness of job, sharp lookouts, prompt reporting, etc.

Convoy HX270 - 10 KTS. - N.Y. to U.K. 56 ships. This ship is # 131, starboard wing, column leader. Escort: 3 HMCS. Weather: Cloudy (low-hanging), visability good.

EWT: 1830
General Quarters until 1905. Broadside guns trained, elevated-depressed (barrels and sight drums). Switches tested - all satisfactory. Weather: Clear. Broken clouds, occasional bright moonlight - full moon.

Diary of the Armed Guard Gunnery Officer on the S.S. Lewis Luckenbach

Mag Temp: Fwd: 44   Aft: 45
Saturday, December 11, 1943

EWT 0630-0705 - General Quarters held - all guns OK. Weather partially cloudy; occasional bright moonlight; visibility fair.
EWT 0800 - Driving rain, sleet, snow; visibility materially cut down.
EWT 0945 - Muster for enlisted crew
EWT 1200 - Sea becoming very rough.
EWT 1204 - SOS received from KGGN, 71.58W, 40.43N - foundering.
EWT 1300 - High waves occasionally breaking over bow and stern.
EWT 1400 - Bow watch moved aft to promenade deck. 50 gas masks issued to Chief Mate McCann for distribution to merchant crew.
EWT 1500 - Great majority of enlisted men very seasick.
EWT 1600 - Apparently lost convoy except for two or three ships and an escort. Seas very rough, wind exceedingly strong with driving rain and snow. Waves breaking over stern. Stern watch moved from gun position to deck. Broadside guns trained and pointed periodically throughout day - found okay.

Mag Temp: Fwd: 42   Aft: 43
Sunday, December 12, 1943

EWT 0400 - Seas somewhat less rough - cloudy - visibility poor. Ship apparently proceeding alone. No other ships in sight. Running lights on. Spoke to Chief Mate on watch about them. Extinguished.
EWT 0645-0730 - General Quarters. Guns all all right. Seas calming. Picked up convoy again.
EWT 1200 - Crew all feeling better again. Guns 1-2-4-6-9 cleaned and greased.
Ralph M. West, Sea 1C reported that during an attack of severe seasickness he lost a three-tooth partial denture from the upper front of his mouth, over the side.

Diary of the Armed Guard Gunnery Officer on the S.S. Lewis Luckenbach

Mag Temp: Fwd: 46   Aft: 45
Monday, December 13, 1943

EWT - 0400 - Weather clear.
EWT - 1200 - Picked up 17 addition- al ships at Halifax, N.S. Escort apparently increased also, akthough exact number not known.
Guns 8 and 10 cleaned and greased.
EWT - 1750 - General Quarters to 1830.
EWT + 1 Hr - 2000 - Finally secured merchant crew list from Purser Roberts showing boat and battle stations. Will correlate it with Navy crew list battle stations.
EWT + 1 Hr - 2400 - Time advanced one hour as of 0200, 12/14/43. Watches' time of duty advanced 20 minutes for each of them starting at 2000 today.

Mag Temp: Fwd: 49   Aft: 48
Tuesday, December 14, 1943

EWT + 1 Hr - 1300 - Boat Drill
EWT + 1 Hr - 1330 - Battle Station Drill

Diary of the Armed Guard Gunnery Officer on the S.S. Lewis Luckenbach

Mag Temp: Fwd: 47   Aft: 47
Wednesday, December 15, 1943

EWT + 1 Hr - 0600 - Rain, sleet, snow, high wind. Barometer falling.
EWT + 1 Hr - 1200 - Position 45-02N 50-24W; course 076.
EWT + 1 Hr - 1400 - Heavy seas breaking over bow. Bow watch secured and moved to promenade deck forward.

Battle helmets have been distributed to Chief Mate McCann, 2nd Mate Roberts, 3rd Mate McPhee and to Captain Olsson.

Mag Temp: Fwd: 42   Aft: 44
Thursday, December 16, 1943

EWT + 1 Hr - 0115 - Distress message received from KCTG to the effect that she is under submarine attack at 48.47N - 22.01W.
EWT + 1 Hr - 0645 - General Quarters to 0710. Guns all ok.
EWT + 1 Hr - 1200 - Position of vessel: 44-38N, 47-20W. Course 098.

British-type battle helmets given to Chief Mate McCann for distribution to the seven members of his emergency party.

Diary of the Armed Guard Gunnery Officer on the S.S. Lewis Luckenbach

Mag Temp: Fwd: 44   Aft: 46
Friday, December 17, 1943

EWT + 1 Hr - 0620-0720 - General Quarters stood. Guns all fully trained and elevated - all OK.
EWT + 1 Hr - 0715 - Biplane - probably Albacore from convoy escort carrier - circled convoy twice.
Capt. Olsson given gas mask, bringing total distributed to 51.

Guns 3,5 and 7 cleaned and lubricated.

Mag Temp: Fwd 40   Aft: 42
Saturday, December 18, 1943

EWT + 1 Hr - 0615-0715 - General Quarters. All guns trained and elevated fully - all OK.
EWT + 1 Hr - 2000 - Time advanced one hour as of 0200, December 19, 1943. Watches time of starting duty advanced 20 minutes for each of them starting at 2000 today.

Diary of the Armed Guard Gunnery Officer on the S.S. Lewis Luckenbach

Mag Temp: Fwd: 47   Aft: 49
Sunday, December 19, 1943

EWT + 2 Hrs - 0640-0720 - General Quarters. All guns fully trained and elevated. All 'OK.
EWT + 2 Hrs - 0715 - Two explosions heard. Presumed to be depth charges Location and distance or cause not determined.
EWT + 2 Hrs - 0810 - Message received from Commodore to effect there are submarines in vicinity. Lookouts and all Navy crew warned to keep especially sharp watch.
EWT + 2 Hrs - 0930 - Commodore signalled emergency turn 45 degrees to starboard.

Mag Temp: Fwd: 47   Aft: 49
Monday, December 20, 1943

EWT + 2 Hrs - 0600-0720 - General Quarters. All guns fully trained and elevated. All OK.
EWT + 2 Hrs - 1230 - Message received from Commodore "Mines reported in vicinity." T. Bowerman, GM2c stationed on bridge with .30 caliber rifle, and lookouts warned. Both .30 cal. Remington Rifles test fired today.
EWT + 2 Hrs - 1535 - Message received from Commodore:"Submarines known to be at position indicated." However, no position was specified. Navy watch and rest of Navy crew

EWT + 2 Hrs - 1130 - Message received from Commodore to effect we are now in submarine zone and column leaders should keep better position.
EWT + 2 Hrs - 1645-1735 - General Quarters and gun drill. 5"51 gun cleaned and lubricated today.

informed and again warned to keep sharp watch.
EWT + 2 Hrs - 1620-1730 - General Quarters.

Diary of the Armed Guard Gunnery Officer on the S.S. Lewis Luckenbach

Mag Temp: Fwd: 46   Aft: 46
Tuesday, December 21, 1943

EWT + 2 Hrs - 0600-0720 - General Quarters. All guns fully trained and elevated. All OK.
EWT + 2 Hrs - 0815 - Commodore signalled emergency turn 45 degrees starboard.
EWT + 2 Hrs - 0820 - Commodore signalled emergency turn 45 degrees starboard.
EWT + 2 Hrs - 0945 - Commodore signalled "Unidentified aircraft approaching." General Quarters called.
EWT + 2 Hrs - 1000 - Signal of Commodore of 0945 hauled down. General Quarters continued until 1100. Gun drills, tracking, etc., on all guns in that hour.
EWT + 2 Hrs - 1055 - Commodore signalled emergency turn 45 degrees port.
EWT + 2 Hrs - 1230 - Message received from Commodore to effect that we might fire our machine guns and "two-pounders" in a safe direction at 1330.
EWT + 2 Hrs - 1300 - Fire, boat, and battle-station drills to 1330.
EWT + 2 Hrs - 1330 - Fired guns #2,3,4,5,6,7,8 (20 MM's) for an approximate total expenditure of 240 rounds. Fired #1 gun (3"50) with 2 anti aircraft shells (2 second setting on fuze) and 3 common rounds. Merchant crew were instructed and participated as loaders on the 20 MM guns during firing. Secured at 1400. No structural defects noted except an observed recoil on the 3"50 fire which was possibly a little too violent. Recoil cylinder on this gun will be checked.
EWT + 2 Hrs - 1615 - General

Continued from previous page
Tuesday, December 21, 1943

duty advanced 20 minutes for each of the three watches starting at 2000 today.
Guns #1,6 and 8 cleaned and lubricated today. 3"50 cleaned, lubricated and bore gauged.

Quarters until 1705.
EWT + 2 Hrs - 2000 - Time advanced one hour as of 0200, December 22, 1943. Watches' time of starting

Diary of the Armed Guard Gunnery Officer on the S.S. Lewis Luckenbach

Mag Temp: Fwd: 42 Aft: 42
Wednesday, December 22, 1943

EWT + 3 Hrs - 0645-0745 - General Quarters. All guns fully trained and elevated. All OK.
EWT + 3 Hrs - 1000-1130 - Progress Test #1 in Seaman 1 cl given to R.H. Williams and R. Young Sea 1cl.
EWT + 3 Hrs - 1400-1500 - Progress Test #1 in Seaman 1cl given to E.W. Westbrook, Sea 1cl.

Mag Temp: Fwd: 45 Aft: 46
Thursday, December 23, 1943

EWT + 3 Hrs - 0645-0740 - General Quarters. All guns fully trained and elevated. All OK.
EWT + 3 Hrs - 1000-1100 - Progress Test #1 in Seaman 1cl given to K. Ward, D. Watkins, and R. West, Sea 1cl.
EWT + 3 Hrs - 1630-1730 - General Quarters.
Guns #3,5,7,2, and 4 cleaned and lubricated today.
Time advanced one hour as of 0200, December 24, 1943. Watches' time of starting duty advanced 20 minutes for each of the three watches starting at 2000 today. Now observing Greenwich Mean Time.

Diary of the Armed Guard Gunnery Officer on the S.S. Lewis Luckenbach

Mag Temp: Fwd: 49 Aft: 48
Friday, December 24, 1943

GMT - 0715-0800 - General Quarters
GMT - 0800 - Flickering light was observed ahead, two points on the port bow. One of the escort went over to investigate and then continued on. When light came abeam it was seen to be in the water. It was probably one attached to a life ring and because of its flickering was believed to be probably a carbide lamp. Ship let it pass to port between columns 12 and 13. Approximate position 55-30N, 09-03W.
GMT - 1430 - Progress Test #1 in Seaman 1cl was given to J.C. Wright and to F.L. Wilson Sea1cl.
GMT - 1730 - General Quarters to 1815.
GMT - 2000 - Time advanced one hour as of 0200, December 25, 1943. Watches time of starting duty advanced 20 minutes for each of the three watches starting at 2000 today. Now observing Greenwich Mean

Mag Temp: Fwd: 47 Aft: 49
Sunday, December 26, 1943

BST - 0800 - Field Day for crews quarters.
BST - 1030 - Inspection of crews quarters. All satisfactory.
BST - 1120 - Officially arrived at port of Cardiff, Wales. Anchored in stream due to fog.
BST - 1430 - T.R. Bowerman GM 2c and Lt. Long, U.S. Army Cargo Security Officer on this ship informed Ensign McCarthy that the after cargo hold of the ship had been rifled and a wooden box broken open from which forty-eight 10-inch commercial phonograph recordings, 25 radio-broadcast transcriptions, and several "tonettes" (small musical instruments) had been taken. This after hold is adjacent to the ship's after magazine and is entered by way of the same hatch. In this connection it is noted that several days before sailing from New York, Ensign McCarthy had noticed that the entrance door to the after hold was

Time plus one hour for British Summer Time.

Mag Temp: Fwd: 48   Aft: 48
Saturday, December 25, 1943

BST 0815 - General Quarters to 0855

5"51 gun cleaned and lubricated today.

ajar and the cargo exposed and informed Lt. Long of that fact. Further inspection several days later showed that nothing had been done about it. Captain Olsson was immediately made cognizant of the loss.
BST - 1430-1630 - A thorough inspection of the quarters, gear, bags and lockers of the U.S. Navy crew was made by Ensign McCarthy. This was done as a result of the incident noted at 1430. Search was negative.
BST - 1630 - U.S. Navy gun crew was warned not to accept anything, under any conditions, or for any reason from the merchant crew; and were warned again of the serious consequences of smuggling articles ashore for themselves or others.
BST - 2000 - Passed through lock and anchored at the buoys at Queens Dock, Cardiff, Wales.

Diary of the Armed Guard Gunnery Officer on the S.S. Lewis Luckenbach

---

Mag Temp: Fwd: 46   Aft: 47
Monday, December 27, 1943

BST - 1030 - Supply Officer came aboard and paid Navy crew.
BST - 1330 - Spoke to Lt. Lyons of the U.S. Naval Port Office, Cardiff, re ship and voyage. Submitted information and repair list.
BST - 1430 - Men mustered on the bridge of the S.S. John Gallup alongside, with the crew of that ship, and were addressed by Lt. Lyons.
BST - 1500 - Signalman 2nd cl. Progress Tests Nos. 1 and 2 given to Oliver C. Kirksey, SM 3c.
Stayed anchored all day in the stream to the buoys. - No cargo worked.

Mag Temp: Fwd: 48   Aft: 48
Tuesday, December 28, 1943

BST

Submitted voyage report to Lt. Lyons of the Cardiff Port Office.

Stayed anchored at buoys - No cargo worked.

Diary of the Armed Guard Gunnery Officer on the S.S. Lewis Luckenbach

---

Mag Temp: Fwd: 48   Aft: 48
Wednesday, December 29, 1943

BST - 2300 - Kirksey, O.C., SM3c was brought aboard by the shore patrol and was charged with speaking and chatting with a girl while he himself was on shore patrol duty. The offence allegedly

Mag Temp: Fwd: 47   Aft: 47
Thursday, December 30, 1943

BST
Stevedores worked 3 1/2 hours moving 102 tons of cargo.

occurred on St. Mary Street in Cardiff about 2130. Kirksey explained to Ensign McCarthy that he knew the girl and had been out with her the night before while on liberty and that she had come up to him tonight and spoken to him. Kirksey was given five days restriction.

Moved today to the quayside. Army stevedores worked six hours removing 222 tons of deck cargo.

Diary of the Armed Guard Gunnery Officer on the S.S. Lewis Luckenbach

Mag Temp: Fwd: 49 Aft: 49
Friday, December 31, 1943

BST - 1500 - West, R.M., Sea1c, while playing in a game of basketball arranged by the U.S. Naval Port Office, Cardiff, turned on his ankle and injured it. Was sent to the U.S. Army Station Hospital #348, APO 872, for treatment of a moderate sprain. He was kept there.

Stevedores worked 8 hours moving 266 tons of cargo.

Mag Temp: Fwd: 45 Aft: 45
Saturday, January 1, 1944

BST
Stevedores worked 4 hours moving 81 tons of cargo.

Diary of the Armed Guard Gunnery Officer on the S.S. Lewis Luckenbach

Mag Temp: Fwd: 47 Aft: 50
Sunday, January 2, 1944

BST
Stevedores worked 5 1/2 hours moving 222 tons cargo.

Mag Temp: Fwd: 48 Aft: 51
Monday, January 3, 1944

BST
Stevedores worked 10 1/2 hours moving 281 tons cargo.

Diary of the Armed Guard Gunnery Officer on the S.S. Lewis Luckenbach

Mag Temp: Fwd: 49 Aft: 48
Tuesday, January 4, 1944

BST
Stevedores worked 10 hours moving 332 tons of cargo.

Mag Temp: Fwd: 51 Aft: 52
Wednesday, January 5, 1944

BST
5"51 gun cleaned and lubricated as was 20 MM # 4.
Stevedores worked 9 1/2 hours moving 265 tons of cargo.

Diary of the Armed Guard Gunnery Officer on the S.S. Lewis Luckenbach

Mag Temp: Fwd: 49 Aft: 49
Thursday, January 6, 1944

BST
Stevedores worked 7 1/2 hours

Mag Temp: Fwd: 48 Aft: 49
Friday, January 7, 1944

BST
Stevedores worked 9 hours moving

moving 146 tons of cargo.	263 tons of cargo.

Diary of the Armed Guard Gunnery Officer on the S.S. Lewis Luckenbach

Mag Temp: Fwd: 47 Aft: 47 Saturday, January 8, 1944 BST Stevedores worked 3 hours moving 110 tons of cargo.	Mag Temp: Fwd: 51 Aft: 50 Sunday, January 9, 1944 BST Stevedores worked 5 hours moving 236 tons of cargo.

Diary of the Armed Guard Gunnery Officer on the S.S. Lewis Luckenbach

Mag Temp: Fwd: 50 Aft: 49 Monday, January 10, 1944 BST Stevedores worked 9 1/2 hours moving 302 tons of cargo.	Mag Temp: Fwd: 50 Aft: 48 Tuesday, January 11, 1944 BST - 1400 - West, R.M., Sea1c, returned to ship and to duty from hospital where he had been undergoing treatment since December 31, 1943. Stevedores worked 2 hours moving 25 tons of deck cargo.

Diary of the Armed Guard Gunnery Officer on the S.S. Lewis Luckenbach

Mag Temp: Fwd: 51 Aft: 48 Wednesday, January 12, 1944 BST Stevedores worked ten hours moving 550 tons of cargo.	Mag Temp: Fwd: 48 Aft: 49 Thursday, January 13, 1944 BST Stevedores worked 6 hours moving 163 tons of cargo.

Diary of the Armed Guard Gunnery Officer on the S.S. Lewis Luckenbach

Mag Temp: Fwd: 54 Aft: 56 Friday, January 14, 1944 BST Stevedores worked 9 hours moving 374 tons of cargo.	Mag Temp: Fwd: 50 Aft: 52 Saturday, January 15, 1944 BST Stevedores worked ten hours moving 262 tons of cargo.

Diary of the Armed Guard Gunnery Officer on the S.S. Lewis Luckenbach

Mag Temp: Fwd: 52 Aft: 51 Sunday, January 16, 1944 BST - 1300 - Smith, R.P., RM 3c, sent to U.S. Army Dispensary, Cardiff, for treatment of infected and swollen right hand. From there he was sent to and admitted to the U.S. Army Station Hospital #348, APO 872, for more extensive	Mag Temp: Fwd: 52 Aft: 49 Monday, January 17, 1944 BST Stevedores worked 22 1/2 hours moving 848 tons.

treatment, on authority of U.S.
Naval Port Office, Cardiff.
Stevedores worked 17 hours moving
517 tons.

Diary of the Armed Guard Gunnery Officer on the S.S. Lewis Luckenbach

Mag Temp: Fwd: 51   Aft: 51
Tuesday, January 18, 1944

BST
Stevedores worked 22 1/2 hours
moving 848 tons.

Mag Temp: Fwd: 51   Aft: 51
Wednesday, January 19, 1944

BST - 1200 Butler, Thomas George,
RM3c, USN, 207 41 97, reported
aboard for duty under orders from
the U.S. Naval Port Officer,
Cardiff, in substitution for Smith,
Richard P., RM3c, USNR, 6601445,
who is left in hospital and detached
from ship. Smith's gear put ashore
in custody of U.S. Naval Port Office
BST - 1200 - Lt. Comdr. Bishop,
officer in charge of shore patrol in
Cardiff came aboard and asked that
the liberty party of Thursday,
January 13 be brought to him
individually for questioning with
regard to an alleged assault by two
American sailors on the proprietor
of the Carleton pub in Cardiff on
January 13. The men were summoned
and after questioning all he took
ashore O.C. Kirksey, SM3c, and K.A.
Ward, Sea1c, to his office for
further questioning, saying that he
was convinced that these two men
were those involved and further that
their offense was concealed and not
reported by the shore patrolman from
this ship on duty that night, R.P.
Smith, RM3c, now in hospital in
Cardiff.
BST - 1600 - Ensign McCarthy went to
the Naval Port Office to get full
particulars from Lt. Comdr. Bishop
re circumstances of entry of 1200.
Found that he had left for the day
and that he had questioned Kirksey
and Ward, took a statement from
them, and then sent them back to
the ship. Ensign McCarthy telephoned
Mr. Bishop and asked him for a copy
of the statement he had taken from
the men. This he refused to do saying that he would take care of
everything by forwarding a copy of
the statement to the Brooklyn Armed
Guard Center where the men would be
disciplined. The men are aboard now
and will be kept aboard until after

Diary of the Armed Guard Gunnery Officer on the S.S. Lewis Luckenbach

Wednesday, January 19, 1944 (Cont)

officials at Brooklyn Armed Guard Center tell me what action to take in the light of the information they presumably will have received by time of arrival in New York.

Stevedores worked 14 1/4 hours moving the remaining 399 tons. Grand total 6500 tons, in 25 days, from day of arrival to today.

Coal slag loaded today: 886 tons in 4 hours.

Mag Temp: Fwd: 51 Aft: 50
Thursday, January 20, 1944

BST - 0000 - Ship restricted preparatory to sailing.

Coal slag loaded today: 1500 tons in 11 1/2 hours. Grand total loaded: 2386 tons.

Diary of the Armed Guard Gunnery Officer on the S.S. Lewis Luckenbach

Mag Temp: Fwd: 50 Aft: 47
Friday, January 21, 1944

BST - 0300 - Cast off from Queens Dock, Cardiff, Wales.
BST - 0415 - Left Cardiff docks.
BST - 1200 - Dropped anchor at Milford Haven, Wales, to form convoy.
BST - 1600 - DEMS enlisted man came aboard to explain target firing on leaving Milford Haven.
BST - 1600 - Zielinski, Robert M., Sea1c, complained of feeling ill. Abdomen tender to touch; nauseated; temperature and pulse normal. Sent to bunk. No medicine or food or drink given. Hot water bottle placed on abdomen.
BST - 1930 - Zielinski called again, said he felt worse. Pain localized to some extent in left abdomen, temperature 101 degrees, pulse strong at 100. Has had no food or drink since breakfast. Physician signalled for from nearby ship.
BST - 2230 - British Naval Control Tug came alongside for Zielinski. Had no doctor aboard. Took him ashore to hospital.

Received word today that we are to sail tomorrow. Conference at Milford Haven at 1100, January 22, 1944.

Mag Temp: Fwd: 51 Aft: 50
Saturday, January 22, 1944

BST
Conference postponed - sailing put off 24 hours.

Received word from British Naval Control that Zielinski would not be able to rejoin ship and that his gear would be called for tomorrow. Packed his gear, tagged it and prepared memorandum to U.S. Naval Port Office, Cardiff, and to Brooklyn Armed Guard Center to be taken off with his gear.

DEMS came aboard and loosened up plug on 5"51 and repaired sight on #2 20MM. Was informed by them would be required to fire all guns on departure. This confirms what Comdr. Pendill, U.S.N. Port Officer, Cardiff, said previously. If refuse to fire, a reprimand will follow - even though target ammunition allowance for period expended.

5"51 cleaned today and lubricated.

Have not been able to get ashore reports on Zielinski and Smith. Will try again tomorrow.

Convoy No.: ONM 221. This ship will have position 113. There will be 19 ships from Milford Haven to be joined at Liverpool by 67 more, when convoy will have 12 columns. Convoy speed scheduled to be 9.5 KTS. Two escorts are listed: HMT Setter from Milford Haven and HMT Aquamarine from Liverpool.

Diary of the Armed Guard Gunnery Officer on the S.S. Lewis Luckenbach

---

Mag Temp: Fwd: 50 Aft: 50
Sunday, January 23, 1944

BST - 1200 - Zielinski was put back aboard ship. Says he was treated as a suspected appendicitis case at the Royal Naval Hospital, Milford Haven, Wales. Was released as recovered today at 1100. No other information was obtainable.
BST - 1330 - Captain informed Ensign McCarthy that he had received orders to sail at 1500.
BST - 1400 - Captain handed Ensign McCarthy revised orders for the target firing on departure. Made every effort to get notices of hospitalization of Smith and Zielinski to U.S. Naval authorities ashore. Not yet successful.
BST - 1600 - Heavy wind and rain. Captain afraid to weigh anchor lest we be thrown on rocks.
BST - 1900 - Rest of convoy gone. Captain has decided to wait until morning and then ask for permission to overtake convoy alone.

Mag Temp: Fwd: 47 Aft: 49
Monday, January 24, 1944

BST - 0800 - Ship weighed anchor and proceeded alone out of Milford Haven to overtake convoy on its way to Liverpool. Captain received orders to do this sometime last night. Sea watches put on.

Have not yet been successful in getting hospitalization notices on Smith and Zielinski ashore. Will try again at Liverpool. If not successful there, must take them to New York.
BST - 1815-1910 - General Quarters
BST - 2110 - Convoy in sight.

Guns were not fired on departure today because ship was late and because sailing was not as originally planned.

Diary of the Armed Guard Gunnery Officer on the S.S. Lewis Luckenbach

---

Mag Temp: Fwd: 48 Aft: 49
Tuesday, January 25, 1944

BST - 0825-0905 - General Quarters.
BST - 1400 - Seas becoming very heavy and wind increasing in force. Forward lookout moved back to bridge and saloon deck.
BST - 1825-1915 - General Quarters.
BST - 2000 - Still accompanying ships of convoy. Have not yet taken position. All ships proceeding in just two columns.

Mag Temp: Fwd: 46 Aft: 47
Wednesday, January 26, 1944

BST - 0845-0925 - General Quarters.
BST - 1400 - Convoy arranged. This ship has taken position 113.
BST - 1845-1925 - General Quarters.

Opportunity has passed to get ashore notices referred to in entry of January 24, 1944. Will have to take them on to New York and submit them there.

Diary of the Armed Guard Gunnery Officer on the S.S. Lewis Luckenbach

Mag Temp: Fwd: 44 Aft: 46
Thursday, January 27, 1944

BST - 0845-0915 - General Quarters.

Time retarded one hour as of 2400. Commencing at 1800 BST time of duty watches retarded 20 minutes for each section.

BST -1/3 Hrs - 1845-1920 - General Quarters.

Mag Temp: Fwd: 43 Aft: 48
Friday, January 28, 1944

GMT - 0930-1005 - General Quarters.
GMT - 1040 - Commodore signalled that enemy submarines are known to be in this vicinity. Condition II put into effect.
GMT - 1400 - Commodore signalled "Submarine sunk." Condition III restored.
GMT - 1830-1915 - General Quarters.

5"51 cleaned and lubricated.

Diary of the Armed Guard Gunnery Officer on the S.S. Lewis Luckenbach

Mag Temp: Fwd: 43 Aft: 45
Saturday, January 29, 1944

GMT - 0815-0955 - General Quarters.
GMT -1/3 Hrs - 1800 - Message from Commodore received to effect that enemy submarines are known to be in vicinity. All lookouts warned accordingly.

Clocks to be retarded one hour as of 2400. Put back 20 minutes for each watch starting at 1800.

GMT -1/3 Hrs - 1815-1855 - General Quarters.

Mag Temp: Fwd: 45 Aft: 47
Sunday, January 30, 1944

GMT-1 Hr - 1030 - Received permission from Commodore to fire 20MM and 5"51 guns at 1100.
GMT-1 Hr - 1100 - Fired 240 rounds from the four starboard 20 MM guns.
GMT-1 Hr - 1115 - Prepared to fire 5"51, and gun misfired. After using all the standard methods of firing without success, it was assumed that a hang fire was in progress, and the gun was secured except for pointer, trainer, gun captain, and battery officer, to see that it was kept trained in a safe direction.
GMT-1 Hr - 1150 - Primer ejected from firing lock of 5"51 without opening breech. It was found to have fired.
GMT-1 Hr - 1155 - 5"51 gun unloaded. Powder bag was thrown over the side and it was observed that the ignition end was partially burned through. It is assumed that the powder had become damp and therefore did not go off. New powder bag was loaded into gun and a new primer inserted. This time the gun fired and was secured. One round expended; one misfire. Bowerman, GM2c, Harper, and Young, Sea1c, and Ens. McCarthy were present during the unloading.
GMT-1 Hr - 1200 - All mounts of guns fired inspected for damage - none found to have been adversely affected by firing.

GMT-1 Hr - 1700 - Clocks to be
retarded one hour as of 2400. Time
for duty of three sections put back
20 minutes as of 1800.
GMT-1 1/3 Hrs - 1810-1845 - General
Quarters.

Noticed that escort was increased by
at least three units - exact number
not known. These include an escort
carrier.

Diary of the Armed Guard Gunnery Officer on the S.S. Lewis Luckenbach

---

Mag Temp: Fwd: 47 Aft: 46
Monday, January 31, 1944

GMT-2 Hrs - 0645-0720 - General
Quarters.
GMT-2 Hrs - 1810-1845 - General
Quarters.

Mag Temp: Fwd: 44 Aft: 45
Tuesday, February 1, 1944

GMT-2 Hrs - 0630-0715 - General
Quarters.
GMT-2 Hrs - 1400 - Storm brewing.
High winds. Waves coming over bow.
Bow watch moved to bridge.
GMT-2 Hrs - 1600 - Gale very severe.
Losing convoy.
GMT-2 Hrs - 1700 - Ships steering
with difficulty. Convoy out of
sight.
GMT-2 Hrs - 1800-1855 - General
Quarters.
GMT-2 Hrs - 2230 - SOS from ship
45, William H. Prescott to effect
that she was breaking in two.

Diary of the Armed Guard Gunnery Officer on the S.S. Lewis Luckenbach

---

Mag Temp: Fwd: 43 Aft: 41
Wednesday, February 2, 1944

GMT-2 Hrs - 0400 - Gale unabated.
GMT-2 Hrs - 0907 - SOS from ship 15
of this convoy - name unknown - to
effect that her starboard side,
forward deck, main deck, between
deck, ship side, and fore and aft
stringer were cracked. She requested assistance. Sustained damage at
0440.
GMT-2 Hrs - 0951 - SOS from ship 15
to effect that she was breaking
constantly and needed assistance.
GMT-2 Hrs - 1200 - Storm abating.
Some ships of convoy in sight.
GMT-2 Hrs - 1700 - Rejoined
Commodore and main body of convoy.
GMT-2 Hrs - 1800-1840 - General
Quarters.

Mag Temp: Fwd: 45 Aft: 43
Thursday, February 3, 1944

GMT-2 Hrs - 0655-0735 - General
Quarters.
GMT-2 1/3 Hrs - 1825-1900 - General
Quarters.

GMT-2 1/3 Hrs - 2400 - Time retarded
one hour. Clocks retarded 20 minutes
for each section of watch
commencing at 1800.

Diary of the Armed Guard Gunnery Officer on the S.S. Lewis Luckenbach

Mag Temp: Fwd: 40 Aft: 41
Friday, February 4, 1944

GMT-3 Hrs - 0615-0705 - General Quarters.
GMT-3 Hrs - 0800 - Noticed that ship was giving off white smoke from her stack. Found it to be due to water having leaked into her fuel tanks - which cannot be corrected until we reach port.
GMT-3 Hrs - 0310 - Radio message from ship 45 of this convoy to effect that she expected to break in two before daylight and was in a heavy gale. (See entry of 2/1/44, 2230.)
GMT-3 Hrs - 0325 - Radio SOS from ship having call letters KIWW: "Lat. 48.10W at 0600 GMT. Vessel breaking in two."
GMT-3 Hrs - 0329 - Radio SOS from KIWW:"Lat 48.10N, Long. 41.10W at 0600 GMT. Vessel breaking in two."
GMT-3 Hrs - 0420 - Radio SOS from KIWW:"Lat 48 degrees 40 North Long. 41 degrees 20 West at 0600 GMT. Vessel breaking in two.

Mag Temp: Fwd: 34 Aft: 33
Saturday, February 5, 1944

GMT-3 Hrs - 0615-0710 - General Quarters.
GMT-3 Hrs 1800-1845 - General Quarters.

Diary of the Armed Guard Gunnery Officer on the S.S. Lewis Luckenbach

Mag Temp: Fwd: 40 Aft: 41
Sunday, February 6, 1944

GMT-3 Hrs - 0630-0720 - General Quarters.
GMT-3 Hrs - 1200 - Present position of this ship is: 43-42N, 51-48W, approximately.
GMT-3 Hrs - 1310 - Mate on watch, Second Mate Roberts, at 1310 observed a life-boat drifting upright in the water about a half-mile off our starboard beam, on the starboard side of our beam ship in column 12.
GMT-3 Hrs - 1340 - At 1340, another drifted past between this column (11) and column 12.
GMT-3 Hrs - 1415 - At 1415 another came by between these columns. The last two were upset. All three boats appeared to be small, double-ended metal boats, painted a very light gray with a black stripe painted across their bottoms about

Mag Temp: Fwd: 38 Aft: 42
Monday, February 7, 1944

GMT-4 Hrs - 0615-0655 - General Quarters.
GMT-4 Hrs - 1530 - Ensign half-masted by order of Commodore. Reason unknown.

one-quarter way from either end.
All boats appeared to be in good
condition and were probably swept
off the decks of some ship during
the recent gale.
GMT-3 Hrs - 1830-1915 - General
Quarters.
GMT-3 Hrs - Clocks retarded one
hour.

Diary of the Armed Guard Gunnery Officer on the S.S. Lewis Luckenbach

Mag Temp: Fwd: 39   Aft: 38
Tuesday, February 8, 1944

GMT-4 Hrs - 0615-0655 - General
Quarters.
GMT-4 Hrs - 1530 - Chief Mate
McCann informed Ensign McCarthy
that the towing spar (fog buoy) was
lost during the night with about
200 feet of line. It had been
streamed during the fog of last
night.
GMT-4 Hrs - 1800-1835 - General
Quarters.
GMT-4 Hrs - 1815 - Three white
flares - probably snowflakes - were
shot into the air about three
columns off our port bow followed
at 1823 by five more in groups of
2-2-1. Significance of these was
not learned.

Mag Temp: Fwd: 38   Aft: 37
Wednesday, February 9, 1944

EWT - 0630-0700 - General Quarters.
EWT - 0900 - About 8 depth charges
were dropped by escort about 3/4
mile off starboard bow. Occasion not
determined.
EWT - 1800-1840 - General Quarters.

Diary of the Armed Guard Gunnery Officer on the S.S. Lewis Luckenbach

Mag Temp: Fwd: 35   Aft: 36
Thursday, February 10, 1944

EWT - 0645-0715 General Quarters.
EWT - 1200 - Two 90 degree course
changes to starboard. 180 degrees
in all. Reason unknown.
EWT - 1620 - 90 degrees turn to
port.
EWT - 1630 - 90 degrees turn to
port.
EWT - 1810-1855 - General Quarters.

Mag Temp: Fwd: 33   Aft: 35
Friday, February 11, 1944

EWT - 1055 - Passed Channel Buoy "C"
(New York).
EWT - 1250 - Officially arrived at
Port of New York.
EWT - 1307 - Dropped anchor about
1 1/2 miles outside Ambrose Light-
ship. Driving snow and sleet.
EWT - 2400 - Still at anchor.

Diary of the Armed Guard Gunnery Officer on the S.S. Lewis Luckenbach

Mag Temp: Fwd: 32   Aft: 31
Saturday, February 12, 1944

EWT - 1000 - Weighed anchor and
proceeded into Harbor.
EWT - 2325 - Came alongside pier at
foot of 31st Street, Brooklyn, N.Y.

Mag Temp: Fwd: 31   Aft: 31
Sunday, February 13, 1944

EWT - 0315 - Submitted Port Watch
list to Lt. Bennett at Port
Director's Office, New York.

Diary of the Armed Guard Gunnery Officer on the S.S. Lewis Luckenbach

Mag Temp: Fwd: 30 Aft: 31
Monday, February 14, 1944

EWT - Port Routine Followed.

Mag Temp: Fwd: 36 Aft: 37
Tuesday, February 15, 1944

EWT - Port routine followed.

Diary of the Armed Guard Gunnery Officer on the S.S. Lewis Luckenbach

Mag Temp: Fwd: 41 Aft: 40
Wednesday, February 16, 1944

EWT - Port Routine Followed.

Mag Temp: Fwd: 40 Aft: 40
Thursday, February 17, 1944

EWT - Port routine followed.

EWT - 1815 - Kirksey, Oliver C., SM3c, 641-14 87, detached for leave. Gee, Raymond H., Sea1c, Seaman Signalman, assigned to unit to replace Kirksey. Gee's Serial number is 917 49 39.

Diary of the Armed Guard Gunnery Officer on the S.S. Lewis Luckenbach

Mag Temp: Fwd: 33 Aft: 32
Friday, February 18, 1944

EWT - Port Routine Followed.

Mag Temp: Fwd: 35 Aft: 35
Saturday, February 19, 1944

EWT - Port routine followed.

Diary of the Armed Guard Gunnery Officer on the S.S. Lewis Luckenbach

Mag Temp: Fwd: 34 Aft: 34
Sunday, February 20, 1944

EWT - Port Routine Followed.

Mag Temp: Fwd: 37 Aft: 37
Monday, February 21, 1944

EWT - Port routine followed.

Diary of the Armed Guard Gunnery Officer on the S.S. Lewis Luckenbach

Mag Temp: Fwd: 35 Aft: 36
Tuesday, February 22, 1944

EWT - Port Routine Followed.

Mag Temp: Fwd: 36 Aft: 35
Wednesday, February 23, 1944

EWT - Port routine followed.

Diary of the Armed Guard Gunnery Officer on the S.S. Lewis Luckenbach

Mag Temp: Fwd: 38 Aft: 42
Thursday, February 24, 1944

EWT - Port Routine Followed.

Mag Temp: Fwd: 39 Aft: 43
Friday, February 25, 1944

EWT - Port routine followed.
EWT - 1830 - Supplies received today.

Diary of the Armed Guard Gunnery Officer on the S.S. Lewis Luckenbach

Mag Temp: Fwd: 40 Aft: 44
Saturday, February 26, 1944

EWT - Port Routine Followed.

Mag Temp: Fwd: 39 Aft: 44
Sunday, February 27, 1944

EWT - Port routine followed.

Diary of the Armed Guard Gunnery Officer on the S.S. Lewis Luckenbach

Mag Temp: Fwd: 41 Aft: 46
Monday, February 28, 1944

EWT - Port Routine Followed.

Mag Temp: Fwd: 40 Aft: 40
Tuesday, February 29, 1944

EWT - Port routine followed.

Diary of the Armed Guard Gunnery Officer on the S.S. Lewis Luckenbach

Mag Temp: Fwd: 37 Aft: 42
Wednesday, March 1, 1944

EWT - Port Routine Followed.

Mag Temp: Fwd: 36 Aft: 41
Thursday, March 2, 1944

EWT - Port routine followed.

Diary of the Armed Guard Gunnery Officer on the S.S. Lewis Luckenbach

Mag Temp: Fwd: 38 Aft: 43
Friday, March 3, 1944

EWT - Port Routine Followed. Expect to receive ammunition tomorrow.
EWT - 1800 - Gunners Mate Bowerman informed Ensign McCarthy that it would be necessary for him to go to court next Monday, March 6, 1944, to press charges against a man who had bothered him in an indecent manner last night and whom he had had arrested. More details will be secured and entered later.
EWT - 1830 - Gunner's Mate Bowerman informed me that he had just found E.J. Talaska, Sea1c, the aft port watch, lying wounded in the aft gun tub with the service pistol beside him, one shell having been discharged. Ambulance was sent for and Port Director's Office notified. My investigation would indicate that the wound was self-inflicted in an attempt at suicide because of domestic troubles. Talaska was examined by a Dr. Montecans of Holy Family Hospital and was taken in an ambulance of that hospital to the U.S. Naval Hospital, Brooklyn, N.Y.

The bullet penetrated the left side below the ribs, travelled upward, and apparently emerged through his back beneath the shoulder blade.
EWT - 2000 - Lt.(J.G.) Palmer B. Kern, of the Operations Office, Armed Guard Center, Brooklyn, NY, arrived and questioned Ensign McCarthy, Gunner's Mate Bowerman, and R.H. Williams, Sea1c, whom

Mag Temp: Fwd: 44 Aft: 45
Saturday, March 4, 1944

EWT - Port routine followed.
EWT - 1000 - Ens. McCarthy with T.R. Bowerman, G.M. 2c, D.M. Lesesne, Sea1c, R.H. Williams, Sea1c, went to Port Director's Legal Office to attend Board of Inquiry in the matter of Talaska's shooting. All four and W.D. Wade, Sea1c are to be detached from the ship on 6 March, 1944, as witnesses.
EWT - 1600 - Received two lots of ammunition aboard:
1. A) 49 cases 20 MM ammunition
   B) 2 cases small arms
   C) 5 units of pyrotechnics
These were delivered aboard by Lt. (J.G.) Breitman of the Port Director's Office for delivery with and for the use of LCT (6) 645 which is part of this ship's cargo.
2. A) 10 rounds 5"51 Com.
   B) 25 rounds 5"51 H.C.
   C) 25 45-sec (5"51) fuzes
   D) 25 nose-det.(5"51) fuzes
   E) 1 fuze removal wrench
   F) 35 rounds 5"51 powder (bags)
   G) 76 " 3"50 AA-fuzed Mark 22-4
   H) 2 "   " short cartridges
   I) 3960 rounds 20MM HET
   J) 8100 "   " HEI
   K) 240 "   " BL&P (Target)
   L) 120 "   " Dummy Drill
   M) 1 box of 3"50 & 5"51 powder samples.
Items A to M are for use on this ship.
All ammunition received today was stowed in the two ships' magazines.

312

Talaska relieved. Mr Kern asked for and was given the gun (S & W - .38 cal., V-52955), belt, holster, and shells, for which he signed a receipt.

Diary of the Armed Guard Gunnery Officer on the S.S. Lewis Luckenbach

Mag Temp: Fwd: 43 Aft: 44
Sunday, March 5, 1944

EWT - 0900 - Ensign Rohde, who is the relieving Armed Guard Commander came aboard for inspection. He was shown the guns, magazines, gear lockers, and other Navy equipment.
EWT - 1530 - Ensign Rohde went ashore. Will take over tomorrow about 1300 with five enlisted replacements.

Mag Temp: Fwd: 43 Aft: 44
Monday, March 6, 1944

EWT - 1200 - Wilderman, Robert Irwin, Sea1c, developed a rash over his face. Was sent to the Armed Guard Center Sick Bay for examination.
EWT - 1600 - Ensign M.E. Rohde, USNR came aboard with five enlisted replacements to relieve Ensign C.G. McCarthy and enlisted men noted in entry of 1000, 4 March, 1944.
EWT - 1615 - Arrangements for relief of command and Ensign Rohde and his crew took over. Relieved officer and men left ship.